D0208646

EXPLORING

Chaos

EXPLORING

Chaos

theory and experiment

Brian Davies

The Advanced Book Program

PERSEUS PUBLISHING
Cambridge, Massachusetts

Many of the designations used by manufacturers and sellers to distinguish their products are claimed as trademarks. Where those designations appear in this book and Perseus Publishing was aware of a trademark claim, the designations have been printed in initial capital letters.

Library of Congress Catalog Card Number: 99-62550
ISBN 0-7382-0090-5

Copyright © 1999 by Brian Davies

All rights reserved. No part of this publication may be reproduced, stored in a retrieval system, or transmitted, in any form or by any means, electronic, mechanical, photocopying, recording, or otherwise, without the prior written permission of the publisher. Printed in the United States of America.

Perseus Publishing is a member of the Perseus Books Group.

Cover design by Bruce W. Bond
Set in 10-point Computer Modern using Textures® for the Macintosh

3 4 5 6 7 8 9—030201
First printing, June 1999
Find us on the World Wide Web at
http://www.perseuspublishing.com

Studies in Nonlinearity
Edited by Robert L. Devaney

to Patricia

Preface

An introduction to non-linear dynamics and chaos is important to many of today's students, not just in the physical sciences, but in a multitude of disciplines where dynamical processes play a vital rôle. The same students, however, are under great pressure to fit numerous other subjects into their university curriculum. Such pressures, operating since secondary college, have already set a pattern: students whose interest is high, whose time is limited, and whose mathematical training is modest. The popularisation of chaos is partly responsible for the interest, it is also responsible for many misunderstandings which need to be dispelled.

This project has evolved from several years of teaching such students. I have tried to develop material which offers opportunity to observe typical non-linear behaviour, and to afford adequate theoretical explanation of key features, using only a minimum of advanced mathematics. For the most part, this means elementary algebra and calculus. As the project unfolded, I became increasingly convinced that students must be enabled to make their own numerical experiments, but that most have neither the time nor the expertise to write their own programs. The present offering, therefore, is more than just a text; I have integrated the theory with software which has been developed in parallel. The intention is that, in as many places as possible, there should be a simple mathematical explanation and appropriate computational tools for each important concept, together with visualisation in a modern graphical environment.

The choice of topics, and the order of their presentation, reflects the tension between the desire to cover the most important parts of the subject and the need to keep the material at an elementary level. Another criterion was that I did not wish too often to go beyond what a reader could reasonably check for him/herself without further theoretical preparation. As well as these considerations, it is hardly necessary to compete with the many excellent advanced books already in print, equally it is not my aim to overlap with other noteworthy books which expound the subject with virtually no mathematics at all. Some of these books, in both categories, are listed in the bibliography; it goes without saying that I owe a debt to each and every one. Because this is an introductory work the bibliography does not contain references to original articles, however a few are scattered throughout the footnotes where it seemed appropriate.

As is often the case, the present book has grown out of lecture notes. In preparing such material for publication it is inevitable that many shortcuts and omissions, which might have been well suited to their original purpose, should be fleshed out, resulting in a considerable expansion of the original. I will not presume to suggest various selections which might be used when teaching an introductory course from this book, except to say that the original course, of about 24 lectures and 10 laboratory sessions, covered most (but certainly not all) of the material in chapters 1–3, a selection from chapters 4–5, and only passing reference to chapter 6.

Students are best able to learn a new subject if they have a sufficient supply of exercises on which to develop their skills. I have accumulated quite a supply of such material over the past few years; these have been incorporated into the text, at the end of each section, together with other material which came to mind while writing the text or developing the software. Doubtless some exercises are derivative of works listed in the bibliography, but it does not seem possible to give adequate credit.

The software, which is freely available for download, is written in Java. This is intended to provide freedom in choosing a platform for its use. In fact, it may be run from within a Java-enabled Web Browser, a mode of deployment which has been popular with many students who were able to use their own personal computers. Their feedback has been invaluable in attempting to make the software as robust and intuitive as possible. There is a price to pay for such a cross-platform choice, particularly the fact that it has not proved convenient to incorporate features whose implementation is critically platform dependent. A more fully featured version is available, written specifically for Apple Macintosh Computers.

I would like to thank Dr. Murray Batchelor, who has been involved with the development of the course for a number of years. In addition I have received many useful comments from Dr. Mark Andrews, who has kindly read the final draft of the manuscript. Many students have also given helpful feedback.

I also owe a great debt to the Australian Apple University Consortium, and Mr. Berrick Krahnen, the AUC local representative, for a great deal of support in relation to software development. In particular, the opportunity to attend two international conferences of software developers has been invaluable, as has been the supply of computing equipment. I have also had much feedback and encouragement from Dr. Neville Smythe and Dr. Ralph Sutherland, both experienced educational software developers.

Brian Davies
Canberra Australia
February 1999

Contents

Chapter 1

Introduction

1.1 Dynamical models

To the Greeks, *chaos* signified the infinite formless space which existed before the universe was created. To the generations of thinkers, philosophers and scientists of the succeeding ages, chaos and formlessness have been the subject of countless assaults in an extraordinary search for understanding of the world in which we live.

In the physical sciences these endeavours have been so successful that we can predict the motion of a space craft so as to enable it to be within a few kilometers of a chosen destination after a journey of several years. This level of prediction comes through the use of a *dynamical model*. The model itself is a conceptualisation in which the state of the system is described by state functions which change in time. A *deterministic* dynamical model is one whose future states are uniquely determined from its present state by prescribed laws of evolution. Using such a model, together with powerful computers to solve the equations which encapsulate the laws, makes possible astounding feats of space travel. Yet they do not permit us to predict the weather!

Even our small corner of the universe — the solar system — is too complex to immediately fit a simple model. The process of modelling sorts out the important facts from those of lesser importance, whereupon an account of only the former is undertaken. For example, a model of the solar system which has been the subject of centuries of investigation considers the sun and planets as point masses moving in otherwise empty space, under the sole effect of mutual gravitational forces.

Population models

Dynamical models have been used for the study of populations of species for more than a century. The following quotation will suffice to introduce the idea[1]

---

[1] David Holton and Robert M. May, "Chaos and one-dimensional maps", in [20], p101.

1

In population dynamics, it is desirable to predict trends in populations due to external influences. One of the simplest population systems is a seasonally breeding organism whose generations do not overlap. ...We seek to understand how the
size x_{t+1} of a population in generation $t + 1$ is related to the
size x_t of the population in the preceding generation. Often
an adjustable parameter appears, accounting for, say, the net
reproductive rate of the population. We may express such a
scalar relationship in general form $x_{t+1} = f(x_t, \lambda)$ ...

The authors go on to discuss some problems with using such a model, but
conclude:

Despite this possibility, there is a rationale for constructing
overly simplified models: to capture the essence of observed
patterns and processes without being enmeshed in the details.

Consider a simple population model for a single species, in which the
reproductive rate[2] is a function $r(x)$ which decreases, with increasing population x, from an initial value $r(0) = r$ to $r(x) = 0$ at some limiting
population number K. If we use x to measure the population as a fraction
of the carrying capacity K, then the point where $r(x) = 0$ will be at $x = 1$.
A simple example is the logistic model, which employs a linear decrease of
$r(x)$ with increasing x:

$$r(x) = r(1 - x), \qquad f(x) = rx(1 - x).$$

Starting from some initial population x_0, this gives rise to the sequence of
populations, at successive generations k,

$$x_{k+1} = rx_k(1 - x_k).$$

Examples of behaviour

Using CHAOS FOR JAVA[3] one can examine the solution in a number of
ways. Figure 1.1 shows the first 50 generations, commencing from an initial
population $x_0 = 1/10$, with four different values of the parameter r. Note
that if $r < 1$ the population gradually dies out, since the reproductive rate
is insufficient for any positive x. Observe the following properties:

---

[2]This simply aggregates the difference between birth and death rates.

[3]Most of the illustrations in this book were produced with this software, which is
free for download. Instructions for obtaining and using it are given in appendix A. You
should always attempt to have it at hand when reading, since only a limited number of
figures can be printed, conveying only a fraction of what can be learned from your own
explorations. In addition, many of the exercises require the use of the software.

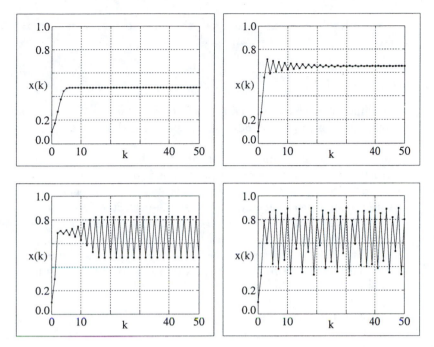

Figure 1.1: Iterations of the logistic map, with parameters (from top left) (i) $r = 1.9$, (ii) $r = 2.9$, (iii) $r = 3.3$, (iv) $r = 3.6$, all with initial value $x_0 = 0.1$.

(i) For $r = 1.9$ the population rises rapidly to a steady value of about 0.47 (47% of the carrying capacity), a figure determined by crowding.

(ii) For $r = 2.9$ the population again stabilises, this time through a sequence of small boom and bust cycles which die out.

(iii) Increasing r to 3.3 changes the behaviour fundamentally. Now the system stabilises on a permanent boom and bust cycle which alternates between good and poor seasons.

(iv) At $r = 3.6$ the behaviour has become extremely complex, with no apparent pattern or simple repetition. It is in fact chaotic.

Imagine the implications for population control policies if such a simple model can generate such disparate outcomes, depending only on the policy settings!

The above figures were produced by the ITERATE(1D) window of CHAOS FOR JAVA with the LOGISTIC MAP selected.[4] Some other interesting values

---

[4]See appendix A.6 for documentation on the ITERATE(1D) window.

for you to look at before proceeding to the next section include $r = 3.5$, 3.83 and 4.0.

Financial models

Dynamical models are not just the preserve of the sciences. Two professors of economics, for example, introduced a paper with the words[5]

> Imagine a bargaining model ... in which each party has been instructed by higher headquarters to respond to each new offer by her opposite number with a counter-offer that is to be calculated from a simple reaction function ... If the perfectly deterministic sequence of offers and counter-offers that must emerge from these simple rules were to begin to oscillate wildly and apparently at random, the negotiations could easily break down as each party ... came to suspect the other side of duplicity and sabotage. Yet all that may be involved, as we will see, is the phenomenon referred to as chaos ...

Needless to say, there is much research on the question of what nonlinear dynamical models and chaos have to say about economics, financial markets,[6] and investment management. In this respect it is interesting to note that Benoit Mandelbrot, who coined the word *fractal*, and whose writings had considerable influence in awakening interest in the present subject, first observed the phenomenon of *scaling* in price changes and income distributions. He stated a pricing principle (hypothesis) as follows (see Mandelbrot [17] chapter 37)

> Scaling principle of price change: When $X(t)$ is a price, $\log X(t)$ has the property that its increment over an arbitrary time lag d, $\log X(t + d) - \log X(t)$, has a distribution independent of d, except for a scale factor.

Fractals are treated briefly in chapter 5 of this book; self-similarity of form under changes of scale is one of their hallmarks. An interesting view of how fractals and chaos theory applies to investment theory, including extensive analyses of financial data, may be found in the book of Peters [25].

---

[5]William J. Baumol and Jess Benhabib, "Chaos: Significance, Mechanism, and Economic Applications", *Journal of Economic Perspectives*, **3**, 77 – 105 (1989).

[6]In 1838, Thomas Tooke wrote that "the money market turns out always to be in unstable equilibrium", an assertion which has been described as an "absurdity" by modern writers. See page 130 for a typical dynamical system which exhibits exactly such behaviour. For the original quotation, see Blatt [8], p7.

1.2   Celestial mechanics

The earliest dynamical systems which were the subject of intensive study are concerned with Isaac Newton's gravitational model of the solar system. A delightful and easily read account of the history of studies into the solar system is given by Ivars Peterson in his book [26]. I shall give only a brief account here.

Newton's theory gave a satisfactory account of a mass of observations, which had been reduced to three laws by Johannes Kepler. Kepler's laws are

(i) Planetary orbits are plane ellipses with the sun at one focus.

(ii) A line joining a planet with the sun sweeps out area at a rate constant in time.

(iii) The square of the periods of the orbits are proportional to the cubes of the mean radii.

One sees that the very statement of the laws already takes us a long way toward reducing the data to a dynamical model. They define the important state variables as the positions and velocities of the solar bodies, and they state some relationships, although no theoretical explanation is offered.

The triumph of Newton's theory is that these laws are explained as the consequence of a simple dynamical model for which he gives the *equations of evolution*. Newton's second law of motion states that the rate of change of momentum of a body is equal to the sum of the forces acting on it; his gravitational theory states that the force acting between any pair is proportional to the product of their masses, inversely proportional to the square of the distance between them, and directed along the line joining them at any instant of time. The constant of proportionality, G, is a *universal constant* of nature.

Newton was acutely aware of various deficiencies of his theory as applied to the solar system in finer detail. In fact he was unhappy about his inability to give a proper account for the observed motion of the moon. There were other discrepancies too, particularly in the motion of the two largest planets, Jupiter and Saturn. In some brilliant work, Pierre Simon de Laplace accounted for this latter as a mutual near resonant interaction resulting in periodic changes which take approximately 900 years for each cycle. So confident was he of the validity of the underlying methods of dynamics that he wrote[7]

> Assume an intelligence that at a given moment knows all the
> forces that animate nature as well as the momentary position

---
[7]Taken from Peterson [26], p229.

of all things of which the universe consists, and further that it is sufficiently powerful to perform a calculation based on these data. It would then include in the same formulation the motions of the largest bodies in the universe and those of the smallest atoms. To it, nothing would be uncertain. Both future and past would be precise before its eyes.

This is an extreme statement of the view that the solar system — even the entire universe — is a predictable *clockwork* system.

Poincaré and the birth of chaos

In November 1890 Henri Poincaré's memoir on the three-body problem (see below for a brief description) was published as the winning entry in an international competition to honour the 60th birthday of King Oscar II of Sweden and Norway.[8] There were four questions from which the contestants might choose; Poincaré's choice was the one whose solution would, it was hoped, lead to a resolution of the question of the stability of the solar system (or rather, the Newtonian model of the solar system). In part, the question read (Barrow-Green [6], p229)

> A system being given of a number whatever of particles attracting one another mutually according to Newton's law, it is proposed ... to expand the coordinates of each particle in a series ... according to some known functions of time ...

Poincaré's winning entry, and the published memoir (which differed significantly from the original due to the discovery of an important error) were on "the problem of three bodies and the equations of dynamics". In fact, his investigations are concerned with the "restricted circular three body problem". This version has two of the bodies, one rather more massive than the other, in circular orbits about their centre of mass, and seeks to explain the motion of a third body whose mass is too small to influence the two primaries. This simplification of the original question — concerned with an arbitrary number of bodies moving in three dimensions — to three bodies moving in a plane, two of them in fixed circular motion, illustrate the importance of simple models to making progress in fundamental understanding. It underscores the comments of Holton and May, made on population models, and quoted above.

A proper exposition of Poincaré's work requires a substantial volume in itself. Here I just mention a few salient points.

---

[8]See the book by June Barrow-Green [6] for a rather complete account of Poincaré's contributions to mathematics and dynamics.

(i) Poincaré gave prominence to the geometric properties of the orbits as smooth curves in space, defined by the evolution of the state variables.

(ii) He showed that by making suitable choices in representing the problem, individual orbits may be investigated via the set of points at which they pierce a two-dimensional *transverse surface*.

(iii) The original dynamics is now encoded as the *map* which relates the successive piercings of this surface, since each is determined from the previous one solely by the equations of motion.

(iv) Periodic orbits show up as isolated points in this map.

(v) Entire families of orbits may now be represented as curves in a surface of section, each point on the curve representing an orbit.

(vi) Certain families of orbits lie on curves which intersect themselves infinitely often in the neighbourhood of a single point.

Thus Poincaré instigated a new way to study dynamical systems which emphasised qualitative and geometric features, not just analytical formulae. His method (ii) is widely used today and is known as the method of *Poincaré sections*.[9]

The study of maps, instituted in (iii) is used in the theory of dynamical systems and chaos. The *homoclinic tangles* identified in (vi) play an important part in advanced studies of chaotic systems. Although I shall not be concerned with the theory of such orbits herein, it is important to understand that it was in the process of exploring the *infinite complexity* of such bizarre objects that Poincaré arrived at the doorway to an appreciation of chaos.

Understandably, Poincaré's work, particularly the memoir of 1890, has drawn unceasing admiration for more than a century. 100 years on, one reviewer wrote that the memoir was[10]

> ... the first textbook in the qualitative theory of dynamical systems ...

1.3   Lorenz: the end of weather prediction?

Despite the importance of Poincaré's work, and other work in the first half of the 20th century, the implications for unpredictable and chaotic

---

[9]In his book "The Essence of Chaos" [16], Edward Lorenz gives a beautifully clear account of the meaning of Poincaré sections without the use of mathematical formulae.

[10]Philip Holmes, "Poincaré, celestial mechanics, dynamical systems theory and chaos", *Physics Reports*, **193**, 137 − 163 (1990).

behaviour were not widely appreciated until the advent of electronic computation. This is hardly surprising, since the fact that usable analytic formulae cannot be found for relatively uncomplicated dynamical models means that a proper appreciation of the nature of their solutions had to await such a development.

Thus it was not until Edward Lorenz' 1963 paper[11] that a new era opened in non-linear dynamics and chaos. Lorenz considered the relatively harmless looking differential equations

$$\frac{dx}{dt} = \sigma(y - x),$$
$$\frac{dy}{dt} = rx - y - xz, \qquad (1.1)$$
$$\frac{dz}{dt} = xy - bz.$$

Here x, y and z are the state variables, σ, b and r are parameters which control the types of behaviour (see below for a brief explanation). Were it not for the two non-linear terms (xz in the second equation and xy in the third), the complete set of solutions would be expressible using only the exponential, sine, and cosine functions, and a few constants easily computed from the coefficients b, σ and r, together with the initial values of x, y and z. That is to say, not only would it be a deterministic dynamical system, but more importantly, all possible behaviour patterns would be simple to understand. One facet I want to emphasise here is that, because of the nature of the equations, were they linear then at most one natural frequency would be required for the description of the motion.

Strange attractors

What Lorenz found are solutions which are *nonperiodic*, that is, they cannot be represented using any finite number of frequencies. These solutions are also *sensitively dependent* on initial conditions, which means that for all practical purposes, prediction of the state of the system is limited to relatively short times. Furthermore, in the regime where chaotic solutions exist, then regardless of the initial conditions, they are all attracted to some region of state space whose dimension is not an integer! It resembles a surface with two wings, but it is more like a fat surface, with an infinite number of sheets. Such objects are generally called *strange attractors*, and again we are confronted with the infinite when examining the behaviour of a simple dynamical system.

---

[11]Edward N. Lorenz, "Deterministic nonperiodic flow", *Journal of Atmospheric Science*, **20**, 130–141 (1963).

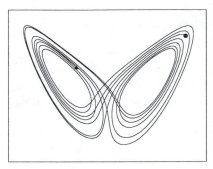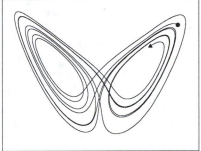

Figure 1.2: Orbits of the Lorenz equations, both with $r = 28$. The initial positions (circle) differ in the fourth significant place, the final positions (triangle) are qualitatively different after a few circuits.

Two typical solutions are shown in figure 1.2, numerically generated by the ODE ORBITS window of CHAOS FOR JAVA.[12] Using Lorenz' choice for the parameters, namely $\sigma = 10$, $b = 8/3$ and $r = 28$, one finds orbits which have become one of the icons of chaos. Each orbit commences from the point displayed as a small circle and ends at the point displayed as a small triangle. The initial position of the two differs only in the fourth significant place of the x-coordinate; it is clear that the final point is on a different wing.

From these static pictures it is not at all evident how the state of the system (which is generated by a continuously travelling point in three-dimensions) moves along its three-dimensional trajectory in time, or even that the orbits are three-dimensional. To see this, you must generate the orbits for yourself using CHAOS FOR JAVA, which will both show you this behaviour and allow you to view the orbits from different view points. You will see that the generating point makes one or more circuits around one of the wings before switching to the other: this process of making circuits then switching continues indefinitely.

The butterfly effect

Lorenz noticed that when he attempted to recompute a given orbit, using the same program on the same computer, he got a different result from the original. This was because his recorded values of x, y and z were less accurate than the internal representation used by the computer, so he was comparing two solutions which differed in their initial state by a small

---

[12]See appendix A.9 for documentation on the ODE ORBITS window.

amount. The surprising effect is that, after a while, the two solutions don't
seem to have much correlation with each other at all.

For example, the two orbits shown in figure 1.2 differ only by a change
of initial values of y in the fourth significant place. Even in the short time
span (20 units) of the displayed orbits, one sees that they no longer agree
except in the most qualitative feature that they are both organised by the
same strange attractor. It is not just the growth of error that is involved.
After all, the simple linear dynamical model $x_{k+1} = rx_k$ has the property
that, if $r > 1$, then an initial difference is magnified by the increasingly
large factor r^k as k increases. However, in this linear model the relative
error remains at the same level of significance for all k, and the qualitative
behaviour of the two solutions is the same in the sense that they look the
same over long intervals of time. What we are facing in equations such
as Lorenz' is the fact that the relative error quickly becomes as large as
the quantities themselves, and that different solutions only have similar
qualitative behaviour over relatively short time intervals. That being said,
a strange attractor does supply a recognisable structure for the solutions.

This effect, *sensitive dependence* of the evolution of a system to the
most infinitesimal changes of initial state is known as the *butterfly effect*,
after the title of a talk by Lorenz:[13]

> Predictability: Does the flap of a Butterfly's Wings in Brazil
> set off a Tornado in Texas?

It encapsulates the question: if Lorenz' equations do not allow long time
prediction, why should more complicated dynamical models of the atmosphere do any better? Debate over such questions continues, as does research into weather and climate prediction. An entire chapter of Lorenz'
book [16] is devoted to an informed but non-technical discussion of the
weather and the implications of chaos for forecasting.

Origin of the Lorenz equations

In the model from which the Lorenz equations are distilled, the focus of
interest is on convective fluid motion driven by heating from below, such as
might occur locally over warm terrain. Lorenz took a set of seven coupled
differential equations (derived by a colleague), ignored four apparently in-
significant variables, and investigated solutions of the remaining three coupled equations. This gave him his first real glimpse of infinitely complex
behaviour in a simple deterministic system.

Of course the original equations for the fluid motion are infinitely complicated, since they must take account of the temperature and movement at

---

[13]The text of the talk is reprinted in Lorenz [16]. He points out that one might equally
well ask if the Butterfly can prevent a tornado in Texas.

every point in the fluid. Lorenz' equations are the simplest possible reduction which retains at least some interesting and representative behaviour. By using a Fourier representation, they impose a simple dependence of temperature variation on height, whose amplitude is measured by the function $z(t)$. Similarly, the intensity of the resulting convective motion and the horizontal temperature gradient are given fixed functional forms, with amplitudes $x(t)$ and $y(t)$. As for the constants, b is related to the horizontal scale of the convective cells, while σ and r encapsulate some important physical properties of the fluid. The main point is that the equations do arise as an extremely simplified dynamical model of a phenomenon which is important in understanding the atmosphere. More importantly, the infinite complexity is not dependent on having an infinitely complicated system.

1.4 Complex behaviour of simple systems

This book is an elementary introduction to the theory of dynamical systems and chaos. The principal aim is to explore the deep relationship between dynamical systems, chaos and fractals, and to uncover structure even where order seems to be absent. We want to understand some of the phenomena which are common across diverse systems, and investigate the mechanisms which make them so. The approach will combine relatively simple mathematics with computer experiments using the program CHAOS FOR JAVA, which has been developed specifically for this purpose.

In the present context, chaos in a dynamical system is a situation where one sees:

(i) Sensitive dependence on the initial conditions, making long-term prediction impossible — the *Butterfly effect*.

(ii) Mixing of the states of the system on ever finer scales so that the trajectories which it may follow become inextricably tangled.

Deterministic dynamical systems may exhibit regular behaviour for some values of their control parameters and irregular behaviour for others. One speaks of *regular* and *chaotic* behaviour in such a system. To quote from an earlier paper of Holmes[14]

> We thus see that deterministic dynamical systems can give rise to motions which are essentially random.

As for the utility of investigating such simple systems, I conclude with another quote from the article by Holton and May

---

[14]Philip Holmes, "A non-linear oscillator with a strange attractor", *Philosophical Transactions of the Royal Society of London*, **A292**, 419–448 (1979).

The development of dynamical systems theory in general, and Lorenz' contribution and May's review[15] in *Nature* in particular, triggered a change in perception: that a large number of complicated equations were not necessary ... for solutions to be chaotic or turbulent-like. Dynamical systems theory has been driven to the forefront of many fields of science with an impressive number and variety of applications.

Exercises

1.1 Experiment with the ITERATE(1D) window of CHAOS FOR JAVA to find different behaviours for the SINE MAP,

$$x_{k+1} = q \sin \pi x_k, \qquad (0 \le q \le 1). \qquad (1.2)$$

In particular, find some values of q for which the population reaches a steady value, some where it undergoes periodic cycles, and some where it appears to be disordered.

Pay attention also to the behaviour near to $q = 0.938$, observing what happens just before this regular behaviour sets in, and what happens as it dissolves into disorder again.

---

[15]Robert M. May, "Simple mathematical models with very complicated dynamics, *Nature*, **261**, 459 – 469 (1976).

Chapter 2

Orbits of one-dimensional systems

This chapter is an investigation of orbits of discrete one-dimensional dynamical systems, particularly properties of stability and periodicity.

2.1 Discrete dynamical systems

I commence with some definitions. While they may seem rather pedantic at this juncture, I want to emphasise the fact that the concept of orbits is independent of such properties as periodicity or stability.

Definition 2.1 (One-dimensional system) *An equation of the form*

$$x_{k+1} = f(x_k; \mu), \tag{2.1}$$

is called a discrete one-dimensional dynamical system, while the quantity x is called the state variable. The coefficient μ, which is not affected by the iteration, is called a control parameter.

A one-dimensional system has only a single state variable, however some have more than one parameter. The function f must have the property that the domain (input) space is *mapped* to itself, so as to allow for iteration; for this reason I shall refer to functions which determine the behaviour of dynamical systems as *maps* rather than functions. Note that the range (output) space can be either a subset of the domain or the whole of it; the essential point is that the range should not exceed the domain.

If more than one state variable is required to model a system, an equation is required for each variable, and the equations take a multi-dimensional form such as the two-dimensional system

$$x_{k+1} = f(x_k, y_k), \qquad y_{k+1} = g(x_k, y_k).$$

Consideration of such systems, and of continuous systems, is deferred to later chapters.

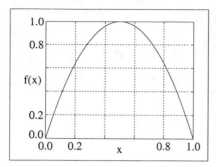 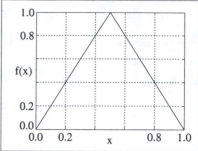

Figure 2.1: The logistic (left) and tent (right) maps at their maximum parameter values, $r = 4$ and $t = 1$, respectively.

Definition 2.2 (Orbit) *The sequence of values x_k, $k = 0, 1, \cdots$, generated by the system (2.1) is called an orbit of the system, while the value x_0 from which the orbit commences is called the initial state.*

Specifying the initial state is often referred to as setting the initial conditions.

Two important systems

I shall show that different models often have identical patterns of behaviour which come from simple properties of the function. For this reason, I shall treat two special one-dimensional examples in much detail, knowing that there are general lessons to be learned. The two are:[1]

(i) The logistic map, already met,

$$f(x) = rx(1 - x), \qquad (0 \le r \le 4). \qquad (2.2)$$

The state variable is x, the control parameter is r.

(ii) The tent map,

$$f(x) = \begin{cases} 2tx, & (x \le \tfrac{1}{2}), \\ 2t(1 - x), & (x \ge \tfrac{1}{2}), \end{cases} \qquad (0 \le t \le 1). \qquad (2.3)$$

Again the state variable is x, but the control parameter is t.

---

[1]Normally a function is denoted by f and its value at x by $f(x)$. Strictly speaking one should write $f : x \to rx(1 - x)$ rather than (2.2) but this is cumbersome for elementary use. The meaning of formulae like (2.2) and (2.3) is that they define the value of f for some specified interval of x. For the second function two formulae are required.

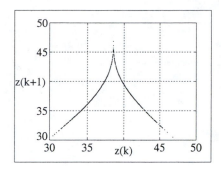

Figure 2.2: Maximum in z return map, Lorenz equations, $r = 28$. Sample size 10^3 points, initial 10 points discarded.

Graphs of the two, at their maximum parameter values, are shown in figure 2.1. Provided the parameters are restricted as indicated, each is a map of the interval $0 \leq x \leq 1$ to itself.

Maximum in z sequence — Lorenz equations[2]

We have already examined some orbits of the Lorenz equations, and noticed how they can circle indefinitely about two organising centres, switching from one to the other erratically. On each circuit they attain a maximum value for the variable z. In fact, it follows from the last of the equations (1.1) that these maxima must occur when

$$\frac{dz}{dt} = xy - bz = 0. \tag{2.4}$$

That is, maxima in z mark the places at which the orbit pierces the surface $z = xy/b$, which is therefore a simple example of a Poincaré transverse surface of section.

Now, because the Lorenz attractor for $r = 28$ is like a thick surface, its intersection with this transverse surface is a thick line, and the information about the points of intersection is almost contained in the maximum z values alone, which I call z_k.[3] For a one-dimensional discrete system $z_{k+1} = f(z_k)$, if one plots pairs (z_k, z_{k+1}) in a plane, they will fall on the graph of f. Therefore, even though the sequence of maximum z values is not exactly one-dimensional, it is instructive to examine such a plot. In fact this was done by Lorenz in his original paper. Figure 2.2 shows the plot of 1000

---

[2]Only the last chapter of this book is concerned with the theory of differential equations. The material in this section may be omitted without loss of continuity.

[3]The corresponding value of the product $x_k y_k$ is given by bz_k. If the points fell on a simple smooth curve in the surface of section this would determine x_k and y_k separately.

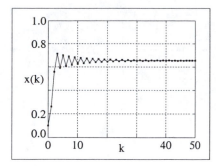 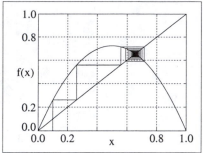

Figure 2.3: Iterations of the logistic map with $r = 2.9$, $x_0 = 0.1$, viewed as a plot of x_k versus k (left) and as a *cobweb* (right). Lines joining successive points serve only as a guide to the eye.

pairs (z_k, z_{k+1}). It gives good motivation for investigating the properties of the tent map.

Unimodal maps

On the interval $0 \leq x \leq 1$, the function (2.2) has zero minimum values at the end points and a maximum of $r/4$ at the mid-point. Similarly for the tent map, which is zero at the end points and has a maximum value $f(1/2) = t$. Therefore these maps have the property of folding the interval, since they are increasing functions of x up to some point $x = x_{\max}$ at which there is a maximum, after which they are decreasing. In fact, when $r > 2$ (for the logistic map) or $t > 1/2$ (for the tent map) they have a stretching action as well: the total length of the image is greater than the length of the original interval, that is, $2f(x_{\max}) - f(0) - f(1) > 1$. Because they are maps and therefore confined always to the same interval, this can only be achieved by folding.

Definition 2.3 (Unimodal map) *A unimodal map of the interval*[4] $I = [a, b]$ *is one which has a single maximum* $x_{\max}$ *in* I.

Note that the derivative of the tent map is not defined at its point of maximum, although it is otherwise continuous, whereas the derivative is everywhere continuous for the logistic map. However, the point of maximum

---

[4]I use the standard notation for intervals of the real line, whereby the endpoints are specified as an ordered pair $a < b$; whether or not they are included is indicated by square or round brackets. For instance, $I = [a, b)$ denotes the set of real numbers x for which $a \leq x < b$. The importance of these distinctions lies in the concepts of *open* and *closed* intervals; the latter contain both boundary points, the former contain neither. In particular (a, b) is open, $[a, b]$ closed; $[a, b)$ and $(a, b]$ are neither open nor closed.

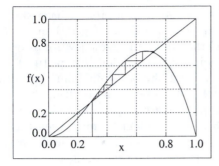
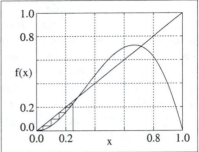

Figure 2.4: Iteration of the map (2.5) with $r = 2.9$. The initial value are $x_0 = 0.3$ (left) and $x_0 = 0.25$ (right).

is a *critical point* in both cases. This is because, in elementary calculus, a critical point is defined as one where the derivative either has the value zero, or is not defined.

Examples of iteration

Let's look at what happens when we iterate the logistic map, starting from the initial value $x_0 = 0.1$, with the parameter choice $r = 2.9$. Figure 2.3 shows two different pictures of the first 50 iterations. One is a plot of x_k as a function of k, in which the actual values are joined by straight lines simply as a guide to the eye. The other is a *cobweb plot*, in which each vertical line guides the eye from x_k to $f(x_k)$, each horizontal line from $f(x_k)$ to x_{k+1}.

These pictures are produced using the ITERATE(1D) and the GRAPH-ICAL ANALYSIS windows of CHAOS FOR JAVA (respectively), so you can reproduce them for yourself and also make further experiments.[5] The cobweb plot shows most clearly what is going on: the state of the system approaches the limiting point at which the graph of $y = f(x)$ intersects the line $y = x$.

Now let's look at a somewhat different unimodal map,[6] defined by the formula

$$f(x) = 27rx^2(1 - x)/16, \qquad (0 \leq r \leq 4) \qquad (2.5)$$

I have chosen the normalising factor $27/16$ so that this is a map of the interval $[0, 1]$ for the same range of parameter values r as for the logistic map $(0 \leq r \leq 4)$. Because of the x^2 term, there may be two non-zero intersections of the graph with the line $y = x$: for $r = 2.9$ they are at $x \approx 0.2863$ and $x \approx 0.7137$.

---

[5] See appendix A.5 for documentation on the GRAPHICAL ANALYSIS window.
[6] Denoted CUBIC #1 MAP in CHAOS FOR JAVA.

Two pictures are displayed in figure 2.4. In the first, I have started the iteration from the initial value $x_0 = 0.3$, a little bigger than 0.2863. However, this point appears to repel the state, and after few iterations it seems to be attracted to the other point of intersection (left picture). To check on this property, I have also started the iteration from the initial value $x_0 = 0.25$, a little smaller than 0.2863. Again it is repelled; this time it is attracted by $x = 0$ (right picture). The latter is also a point at which the map intersects with the line $y = x$. For the logistic map, even though we started close to it, it acted as a repeller and was hardly noticed; for this new map it is a point of attraction so it makes its presence felt.

Exercises

2.1 Solutions of the Lorenz equations orbit around two centres, switching from one to the other irregularly. In 1976, Otto Rössler suggested investigating the equations

$$\frac{dx}{dt} = -y - z,$$
$$\frac{dy}{dt} = x + ay, \tag{2.6}$$
$$\frac{dz}{dt} = a + z(x - c),$$

which do not arise from a physical model, but which have the simple property that their solutions circle the vertical (z) axis, lying close to the x-y plane much of the time. Observe that the only non-linearity is the innocent looking term zx in the last equation. Rössler chose $a = 1/5$, and this is the default choice in CHAOS FOR JAVA. Use the RETURN MAPS[7] window with $c = 5.7$ to view the maximum in x return map for these equations. Compare with figure 2.2 for the Lorenz equations.

2.2 Show that one orbit of the tent map with $t = 1$ is

$$2/5, 4/5, 2/5, 4/5, \cdots$$

i.e., an orbit which repeats itself exactly every second iteration. Try to observe it using the ITERATE(1D) window of CHAOS FOR JAVA.

2.3 Consider the map[8]

$$f(x) = rx(1 - x^2)/\sqrt{3}, \qquad (0 \le r \le 4.5). \tag{2.7}$$

Show that f is a unimodal map of the interval $[0, 1]$ to itself for the given range of the parameter r.

---

[7]See appendix A.11 for documentation on the RETURN MAPS window.
[8]Denoted CUBIC #2 MAP in CHAOS FOR JAVA.

2.4 The CUBIC #3 MAP is defined by[9]

$$f(x) = x(1 - p + px^2), \qquad (0 \le p \le 4). \qquad (2.8)$$

It is not unimodal, but it is an *antisymmetric function*, i.e.

$$f(-x) = -f(x).$$

(i) Find the positions and number of the minima and maxima of f.

(ii) Show that f maps the interval $[-1, 1]$ into itself for the given range of the parameter p.

(iii) Show that, as a consequence of the *symmetry*, if $x_0, x_1, x_2, \cdots$ is an orbit, then so is $-x_0, -x_1, -x_2, \cdots$.

2.2   Fixed points and stability

Points of intersection in the x-y plane of the two curves $y = f(x)$ and $y = x$ are evidently of great importance, which warrants some definitions.

Definition 2.4 (Fixed point) *Any value x^* for which $f(x^*) = x^*$ is called a fixed point of f.*

Definition 2.5 (Stable and unstable fixed point) *A fixed point x^* is stable if it belongs to an interval $I = (a, b)$, such that for any x_0 in I, the orbit which commences from x_0 converges to x^* as k increases toward infinity; it is unstable if it is ejected from I as k increases toward infinity.*

A stable fixed point will also be called an *attractor*, an unstable fixed point a *repeller*. A fixed point may also be stable in some weaker sense (the definition I have given is generally called asymptotic stability). For example, iterates may stay close to x^* provided they start close enough, without ever approaching x^* more closely. In the context of fixed points, I shall treat only asymptotic stability.

Definition 2.6 (Basin of attraction) *The set of all initial states whose orbits converge to a given attractor is called the basin of attraction.*

---

[9]You may be wondering how many CUBIC MAPS are going to appear. A little thought shows that this should be the last, although none of them is completely general. The generic cubic function $f(x) = a_0 x^3 + a_1 x^2 + a_2 x + a_3$ may be classified according as a_0 is either (i) negative, the minimum is followed by the maximum, or (ii) positive, the maximum is followed by the minimum. The CUBIC #1 and CUBIC #2 MAPS are of type (i), and may be used to provide unimodal maps differing from the LOGISTIC MAP, the CUBIC #3 MAP is of type (ii), leading to many interesting properties. In addition, the CUBIC #2 and CUBIC #3 MAPS were chosen to be antisymmetric functions.

A crucial part of definitions 2.5 and 2.6 is a knowledge of the behaviour of a dynamical system in the long run, expressed in mathematical terms by statements like "as k increases toward infinity". What will become increasingly clear, as we delve into some of the theory of dynamical systems, is that in many situations it is impossible to give an analytic argument which clearly determines whether or not a system does enjoy a particular property, when the definition depends on an infinite limit. The title of this book is therefore no accident: investigating chaos in dynamical systems often reduces to an exploration of the infinite, using numerical tools which are manifestly finite.

Stability analysis

How can one check the stability of a fixed point from the properties of the map alone? The usual answer is that it depends on the first derivative of the map. However, to make life easier, I shall assume that the maps we consider are *smooth* in the vicinity of any fixed point, that is, the function has continuous derivatives of all orders. In fact, I shall generally consider maps which are smooth in the whole interval on which they act, although some maps such as the tent map will have isolated non-conforming points. This will not matter provided we do not wish to investigate fixed point which coincide with these bad points, at least not using the derivative test!

Linear approximation

Consider a fixed point x^* of a smooth map f. Let $\delta_k = x_k - x^*$ denote the difference between the kth point on the orbit and the fixed point. I want to investigate how it compares with the next difference $\delta_{k+1} = x_{k+1} - x^*$. Using linear approximation,[10]

$$\delta_{k+1} = f(x_k) - x^* = f(x^* + \delta_k) - x^*$$
$$\approx f(x^*) + \delta_k f'(x^*) - x^* = \delta_k f'(x^*).$$

An important feature is that δ_{k+1} will have the same sign as δ_k if $f'(x^*)$ is positive, the opposite sign if $f'(x^*)$ is negative.

How good is the approximation? The answer is that, for a smooth map, one may in fact write an exact equation

$$f(x^* + \delta_k) = x^* + \delta_k f'(x^{**}), \tag{2.9}$$

where x^{**} is a point at which a tangent to the curve is parallel to the chord which joins (x^*, x^*) and $(x^* + \delta_k, f(x^* + \delta_k)) = (x^* + \delta_k, x^* + \delta_{k+1})$. There

---

[10]Note that I have opted for the notation f' rather than df/dx for the derivative, although the latter will be used for applying the chain rule of differentiation.

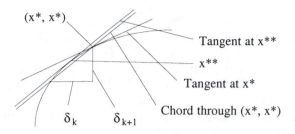

Figure 2.5: Linear approximation by a tangent and a chord.

must be such a point, no further distant from x^* than $|\delta_k|$, and therefore x^{**} is in the interval $I = [x^* - |\delta_k|, x^* + |\delta_k|]$. These features are illustrated in figure 2.5; I has been chosen symmetrically because the iterations will switch from side to side if $f'(x^*)$ is negative.

Derivative test

From (2.9) there are two possibilities of interest:[11]

(i) x^* and x_k belong to an interval I in which $|f'(x)| < 1$. Denoting the maximum value of $|f'(x)|$ on I by M, we have

$$|\delta_{k+1}| \leq M|\delta_k|.$$

This says that the new iteration is within the interval I, and closer to x^* than the original. We may repeat the argument, giving

$$|\delta_{k+2}| \leq M|\delta_{k+1}| \leq M^2|\delta_k|.$$

and further, to get

$$|\delta_{k+l}| \leq M^l|\delta_k|,$$

after l steps. Since $M < 1$, the sequence of values δ_{k+l} converges to zero and the fixed point is stable.

(ii) x^* and x_k belong to an interval I in which $|f'(x)| > 1$. Denote the minimum value of $|f'(x)|$ on I by M, then

$$|\delta_{k+1}| \geq M|\delta_k|.$$

This says that the new iteration cannot be as close as the first. Moreover, no matter how close to x^* we start the iteration, it shows that the orbit moves away by a factor at least as big as M at each step until it is ejected from the interval.

---

[11] There is also the *marginal case*, when $|f'(x^*)| = 1$. See, however, exercise 2.12.

Let's put all this together. Given a fixed point x^* of a smooth map, at which $|f'(x^*)| \neq 1$, then there is an interval containing x^* in which either $|f'(x)| < 1$ or $|f'(x)| > 1$, according as $|f'(x^*)| < 1$ or $|f'(x^*)| > 1$. So the stability of the fixed point is completely determined by the value of $|f'(x^*)|$. For simplicity I have been writing $f(x)$ rather than $f(x; \mu)$ when indicating the variables on which f depends, and this should be kept in mind when considering an expression for $f'(x^*)$. It is still a function of the parameter(s), because both f and x^* depend on them.

Note also the fact that the important qualitative difference between having iterations stay on the same side of x^*, or alternate from side to side, is determined by the sign of $f'(x^*)$.

Fixed points of the logistic map

For the logistic map (2.2) the fixed point equation $x = f(x)$ is the quadratic equation

$$x - rx(1 - x) = x(rx - r + 1) = 0,$$

whose two solutions are $x_0^* = 0$ and $x_1^* = (1 - 1/r)$. For $0 < r < 1$, x_1^* is not in the interval $[0, 1]$ so there is only one fixed point,[12] x_0^*. Therefore, the formulae we seek are

$$
\begin{aligned}
x_0^* &= 0, & (0 \leq r \leq 4), \\
x_1^* &= 1 - 1/r. & (1 \leq r \leq 4).
\end{aligned}
\qquad (2.10)
$$

Since $f'(0) = r$, x_0^* is a stable fixed point in the range $0 \leq r < 1$ and unstable if $1 < r \leq 4$. For the other fixed point x_1^*,

$$f'(x_1^*) = 2 - r.$$

So x_1^* is a stable fixed point in the range $1 < r < 3$, but unstable in the range $3 < r \leq 4$, for which both fixed points are unstable. Instability is reached because the value $f'(x_1^*)$ passes through the value -1.

Exercises

2.5 Consider the CUBIC #2 MAP of exercise 2.3. Using elementary algebra, solve the fixed point equation, and show that there is only one fixed point ($x_0^* = 0$) for $0 \leq r < \sqrt{3}$, but that there are two fixed points when $\sqrt{3} < r \leq 4.5$. Give a formula for the new point x_1^*.

---

[12]Of course the other solution is relevant if we remove the restriction $0 \leq x \leq 1$. In fact, its properties for $0 \leq r \leq 1$ are germane to the question of how the stability of both fixed points changes at $r = 1$, even in the present case.

2.6 Consider the CUBIC #1 MAP of equation (2.5). Using elementary algebra, solve the fixed point equation, and show that there is only one fixed point $(x_0^* = 0)$ for $0 \le r < 64/27$, but that there are three fixed points for $64/27 \le r \le 4$. Give a formulae for the new pair $x_{\pm}^*$.

2.7 Consider the CUBIC #1 MAP map, whose fixed points were found in the previous exercise. Use the GRAPHICAL ANALYSIS window of CHAOS FOR JAVA[13] to tabulate $x_{\pm}^*$ and $f'(x_{\pm}^*)$ for values of $r = 2$ to $r = 4$ in steps of 0.1. Use your data to graph the position of the fixed points in the x-r plane and indicate where they are stable and where they are unstable, using (for example) a blue or red pen when joining the points.[14]

2.8 Consider the CUBIC #2 MAP map, whose fixed points were found in exercise 2.5. Using elementary calculus, derive a formula for $f'(x_1^*)$ as a function of r, and show that x_1^* is stable for $\sqrt{3} < r < 2\sqrt{3}$ and unstable for $2\sqrt{3} < r \le 4.5$.

2.9 The SINE MAP was investigated in exercise 1.1 using the ITERATE(1D) window of CHAOS FOR JAVA.

(i) Show that it has a single fixed point $x_0^* = 0$ for $q < 1/\pi$, and that when $q > 1/\pi$ there is an additional non-zero fixed point given as the solution to the transcendental equation $x^* = q \sin \pi x^*$ (which has no explicit solution in simple form).

(ii) Show that x_0^* is stable for $q < 1/\pi$, unstable for $1/\pi < q \le 1$.

(iii) Use the GRAPHICAL ANALYSIS window of CHAOS FOR JAVA to tabulate the fixed point x_1^* and the derivative value $f'(x_1^*)$, for values of $q = 0.3$ to $q = 1.0$ in steps of 0.05.

(iv) Use your data to graph the position of the fixed points x_0^*, x_1^* in the x-q plane, and indicate where they are stable and where they are unstable.

2.10 The CUBIC #3 MAP was defined in exercise 2.4. Obviously it has three fixed points, $x_0^* = 0$ and $x_{\pm}^* = \pm 1$. Show that x_0^* is stable for $0 \le p < 2$, unstable for $2 < p \le 4$. Show also that $x_{\pm}^*$ are unstable for all $p > 0$.

---

[13] Appendix A.5 has details of using the GRAPHICAL ANALYSIS window for this purpose.
[14] This is an example of a *bifurcation diagram*, the subject of the next chapter.

2.11 The logistic map with $r = 2$ has a stable fixed point $x_1^* = 1/2$. Using elementary algebra, show that the distance $\delta_k = x_k - x_1^*$ behaves as $\delta_{k+1} = K\delta_k^2$, and find the constant K. Explain why the convergence is so extraordinarily fast[15] for this particular value of r.

2.12 At $r = 3$ the fixed point $x_1^* = 2/3$ of the logistic map is marginally stable, and the derivative test does not determine its stability.

(i) Show that

$$\delta_{k+1} = -\delta_k + 3\delta_k^2,$$

which shows that the iterations oscillate from side to side while getting slowly closer. Using this result, show further that

$$\delta_{k+2} \approx \delta_k - 12\delta_k^3,$$

which indicates how extraordinarily slow convergence is.

(ii) To make further progress, notice that δ_k varies only slowly with increasing k, so one can treat the equation approximately as a differential equation, with k as a continuous variable, and $(\delta_{k+2} - \delta_k) \approx 2d\delta/dk$. Show that this gives

$$\frac{d\delta}{dk} \approx -6\delta^3,$$

and that the solution is

$$\frac{1}{12\delta^2} \approx k - K,$$

where K is a constant of integration. This implies the *scaling relation* $\delta \approx k^{-1/2}$, $k \to \infty$.

(iii) Use the ITERATE(1D) window of CHAOS FOR JAVA to observe the convergence of iterations for $r = 3$. By zooming in on the vertical scale and making measurements, verify the scaling relation just derived.

2.3   Some orbits of the tent map

For the tent map (2.3) with $0 \leq t \leq 1$, one solution of the fixed point equation is $x_0^* = 0$. The derivative is $f'(0) = 2t$, so x_0^* is stable for $0 \leq t < 1/2$ and unstable for $1/2 < t \leq 1$. For $t > 1/2$, there is an additional solution given by the intersection of the lines $y = x$ and $y = 2t(1 - x)$ (see equation (2.3)). The solution is

$$x_1^* = \frac{2t}{1 + 2t}, \qquad t \geq 1/2. \tag{2.11}$$

---

[15] This is known as *quadratic convergence*.

There is a vital point to note if you are going to avoid serious problems when finding formulae for fixed points. The solution is obtained by equating two formulae, that is, by solving $x^* = 2t(1 - x^*)$. Now the two lines intersect, at the point (2.11), for every value of t in the range $0 \leq t \leq 1$. However, the formula $f(x) = 2t(1 - x)$ used for the tent map only applies if $x \geq 1/2$, so this restriction must also be applied to the solution x_1^*. The condition $x_1^* \geq 1/2$ is equivalent to $t + 1/2 \leq 2t$, or $t \geq 1/2$, so all is well provided we use the formula correctly. As for stability,

$$f'(x_1^*) = -2t, \qquad t > 1/2.$$

It follows that x_0^* and x_1^* are both unstable for $1/2 < t \leq 1$. Note that if $t = 1/2$, the derivative test does not apply,[16] because the tent map is not differentiable at $x = 1/2$.

Unstable orbits

For $0 \leq t < 1/2$, any point x_0 in the interval $0 < x_0 \leq 1/2$ is attracted to the fixed point $x_0^* = 0$. If it is in the interval $1/2 \leq x_0 \leq 1$, it is mapped immediately to a value x_1 in the interval $0 \leq x_1 < 1/2$, after which it is attracted to $x_0^* = 0$.

As the value of t is increased, the tent map makes a sudden transition from total stability to total instability. If $1/2 < t \leq 1$, any point x_0 in the interval $0 < x_0 < 1/2$ is repelled by the fixed point x_0^*, steadily increasing in value by the factor $2t > 1$ until it attains a value $\geq 1/2$. At this juncture it is in the interval $1/2 \leq x \leq t$, where the map is defined by a different formula.[17]

What is its fate under subsequent iteration? The fixed point x_1^* is itself in the interval $1/2 < x_1^* < t$ with $f'(x_1^*) = -2t < -1$. Therefore the iterations alternate from one side of x_1^* to the other while getting further away, each time by the factor $2t > 1$. However, f is a decreasing function for $1/2 < x_1^* \leq t$, and its minimum value on this interval is

$$f(t) = 2t(1 - t) < 1/2.$$

So the iteration must eventually escape back to $x < 1/2$.

To put all this together, first define two intervals[18]

$$I_1 = [2t(1 - t), 1/2), \qquad I_2 = [1/2, t].$$

Then I have shown that, for any starting point except the fixed points x_0^* and x_1^*, or the end point $x = 1$, the iterations will be attracted into I_1

---

[16] If $t = 1/2$, any $0 \leq x \leq 1/2$ is marginally stable, but not asymptotically stable.

[17] The case $t = 1$ is somewhat special because any orbit which attains the value $1/2$ will go to the unstable fixed point 0 (via the value 1) and remain there for all time.

[18] Recall footnote 4 on page 16 for the convention on writing intervals of the real line.

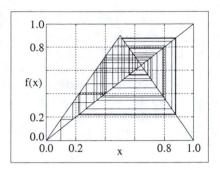

Figure 2.6: Iteration of the tent map, $t = 0.9$, $x_0 = 0.1$.

or I_2, after which they keep switching between the two; they can never stay indefinitely in either. Figure 2.6 displays 32 iterations of the tent map with $t = 0.9$, starting from $x_0 = 0.1$. The switching behaviour is seen quite clearly. The same argument applied to figure 2.2 helps explain the switching behaviour of the Lorenz attractor.

Period 2 orbit of the tent map

Consider the orbit of the tent map, with $t > \frac{1}{2}$, with initial value $x_0^* = 2t/(1 + 4t^2)$. It is easy to check[19] that that this formula gives a value in the interval $x_0^* < \frac{1}{2}$ for any $t > \frac{1}{2}$, since

$$\frac{1}{2} - x_0 = \frac{1 + 4t^2 - 4t}{2(1 + 4t^2)} = \frac{(1 - 2t)^2}{2(1 + 4t^2)} > 0.$$

After one iteration,

$$x_1^* = 2tx_0^* = \frac{4t^2}{1 + 4t^2} > \frac{1}{2}.$$

For the next iteration, $x_2^* = 2t(1 - x_1^*) = x_0^*$. So the system alternates between just two states, and the complete orbit is simply $x_0^*, x_1^*, x_0^*, x_1^*, \cdots$. This is known as a periodic, or period 2, orbit.

Now let's attempt to observe this orbit numerically for $t = 0.9$. To 9 decimal places, the formula for the orbit gives

$$x_0^* \approx 0.424528302, \qquad x_1^* \approx 0.764150943. \tag{2.12}$$

I have shown in figure 2.7 what ITERATE(1D) window of CHAOS FOR JAVA finds. The left hand picture uses the initial value $x_0 = 0.424528302$ from (2.12), the right hand one $x_0 = 0.424528303$, a change of one unit in the

---

[19]This check is essential so as to decide the correct formula to use for $f(x_0^*)$.

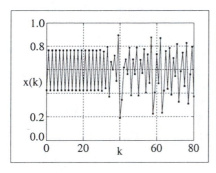 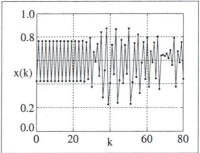

Figure 2.7: Iteration of the tent map with $t = 0.9$, starting near an unstable period 2 orbit: $x_0 = 0.424528302$ (left), $x_0 = 0.424528303$ (right).

ninth decimal place. After about 30 iterations the numerically computed orbits depart from periodic behaviour on a scale which one can easily distinguish in the figure, and at the end of 40 iterations they have returned to a state of apparent chaos. Furthermore, there is no discernible relationship between the two orbits once this happens, apart from the continual switching from side to side. Lorenz describes the situation as follows ([16] page 8, Lorenz' own emphasis)

> Returning to chaos, we may describe it as behaviour that *is* deterministic, or is nearly so if it occurs in a tangible system that possesses a slight amount of randomness, but does not *look* deterministic. This means that the present state completely or almost completely determines the future, but does not appear to do so. How can deterministic behaviour look random? ...almost, but not quite, identical states occurring on two occasions will *appear* to be just alike, while the states that follow, which need not be even nearly alike, will be observably different. In fact, in some dynamical systems it is normal for two almost identical states to be followed, after a sufficient time lapse, by two states bearing no more resemblance than two states chosen at random from a long sequence. Systems in which this is the case are said to be *sensitively dependent on initial conditions.*

The orbits shown in figure 2.7 differ not only in their initial states, but also in the effect of numerical error at each computational step. Because these are small ($\approx 10^{-15}$ per step in the example here) the system almost completely determines its future at each step. I shall return to a discussion of these questions on page 41, particularly the relationship between computed orbits and exact formulae.

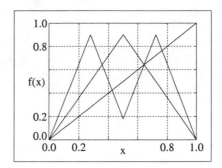

Figure 2.8: Second composition of the tent map, $t = 0.9$.

2-fold composition map

The behaviour shown in Figure 2.7 is just a manifestation of the fact that we attempted to observe an unstable orbit. Since straightforward computation fails, I turn to theoretical investigation.

Iterating the map twice results in the sequence

$$x_0 \rightarrow x_1 = f(x_0) \rightarrow x_2 = f(x_1) = f(f(x_0)).$$

I shall write a subscript to denote the function of a function $f(f(x))$ or *function composition* $(f \circ f)(x)$, i.e.,

$$f_2(x) = f(f(x)) = (f \circ f)(x),$$

and call it the *second composition* of the map f. The notation $(f \circ f)$ is more precise, but I prefer to use f_2 in anticipation of the fact that we shall need n-fold compositions; f_n is much easier to write, and work with, than $(f \circ f \circ \cdots \circ f)(x)$.

The importance of this new map follows from the following observations:

(i) Fixed points of f must be fixed points of f_2: if $f(x^*) = x^*$, then

$$f_2(x^*) = f(f(x^*)) = f(x^*) = x^*.$$

(ii) If x_1^* is a fixed point of f_2 which is not a fixed point of f, then $x_2^* = f(x_1^*)$ has the same property. To see that, note that

$$f_2(x_2^*) = f_2(f(x_1^*)) = f(f_2(x_1^*)) = f(x_1^*) = x_2^*.$$

(iii) Pairs of fixed points of f_2, x_1^*, $x_2^* = f(x_1^*) \neq x_1^*$ are period 2 orbits, since

$$f(x_2^*) = f_2(x_1^*) = x_1^*.$$

To visualise the second composition of the tent map with $t > 1/2$, divide the interval $[0, 1]$ into left (L) and right (R) half intervals. For x in L, $f(x) = 2tx$, which takes its values in L, as x increases from 0 to $1/4t$, and then in R. So $f_2(x) = f(2tx)$ at first increases from 0 to a maximum value $f(1/2) = t$, and then decreases to the value $f(t)$. Similarly, when x is in R, $f(x) = 2t(1 - x)$ which decreases from t to 0, and $f_2(x)$ runs through its values in the reverse direction: first increasing from $f(t)$ to $f(1/2)$ again, and then decreasing back to zero. The situation for $t = 0.9$ is shown in figure 2.8. We can see the fixed point and the period 2 orbit quite clearly in this graph. Moreover, we can see that the derivative of f_2' satisfies $|f_2'(x^*)| > 1$ for each of them. One also sees that there is no possibility for further periodic orbits of period 2, since there are only four fixed points of f_2. Two of these are the fixed points of f, the other two constitute the periodic orbit found above.

Exercises

2.13 Derive the formulae which define the second composition f_2 of the tent map for arbitrary $0 \le t \le 1$, carefully delineating the intervals (of x) in which each should be used. How many formulae are needed for $t \le 1/2$? How many for $1/2 < t \le 1$?

2.14 Solve for the intersection with the graph $y = x$ for each of the four formulae in the previous exercise, and show that they give the position of the two fixed points and the period 2 orbit correctly.

(i) There is nothing wrong with the formulae for $t < 1/2$, although the tent map has only the trivial fixed point x_0^* in this case. Carefully reconcile the formulae with this fact.

(ii) It is essential to try to make independent checks of formulae obtained in investigating any problem, even though one formula can be worth a ream of numerical data. Use the GRAPHICAL ANALYSIS window of CHAOS FOR JAVA to make numerical checks of your formulae for at least the values $t = 0.3$, $t = 0.6$ and $t = 0.8$.

2.15 For some values of p, the CUBIC #3 MAP has a *symmetric*[20] period 2 orbit consisting of a pair of points $(+x^*, -x^*)$, which may be found by solving the equation
$$f(x^*) = -x^*.$$

Using elementary algebra, determine a formula for x^*, and the range of parameter values for which the orbit exists.

---

[20]See exercise 2.20 for the general definition.

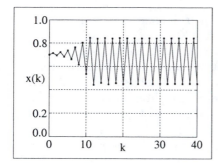 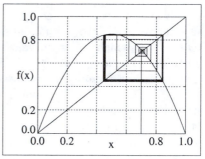

Figure 2.9: Iteration of the logistic map, $r = 3.4$, $x_0 = 0.7$, indicating possible convergence to a period 2 orbit

2.4   Period doubling of the logistic map

What happens for the logistic map when $r > 3$? Both of its fixed points are unstable in this range, but it does not behave like the tent map. Figure 2.9 shows an example of iterations of the logistic map, starting from the initial value $x_0 = 0.7$, with the parameter choice $r = 3.4$. x_0 is quite close to the fixed point $x_1^* \approx 0.7059$, but the iterations move quickly away, and appear to converge to a rectangular path on the cobweb plot — a periodic orbit of period 2. I shall show that this is indeed the case.[21] For the picture shown in figure 2.9, it is easy to find numerical values using a facility in the GRAPHICAL ANALYSIS window of CHAOS FOR JAVA for finding fixed points. They are (rounded to 5 decimal places)

$$x_-^* \approx 0.45196, \qquad\qquad x_+^* \approx 0.84215.$$

These values have the property (to within the accuracy given) $f(x_-^*) = x_+^*$, $f(x_+^*) = x_-^*$.

Formula for the orbit

Now let's find the fixed point of the second composition map $f_2(x) = f(f(x))$ of the logistic map. Substituting $f(x) = rx(1-x)$ for x into $f(x)$ itself, we get[22]

$$f_2(x) = r^2 x(1-x)(1 - rx + rx^2).$$

---

[21] As suggested by the section title, this is a phenomenon known as a *period doubling bifurcation*, a topic which is treated in detail in Chapter 3. You need to understand the present simple example thoroughly as a prelude to understanding the general case.

[22] This simple substitution is possible only because the map is defined by a single formula over the entire interval.

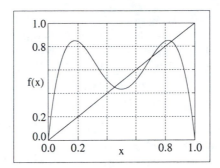

Figure 2.10: Second composition of the logistic map, $r = 3.4$.

A graph of f_2 when $r = 3.4$ is shown in figure 2.10. To find an exact formula for the fixed points, we must solve the equation $f_2(x) = x$, which is equivalent to solving the polynomial equation $\phi_2(x) = x - f_2(x) = 0$. $\phi_2(x)$ is a fourth order polynomial and we want to factor it.

Recall (page 28) that fixed points of f must be fixed points of f_2. So two factors of $\phi_2(x)$ must be x and $(x - 1 + 1/r)$, since the fixed points of f are $x_0^* = 0$ and $x_1^* = (1 - 1/r)$. Using this knowledge, or alternatively, using a computer algebra package,

$$\phi_2(x) = x(1 - r + rx)(1 + r - rx - r^2 x + r^2 x^2). \tag{2.13}$$

The new fixed points are the roots of the quadratic factor $(1 + r - rx - r^2 x + r^2 x^2)$. Calling them $x_\pm^*$, and using the formula for solution of a quadratic,

$$x_\pm^* = \frac{1 + r \pm \sqrt{r^2 - 2r - 3}}{2r}. \tag{2.14}$$

The quantity under the square root sign factors as $r^2 - 2r - 3 = (r+1)(r-3)$. It must not be negative for real solutions, which gives the condition $r \geq 3$ for the existence of the new fixed points $x_\pm^*$. So we have found the pair of points which were observed experimentally.

Stability of period 2 orbits

The investigation of the stability of period 2 orbits may be reduced to an investigation of the stability of fixed points of f_2. Suppose that x_0^*, x_1^* is a period 2 orbit of a map f which is smooth, at least in two intervals I_0 and I_1 which contain the point x_0^* and x_1^* respectively.

(i) Suppose that the orbit is stable, so that a trajectory starting from any x_0 in I_0 converges to the periodic orbit. Then the sequence of values

$x_0, x_2, x_4, \cdots$ converge to x_0^*, with the alternating values $x_1, x_3, x_5, \cdots$ converging to x_1^*. The actual orbit under consideration consists of two subsequences (the even and the odd members) each of which converges to one of the points x_0^*, x_1^*.

This shows that both points on a stable period 2 orbit are stable fixed points of the second composition map f_2.

(ii) Suppose that x_0^* and x_1^* are stable fixed points of the second composition map f_2, and that $x_1^* = f(x_0^*)$, $x_0^* = f(x_1^*)$. Suppose also that the map f is smooth in intervals I_0 and I_1 containing the two fixed points. Then we may choose an interval containing x_0^*, also contained in I_0, from which all orbits of the second composition map converge to the fixed point x_0^*. Label the points in such an orbit of f_2 as $x_0, x_2, x_4, \cdots$, and define odd-numbered points by $x_1 = f(x_0)$, $x_3 = f(x_2)$, $x_5 = f(x_4), \cdots$. Because the even numbered points are an orbit of f_2, it follows that $x_2 = f(x_1)$, $x_4 = f(x_3)$, $x_6 = f(x_5), \cdots$, that is, the totality of points thus defined are a single orbit of f. Because the map f is smooth, the odd-numbered points converge to x_1^*, so that this orbit of f converges to the period 2 orbit x_0^*, x_1^*.

This shows that a pair of stable fixed points of f_2, which map to each other under f, constitute a stable period 2 orbit of f. Note that we needed something extra (smoothness) to make the argument work in this direction.

Derivative test for period 2 orbit

Now let's apply the derivative test to the pair x_0^* and x_1^*. First we need the derivative. Recall the chain rule for a function of a function, $f(g(x))$:

$$\frac{df}{dx} = \frac{df}{dg}\frac{dg}{dx} = f'(g(x)) \cdot g'(x).$$

In the present case f and g are the same, and we get

$$f_2'(x) = f'(f(x)) \cdot f'(x).$$

Now we must find the value of f_2' at each of the two fixed points. The important fact is that $f(x_0^*) = x_1^*$, and conversely, so that

$$f_2'(x_0^*) = f'(x_1^*) \cdot f'(x_0^*) = f_2'(x_1^*). \tag{2.15}$$

This is in line with what we already know: the two fixed points together form an orbit, and since stability is a property of the orbit, not just some of its points, it must be a simultaneous property of both fixed points of f_2.

What we have here is that the derivative used to test the stability of these fixed points involves the same value at each of them, simply because they are part of an orbit. The conclusion is that a period 2 orbit x_0^*, x_1^* is stable if $|f'(x_0^*)f'(x_1^*)| < 1$ and unstable if $|f'(x_0^*)f'(x_1^*)| > 1$.

Logistic map — stability of the period 2 orbit

A simple calculation gives

$$f_2'(x_\pm^*) = 4 + 2r - r^2. \tag{2.16}$$

This is a decreasing function of r for $r > 1$. $f_2'(x_\pm) = 1$ when $r = 3$ and $f_2'(x_\pm) = -1$ when $r = 1 + \sqrt{6} \approx 3.4494897$. $f_2'(x_\pm) < -1$ for $r > 1 + \sqrt{6}$. The conclusion is that the period 2 orbit is stable in the range $3 < r < 1 + \sqrt{6} \approx 3.4494897$ and unstable beyond that point.

Exercises

2.16 Derive the formula (2.16) for $f_2'(x_\pm^*)$, and show that it is a decreasing function of r when $r > 1$. Show also that it has the stated particular values: (i) $f_2'(x_\pm^*) = 1$ if $r = 3$, (ii) $f_2'(x_\pm^*) = -1$ if $r = 1 + \sqrt{6}$. Find the value of r for which $f_2'(x_\pm^*) = 0$.

2.17 The CUBIC #3 MAP has a symmetric period 2 orbit $(+x^*, -x^*)$ found in exercise 2.15. Using equation (2.15) evaluate $f_2'(\pm x^*)$ as a function of p, and show that this orbit is stable for $2 < p < 3$ and unstable for $3 < p \le 4$. Show also that the orbit becomes unstable because $f_2'(x^*)$ passes through the critical derivative value $+1$. Compare this with the mechanism whereby the period 2 orbit of the logistic map becomes unstable.

2.18 The CUBIC #2 MAP (2.7) may be regarded as a map of the real numbers into themselves, in which case the fact that it is an antisymmetric function can be important.

(i) Show that it has a symmetric period 2 orbit $(+x^*, -x^*)$ where

$$x^* = \sqrt{1 + \sqrt{3}/r},$$

and that this orbit is unstable for all $r > 0$.

(ii) Show that the function has a local maximum at $x = 1/\sqrt{3}$, with a corresponding local minimum at $x = -1/\sqrt{3}$, and find their values.

(iii) Use this result to show that f is a map of the interval $[-x^*, x^*]$ to itself for $0 \le r \le 3\sqrt{3}$.

2.5   Periodic orbits and compositions

Definition 2.7 (Periodic orbit) *A periodic orbit of period n is a sequence $\{x_0^*, \cdots, x_{n-1}^*\}$ for which*

$$x_1^* = f(x_0^*), \quad x_2^* = f(x_1^*), \quad \cdots \quad x_{n-1}^* = f(x_{n-2}^*), \quad x_0^* = f(x_{n-1}^*),$$

with the property also that all the points are distinct from each other.

By this definition a fixed point is also a period 1 orbit.

Definition 2.8 (Stable orbit) *A periodic orbit is stable if each point on it belongs to some interval such that every orbit starting from an arbitrary point in the interval converges to the periodic orbit.*

Such an orbit will also be called a *periodic attractor*. Moreover, the set of initial values from which iterations converge to a periodic attractor are called its basin of attraction.

Definition 2.9 (Composition of a map) *The n-fold composition f_n of the map f is defined inductively by*

$$f_n(x) = f_{n-1}(f(x)).$$

Obviously each member x_k^* of a periodic orbit is a fixed point of the n-fold composition f_n. Because of the requirement that all the points be distinct, they cannot be fixed points of any composition f_m for which $m < n$. This gives an alternative method of defining a periodic orbit; any fixed point x^* of the n-fold composition f_n, which is not a fixed point of f_m for all $m < n$, generates a period n orbit.

The definitions may be used to construct a catalogue of the number of periodic orbits of a map. As an example, a table of periodic orbits of the logistic map is given in table 2.1. The second column gives the number of fixed points of f_n, obtained using CHAOS FOR JAVA; the next is the number of fixed points which belong to periodic orbits of period $m < n$ where m divides n. The difference between the two, which must be a multiple of n, is the number of fixed points which belong to period n orbits, as given in the last two columns.

Derivative of f_n

It is obvious that the arguments relating the stability of period 2 orbits with the stability of the corresponding fixed points of f_2 will extend to period n orbits and the stability of the corresponding fixed points of f_n. We need a general formula for the derivative of an n-fold composition f_n. It is quite

n	fixed points	period $m < n$	new points	period n
1	2	–	2	2
2	4	2	2	1
3	2	2	–	–
4	8	4	4	1
5	2	2	–	–
6	16	4	12	2
7	2	2	–	–
8	32	8	24	3

Table 2.1: Table of orbits, LOGISTIC MAP, $r = 3.7$.

simple: if $x_i, x_{i+1}, \cdots, x_{i+n-1}$ are n successive iterates of the map starting with x_i, then

$$f'_n(x_i) = \prod_{j=0}^{n-1} f'(x_{i+j}) = f'(x_i) \cdot f'(x_{i+1}) \cdots f'(x_{i+n-1}). \qquad (2.17)$$

This is the product of derivatives of f at each of the n successive places visited, starting from x_i.

The demonstration of this claim uses mathematical induction. I shall show that if it is true for some number n, then it is true for the next number $n + 1$. It has already been proved for $n = 2$ (page 32). For $n = 3$, $f_3(x) = f_2(f(x))$, and the chain rule for differentiation gives

$$f'_3(x_i) = f'_2(f(x_i)) \cdot f'(x_i) = f'_2(x_{i+1}) \cdot f'(x_i) = f'(x_{i+2}) \cdot f'(x_{i+1}) \cdot f'(x_i).$$

For arbitrary n, $f_n(x) = f_{n-1}(f(x))$ and the same argument gives

$$\begin{aligned} f'_n(x_i) &= f'_{n-1}(f(x_i)) \cdot f'(x_i) \\ &= f'_{n-1}(x_{i+1}) \cdot f'(x_i) \\ &= f'(x_{i+n-1}) \cdots f'(x_{i+1}) \cdot f'(x_i), \end{aligned}$$

as required.

It follows from the formula for $f'_n(x)$ that points on a periodic orbit all have the same stability, since the values of the derivatives $f'(x_i^*)$ which go into the calculation of $f'_n(x_i^*)$ are evaluated at precisely every point of the periodic orbit, each once and once only. This is independent of where we start on the orbit, because it is periodic. So we have a simple derivative test: a periodic orbit is stable, or unstable, according as the product of the derivatives $f'(x_i^*)$ taken over the orbit has magnitude less than, or greater than, unity.

Exercises

2.19 Use the GRAPHICAL ANALYSIS window of CHAOS FOR JAVA to make a table of the orbits of the TENT MAP for $t = 0.9$ up to period 8.

2.20 From exercise 2.4 we know that if $x_0, x_1, \cdots$ is an orbit of the CUBIC #3 MAP (2.8) then so is $-x_0, -x_1, \cdots$. This allows us to classify periodic orbits of an antisymmetric map: they are *symmetric* if they have the property that whenever x^* is a point on the orbit, so is $-x^*$.

(i) Show that the n-fold compositions of the CUBIC #3 MAP are antisymmetric, $f_n(-x) = -f_n(x)$.

(ii) Show that for a period n orbit to be symmetric, n must be an even integer.

(iii) Writing $n = 2m$, show further that for any point x_i^* on such an orbit, $x_{i+m}^* = -x_i^*$.

2.21 If B is a basin of attraction of a fixed point x^*, then for any x in B, $f_n(x) \to x^*$ as $n \to \infty$. Graphically this means that B appears, in the graph of f_n, as horizontal line segments at height x^*, for sufficiently large n.

(i) Use the GRAPHICAL ANALYSIS window of CHAOS FOR JAVA to simultaneously view f and f_n for the logistic map at $r = 2.5$, for increasing values n. What basin of attraction does this indicate for the fixed point?

(ii) Repeat the experiment for $r = 3.3$. What basins do you observe, and what is the basin of attraction of the period 2 orbit?

(iii) Repeat for $r = 3.5699456$, selecting[23] $n = 2, 2^2, \cdots 2^{15} = 32768$. Pay particular attention to the fixed point near to $x = 0.5$, zooming in to see the detail.

2.22 This exercise is similar to the previous one, but involves the CUBIC #1 MAP of equation (2.5), whose fixed points were found in exercise 2.6.

(i) Use the GRAPHICAL ANALYSIS window of CHAOS FOR JAVA to simultaneously view f and f_n at $r = 3$, for increasing values n. What basin of attraction does this indicate for the fixed points?

(ii) What rôle does the unstable fixed point of f appear to play in this?

---

[23] The reason for these choices will become clear in section 3.5.

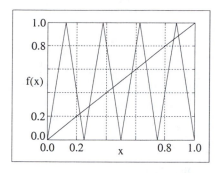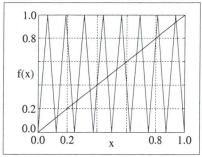

Figure 2.11: Third and fourth compositions of the tent map at the maximum parameter value $t = 1$.

2.6 The fully chaotic tent map

For the tent map with $t = 1$, the graph of f_2 is a double tent. It is easy to analyse this case. Each of the two intervals $L = [0, 1/2]$ and $R = [1/2, 1]$ is mapped to the whole interval $[0, 1]$ under the first (inner) mapping of $f(f(x))$, so there is a complete tent on each half. The difference between the present case with $t = 1$, and the earlier more general discussion for $1/2 < t < 1$, is that the new maxima and minima are all 0 and 1.

Similarly, for f_3 we get four copies of the tent map, each one-quarter of the original length, since the inner mapping sends each of L and R to the entire interval, after which f_2 acts to produce a double tent on each. The general picture is clear: the graph of f_n has 2^{n-1} replicas of the tent map, consisting of 2^n straight line segments which join alternating values of 0 and 1. Examples for $n = 3$ and 4 are displayed in figure 2.11.

Periodic orbits of the tent map

Remember that I am restricting this analysis to the case $t = 1$. It is clear from the foregoing that the n-fold composition f_n has 2^n fixed points, of which one is $x_0^* = 0$. For $n = 1$ there are two period 1 orbits, $x_0^* = 0$ and $x_1^* = 2/3$. Since f_2 has four fixed points, of which two are new, the new pair is a single period 2 orbit, $(2/5, 4/5)$.

Now consider $n = 3$. f_3 has eight fixed points. Of the previous n values considered, only $m = 1$ divides $n = 3$; so only two fixed points are among these eight. The other six must therefore be two period 3 orbits. In fact they are given by $(2/9, 4/9, 8/9)$ and $(2/7, 4/7, 6/7)$, as you can easily check.

For $n = 4$, there are 16 fixed points, of which two belong to $n = 1$ and two more to $n = 2$. This leaves 12 points, which must constitute three distinct period 4 orbits. One of them is $(2/17, 4/17, 8/17, 16/17)$, and I leave it as an exercise to find the other two.

For arbitrary n, we see from this pattern that there is at least one period n orbit, given by the sequence $(2/(2^n + 1), 4/(2^n + 1), \cdots, 2^n/(2^n + 1))$. However, there will be many more. The important conclusion is that there are periodic orbits of every period. None of these periodic orbits contains the point 0, $1/2$ or 1, so the derivative test applies. But $f'(x^*) = \pm 2$, giving $f'_n(x^*) = \pm 2^n$, and they are all unstable. This is one of the hallmarks of chaos — infinitely many unstable periodic orbits.

Dense periodic and eventually periodic orbits

I turn now to another important property of these unstable orbits: they are *dense* in the state space. By this I mean that, for any choice x_0 of initial state, and any choice of a distance δ, no matter how small, there are points on unstable orbits within the distance δ of x_0.

Not all of these orbits are periodic. Consider the orbit which commences from the initial value $x_0 = 5/9$; the iterations go as follows:

$$5/9 \xrightarrow{f} 8/9 \xrightarrow{f} 2/9 \xrightarrow{f} 4/9 \xrightarrow{f} 8/9 \cdots$$

We see that, although $5/9$ is not on a periodic orbit, the iterations join a period 3 orbit after just one step.

Definition 2.10 (Eventually periodic orbit) *An orbit which joins a periodic orbit after a finite number of iterations, but which is not a periodic orbit, is called an eventually periodic orbit.*

Next, consider any rational number in the interval $0 < x < 1$; that is, $x = m/n$ where $0 < m < n$. Since $t = 1$, $f(m/n)$ is given by either $2m/n$ (if $m \leq 2n$) or $2(n - m)/n$ (if $m > 2n$). The point is that x is mapped to another rational number with the same denominator. Since there are only $n - 1$ rationals in the interval $(0, 1)$ with denominator n, we conclude that every rational number is either on a periodic orbit, or on an eventually periodic orbit. Again, consider any irrational number in the interval $0 < x < 1$; that is, $x \neq m/n$ for any integers m, n. Then $(1 - x)$ and $f(x)$ are also irrational numbers, so orbits of rational and irrational numbers are quite distinct.

Orbits of irrational numbers cannot be periodic. To see this, notice that after each iteration, x_k is mapped either to $x_{k+1} = 2x_k$ or $x_{k+1} = 2 - 2x_k$, both of which are integer linear combinations of x_k. So, after n iterations, where n is the period, we have

$$x_n = \pm 2^n x_0 + N = x_0,$$

for some integer N. Solving for x_0 gives

$$x_0 = \frac{N}{1 \mp 2^n}, \qquad (2.18)$$

which is a rational number. It follows also that irrational orbits cannot be eventually periodic.

The important conclusion is that the tent map with $t = 1$ is chaotic. There are a *countable*[24] set of orbits, whose initial values are the rational numbers, all of which are eventually periodic, and an *uncountable* number of orbits, whose initial values are irrational numbers, all of which are not eventually periodic. The unstable periodic orbits lurk in the background, never being observed in simple numerical experiment, always creating chaos, nevertheless they constitute a set of *measure zero* in the totality of orbits.

One observation which I want to make at this point is that, for the purpose of computation, all numbers are rational, since computation is limited to finite numerical accuracy. This raises the question of whether one can draw any firm conclusions from numerical computation. As an interim comment, note that for computations done to 15 decimal places of accuracy, we should not expect to have numerical recurrence on a scale of less than (say) $10^{12} - 10^{14}$ iterations. But numerical experiments rarely go beyond 10^8 iterations.

Sensitive dependence and mixing

Consider the collection of all orbits which start from some interval $a < x_0 < a + \delta$. From properties proved for the composition map f_n, it is clear that there will be some integer N so that the set of values taken by f_n, as x_0 ranges through the interval $a < x_0 < a + \delta$, is the whole interval $[0, 1]$ whenever $n > N$. This happens no matter how small the interval length δ is chosen to be. It is an example of *mixing* behaviour. Nearby orbits separate by a factor 2 per iteration, but because the system is bounded this can continue only by mixing of orbits. At each iteration the interval is stretched to twice its length and then folded back on itself to fit. The consequence is that, after a sufficient number of iterations, the error is of the same order as the state variable itself. The relative error increases to 100%! The paradigm is commonly known as the baker's transformation, since it is exactly analogous to rolling and folding dough.

---

[24] Recall that a countable set is one which can be enumerated using the positive integers as index, that is, a complete list $\{a_1, a_2, \cdots\}$ of its members is possible. For example, the set of positive rational numbers m/n $(m, n > 0)$ may be listed in this way: set $a_1 = 1/1$, $a_2 = 2/1$ $a_3 = 1/3$, then list the three fractions for which $m + n = 3$, then the four for which $m + n = 4$, and so on, every member of the set appears on this list. A set is uncountable if no such enumeration is possible; it is a standard result that any interval of the real line is uncountable.

Exercises

2.23 A systematic way to look for periodic orbits of a unimodal map is to first classify them by sequences[25] $LRRRLR\cdots$ according as the x values fall to the left (L) or right (R) of the maximum of f. Thus, for the tent map with $t = 1$, there is one period 2 orbit LR and two[26] period 3 orbits LLR and LRR. Find the two period 3 orbits. (That is, let x_0 be an unknown point in L, calculate x_1, x_2, x_3 for the assumed orbit classification, then determine x_0 by the condition $x_3 = x_0$.

2.24 Investigate period 3 orbits of the tent map for arbitrary t, as follows.

(i) Use the GRAPHICAL ANALYSIS window of CHAOS FOR JAVA to investigate the behaviour of the third composition map as t is increased from $t = 1/2$ to $t = 1$. Estimate the critical value of t for which period 3 orbits first appear.

(ii) Use the method of the previous exercise to find formulae for the two types of period 3 orbit (LLR and LRR).

(iii) Using the consistency of these formulae with the assumptions made to find them, show that the critical value for the appearance of period 3 orbits is

$$t^* = \frac{1 + \sqrt{5}}{4}.$$

2.25 Find all the period 4 orbits of the tent map with $t = 1$, using the method of the previous exercises.

2.26 The graph of f_n for tent map at $t = 1$ has 2^n straight line segments, half of slope 2^n, the other half of slope -2^n.

(i) Derive the equations of each of the straight line sections.

(ii) By solving the fixed point equation for each of the above lines, give an explicit formula for the 2^n fixed points of f_n, and hence verify the result (2.18) found above for rational orbits.

---

[25] This is the idea behind the method of *symbolic dynamics*, see (for example) the book by Robinson [28]. For the tent map with $t = 1$ the dynamics can also be reduced to base 2 arithmetic; see pages 153ff. for a brief excursion into these ideas.

[26] Because of periodicity, LLR is equivalent to LRL and RLL, similarly LRR is equivalent to RLR and RRL.

2.27 Consider a "3 part" tent map[27] of the interval $[-1, 1]$ defined by the formulae

$$f(x) = \begin{cases} 3t(x + \frac{2}{3}), & (x \leq -\frac{1}{3}), \\ -3tx, & (-\frac{1}{3} \leq x \leq \frac{1}{3}), \\ 3t(x - \frac{2}{3}), & (x \geq \frac{1}{3}), \end{cases} \qquad (2.19)$$

where $0 \leq t \leq 1$.

(i) It was proved in exercise 2.4 that for an antisymmetric map, if $x_0, x_1, x_2, \cdots$ is an orbit, then so is $-x_0, -x_1, -x_2, \cdots$. Show that f is antisymmetric, so that its orbits enjoy this symmetry.

(ii) Show that there is only one fixed point for $0 < t < 1$, and investigate its stability as a function of t.

(iii) Investigate the period 2 orbits for $t = 1$, and group them according to their symmetry.

(iv) Investigate the period 2 orbits for arbitrary t, and find the critical t values at which each first appears.

2.28 Consider the TENT #3 MAP of the previous exercise, with $t = 1$.

(i) Show that f_n has 3^n fixed points.

(ii) Catalogue the periodic orbits, up to period 6, as in table 2.1.

(iii) Show that orbits are all rational or all irrational numbers, exactly as for the tent map with $t = 1$.

(iv) Show that for any initial point x_0 and for any arbitrarily small distance δ the set of orbits which originate within the interval $(x_0 - \delta, x_0 + \delta)$ eventually spread over the entire interval $[-1, 1]$.

2.7 Numerical versus exact orbits

It would be remiss to continue a synthesis of analysis and numerics without addressing the question of what relationship, if any, exists between them. This is particularly urgent, since I want to introduce two vital tools for the analysis of non-linear systems, Fourier analysis and Lyapunov exponents. Both have an appropriate theoretical basis, but in practice they are applied using extensive computation on a given system, and we need to know that

---

[27]This is the TENT #3 MAP of CHAOS FOR JAVA.

such numerical results will have some meaning. There are some general results about this question, which go under the title of *shadowing theorems*. Basically, numerically computed orbits are shadowed by exact orbits, in the sense that there are always exact orbits close to computed ones, even over long time intervals. More precisely, if $\bar{x}_0, \cdots, \bar{x}_k$ is numerically computed, with typical error at each step in the order of ϵ, then there is an exact orbit $z_0, \cdots, z_k$ for which $|\bar{x}_i - z_i| \approx \epsilon$ for $i = 0, \cdots, k$. Note that $\bar{x}_0 \neq z_0$: the shadow really is a different orbit.

Such a statement is not as strong as one might like, but at least it says that numerics do approximate some actual behaviour of the mathematical model under study. For example, our earlier unsuccessful attempt (page 27) to reproduce an unstable period 2 orbit numerically produced something which was close to an actual orbit, but not close to the period 2 orbit we set out to find.

Accumulation of errors for the tent map

Suppose that x_k is an orbit of the tent map with $t = 1$, that is, it exactly satisfies

$$x_{k+1} = \begin{cases} 2x_k, & (x_k \leq \frac{1}{2} \\ 2 - 2x_k, & (x_k \geq \frac{1}{2}) \end{cases}$$

Let's represent our attempt to calculate this numerically by the sequence $\bar{x}_k$. The numerics begins with

$$\bar{x}_0 = x_0 + \epsilon_0,$$

where ϵ_0 is the error in representing x_0 numerically. After the first iteration

$$\bar{x}_1 = f(\bar{x}_0) + \epsilon_1,$$

where ϵ_1 is the error in calculating $f(\bar{x}_0)$. The difference between exact and numerical values has now grown to $\bar{x}_1 - x_1 = \pm 2\epsilon_0 + \epsilon_1$, and the $\pm$ sign is determined according as $\bar{x}_0 < \frac{1}{2}$ or $\bar{x}_0 > \frac{1}{2}$.

After k steps we have

$$\bar{x}_k - x_k = \pm 2^k \epsilon_0 \pm 2^{k-1} \epsilon_1 \pm \cdots + \epsilon_k,$$

where the $\pm$ sign in front of each ϵ_i is determined by the number of times the iteration has involved $\bar{x}_i > \frac{1}{2}$ since that error was first introduced. We can see the difference growing rapidly until there is no apparent relationship between the two sequences — sensitive dependence on initial conditions.

An orbit in the shadow

To keep track of the source of errors, I have used the symbols ϵ_i above. But all these errors have the same numerical origin, and they will all be measured in units of some small quantity ϵ related to the computational process. The relation of x_k to x_0 is determined by the continuous function f_k. Continuity means that we may examine other exact orbits commencing from values z_0 in the vicinity of x_0, and look for a value for which z_k is close to the computed value $\bar{x}_k$, even though x_k is not close!

As a first step, if $\bar{x}_1 \neq x_1$, then it is easy to find a z_0 near to x_0 such that $\bar{x}_1 = z_1$. Furthermore, because past errors double at each iteration, the distance between z_0 and x_0 will be only about $\epsilon/2$. At the next iteration, $\bar{x}_2$ will differ from both x_2 and z_2, although for the latter the difference will only be because of the error introduced at the second step. At this point, we replace z_0 by z_0^{new}, chosen so that $\bar{x}_2 = z_2^{\text{new}}$ (which of course means that we no longer have agreement at the first iteration). To do this we must shift the second iteration by an amount of the order ϵ. Once more the magnification factor comes to the rescue with respect to the previous iterations: the shift from z_1 to z_1^{new} is in the order of $\epsilon/2$, and the shift from z_0 to z_0^{new} is in the order of $\epsilon/4$.

Now the process of finding the shadowed orbit is clear. We repeatedly refine the choice of z_0, applying at the kth step the condition

$$z_k^{\text{new}} - \bar{x}_k = 0.$$

This will involve shifting the previous z_{k-1} by about $\epsilon/2$, the previous z_{k-2} by about $\epsilon/4$, right back to a shift in the previous z_0 by about $\epsilon/2^k$. All of these shifts are cumulative, but in a controlled fashion, since

$$1 + \frac{1}{2} + \frac{1}{2^2} + \cdots + \frac{1}{2^k} < 2$$

for any k. So, for any k, we may find an exact orbit $z_0, \cdots, z_k$ which is close to the numerically computed orbit $\bar{x}_0, \cdots, \bar{x}_k$, at each step.

This argument can be made precise (by which I mean that the estimates are replaced by precise inequalities), and can be extended to a wider class of problems than just the tent map. They show that any numerically computed orbit of a wide class of maps is shadowed by a real orbit, whose distance away at each iteration is of the order of the numerical error committed at each step. However, the shadow may not be what we set out to approximate, particularly in the case of unstable periodic orbits, for which more sophisticated computational techniques are required. Moreover, since the errors depend on the computational details, so does the numerically observed orbit For example, even the difference between evaluating $rx(1-x)$ as $r \cdot x \cdot (1-x)$ or $r \cdot (x - x \cdot x)$ is sufficient to give quite different orbits for a value of r where the system is chaotic. For this reason it is vital to have some measurable quantities which depend on long term behaviour and which are not sensitive to detail which cannot be reproduced.

2.8   Fourier analysis of an orbit

Joseph Fourier introduced the technique of representing a function as a linear combination, or superposition, of trigonometric functions.[28] It applies both to continuous functions and to discrete ones. If a signal is periodic[29] then the spectrum contains the basic frequency plus integer multiples thereof — the *harmonics*. This is a familiar everyday idea, for example, in acoustics.

The discrete case is appropriate for discrete dynamical systems. The theoretical basis, which depends on the discrete orthogonality of the sine and cosine functions, is probably unfamiliar to you, even if you have studied the topics of Fourier series and/or integrals elsewhere. But it is easy to understand the meaning of Fourier analysis, and what it says about the *frequency domain*. Since actual calculations are always done using a computer package, I shall concentrate on meaning and interpretation rather than theory, although a brief theoretical account is given in appendix B.

First, consider a period 2 orbit, with $x_k = x_0^*$ for even k, $x_k = x_1^*$ for odd k. Since $\cos \pi k = +1$ for even k and -1 for odd k, it is obvious that we can represent the orbit using just two cosine functions:

$$x_k = a_0 \cos(0) + a_{1/2} \cos\left(2\pi \cdot {}^1\!/_2 \cdot k\right).$$

I have written $2\pi \cdot {}^1\!/_2$ rather than simply π to show quite explicitly that the period 2 component of the orbit has frequency $^1\!/_2$, in the time unit of the iteration process. Formulae for the amplitudes a_0, $a_{1/2}$ are

$$a_0 = {}^1\!/_2(x_0^* + x_1^*), \qquad a_{1/2} = {}^1\!/_2(x_0^* - x_1^*).$$

From this point of view, we regard the data as having a zero-frequency component of amplitude a_0 and an oscillating component of amplitude $a_{1/2}$, whose frequency is half the frequency of iteration.

Period 4 is almost as simple. This time we need to know the behaviour of $\cos \pi k/2$ and $\sin \pi k/2$. Starting with $k = 0$ they generate the sequences

---

[28] The story of Fourier's discovery is an interesting tale of the human side of scientific research. It took him from 1807 to 1824 to bring his work to publication, despite much earlier recognition!

[29] A periodic orbit has been defined as one which repeats itself exactly after some minimum number of iterations n: $a_{k+n} = a_k$. A continuous function is periodic if it repeats itself after some minimum time T: $f(t + T) = f(t)$. However, continuous functions are not the subject of this section.

$1, 0, -1, 0, \cdots$ and $0, 1, 0, -1, \cdots$, which have period 4, or frequency $\frac{1}{4}$. From this, it is easy to work out that a period 4 orbit has the representation

$$
\begin{aligned}
x_k = a_0 &+ a_{1/4} \cos\left(2\pi \cdot \frac{1}{4} \cdot k\right) \\
&+ b_{1/4} \sin\left(2\pi \cdot \frac{1}{4} \cdot k\right) + a_{1/2} \cos\left(2\pi \cdot \frac{1}{2} \cdot k\right),
\end{aligned}
\tag{2.20}
$$

where

$$
\begin{array}{ll}
a_0 = \frac{1}{4}(x_0 + x_1 + x_2 + x_3), & a_{1/4} = \frac{1}{2}(x_0 - x_2), \\
a_{1/2} = \frac{1}{4}(x_0 - x_1 + x_2 - x_3), & b_{1/4} = \frac{1}{2}(x_1 - x_3).
\end{array}
\tag{2.21}
$$

Again the interpretation is that of frequency components, this time at one-quarter and one-half of the iteration frequency.

For a period 3 orbit

$$
x_k = a_0 + a_{1/3} \cos\left(2\pi \cdot \frac{1}{3} \cdot k\right) + b_{1/3} \sin\left(2\pi \cdot \frac{1}{3} \cdot k\right),
\tag{2.22}
$$

with

$$
\begin{aligned}
a_0 &= \frac{1}{3}(x_0 + x_1 + x_2), \\
a_{1/3} &= \frac{2}{3}\left(x_0 + \cos(2\pi \cdot \frac{1}{3}) \cdot x_1 + \cos(2\pi \cdot \frac{2}{3}) \cdot x_2\right), \\
b_{1/3} &= \frac{2}{3}\left(\sin(2\pi \cdot \frac{1}{3}) \cdot x_1 + \sin(2\pi \cdot \frac{2}{3}) \cdot x_2\right).
\end{aligned}
\tag{2.23}
$$

This follows after substituting the previous formulae (2.22) for x_k into the right hand sides of (2.23) and then using the values of the trigonometric functions:

$$
\begin{array}{ll}
\sin \frac{2\pi}{3} = \sqrt{3}/2, & \cos \frac{2\pi}{3} = -\frac{1}{2}, \\
\sin \frac{4\pi}{3} = -\sqrt{3}/2, & \cos \frac{4\pi}{3} = -\frac{1}{2}.
\end{array}
$$

General representation

There are general principles emerging from these simple examples.

(i) From an orbit of length N we expect to be able to calculate the coefficients of about $N/2$ cosine functions and about $N/2$ sine functions by solving N linear equations for N unknowns.

(ii) The observable frequency components will be in the range 0 to $\frac{1}{2}$, since we cannot observe periodic components whose variation is faster than that in a discrete process.

That is, it is a reasonable hypothesis that if we have a data set x_k, $k = 0, \cdots, N-1$, there is a trigonometric representation

$$
x_k = \sum_m \left[a_{m/N} \cos\left(2\pi \cdot \frac{m}{N} \cdot k\right) + b_{m/N} \sin\left(2\pi \cdot \frac{m}{N} \cdot k\right) \right],
\tag{2.24}
$$

where the sum is taken over $0 \leq m \leq N/2$.

From now on I assume that N is an even number, so that the maximum value of m is $N/2$, an integer. This is no real restriction, since we shall make N large in typical computations, and there are other reasons to make N divisible by small numbers, particularly powers of 2. The frequencies which may be detected in a finite-length sample (even N) are

$$m/N = {}^0\!/_N, {}^1\!/_N, {}^2\!/_N, \cdots, {}^1\!/_2,$$

that is, a discrete set of frequencies from 0 to $1/2$ in steps of $1/N$.

Amplitude and phase

Observe that terms with frequency m/N come in sine and cosine pairs, except for the frequencies 0 and $1/2$. The precise reasons are given in appendix B; briefly it comes from the fact that if an even number of points are equally spaced around a circle, all but two of them will be symmetrically placed with respect to an axis of symmetry drawn through a selected diametrically opposite pair.

Using the trigonometric identity $\cos(\theta - \phi) = \cos\theta\cos\phi + \sin\theta\sin\phi$, such pairs may always be combined to single cosine terms, with amplitude $A_{m/N} = \sqrt{a_{m/N}^2 + b_{m/N}^2}$ and phase $\phi_{m/N}$, to give a simpler general form than equation (2.24), namely

$$x_k = \sum_m A_{m/N} \cos\left(2\pi \cdot m/N \cdot k - \phi_{m/N}\right). \tag{2.25}$$

I spare the details; the point is that it is possible. I shall use the representation by amplitude and phase, since they give independent information which have quite different significance. In fact, we shall be interested solely in the amplitude when analysing orbits of dynamical systems.

Periodic extension

Suppose we take a sample of length N from an arbitrary, but longer, orbit, compute the amplitudes and phases, then try to use this spectral data to reconstruct the original data. What do we get? The answer is that we can reconstruct, from the spectral data, a period N orbit which agrees exactly (or at least to within numerical error) with the sample data itself, but has no necessary connection with any other point on the orbit. The reconstruction provides a *periodic extension* of the observed data.

Fourier analysis gives information about the frequency content of a given sample from a given orbit; it does not provide a mechanism for prediction,

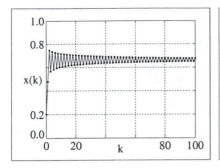 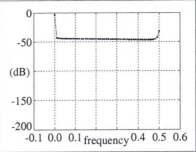

Figure 2.12: 100 iterations of the logistic map, $r = 2.99$, $x_0 = 0.2$, and the Fourier amplitudes of the same 100 points.

particularly of unstable or chaotic orbits! Furthermore, since the information content comes solely from the sample, it is important to work with sufficiently large samples so as to get reliable results.

Logarithmic amplitude scale

In a typical calculation, there will be significant amplitudes which are very small compared with the largest one — typically ratios as small as $10^{-8} \sim 10^{-12}$ can affect interpretation of the spectrum. In order to see such information on a graph, it is necessary to display the amplitudes using a logarithmic scale. There is an established unit of measurement for this purpose:

Definition 2.11 (Decibel) *If A is a positive number, then its decibel (dB) value is calculated as $20 \log A$, where the logarithm is taken to the base 10.*

Since $\log 2 \approx 0.3$, each doubling or halving of an amplitude shows up as an increase or decrease of about 6dB on this scale. Now let's look at some actual computations.[30]

First, figure 2.12 shows the spectrum[31] generated by the first 100 iterations of the logistic map, starting from $x_0 = 0.2$, with $r = 2.99$, alongside the actual iterations. Because r is close to the critical value $r = 3$, convergence is quite slow.

(i) Observe that the zero-frequency component is dominant. This is in accordance with the fact that the map has a stable fixed point ≈ 0.66 at this value of r.

---

[30] See appendix A.4 for documentation on the FOURIER ANALYSIS window.

[31] For visual clarity, the frequency scale is chosen from -0.1 to 0.6. When interpreting such figures remember that possible frequencies are restricted to the range 0.0 to 0.5.

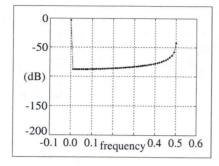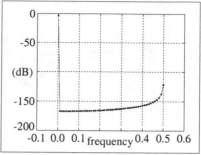

Figure 2.13: Fourier analysis of 100 iterations of the logistic map, $r = 2.99$, $x_0 = 0.2$, showing the effect of first discarding 100 points (left) and 1000 points (right). Compare with figure 2.12.

(ii) There is a pronounced period 2 transient, which is reflected by an obvious peak in the spectrum at the corresponding frequency 1/2.

(iii) All frequency components are significant, due to the fact that the state of the system is one of continual significant change during this initial phase.

Second, figure 2.13 shows the effect of waiting some time for the iterations to approach the fixed point more closely. Both examples use the previous sample size of 100 points, the first after discarding 100 iterations, the second after discarding 1000. It is evident that the Fourier amplitudes are converging to a state where only A_0 is non-zero, as should be.

Fast Fourier Transform

Calculating each of the $N/2$ coefficients $A_{m/N}$ and $\phi_{m/N}$ requires a sum over all N values x_k. This seems to imply a calculation whose time increases proportionally to N^2. The *Fast Fourier Transform* (FFT) algorithm is a particularly clever and efficient way of building up the computation using a *divide and conquer* strategy, which requires an amount of computation which grows only in proportion to $N \ln N$, a dramatic improvement for large sample sizes. Some details are given in appendix B.

For real efficiency the FFT requires that N have only small prime numbers as divisors. The most efficient choice is to make N a power of 2. For example, if $N = 2^m$, the FFT requires m recursive steps, for each of which the number of calculations is proportional to N, giving a total count proportional to $Nm \approx N \ln N$. There are, however, other important factors to be taken into account when selecting sample sizes.

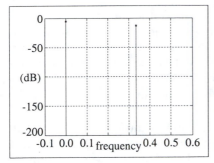 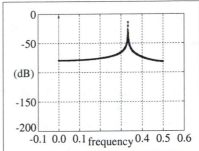

Figure 2.14: Fourier amplitudes of iterations of the logistic map, $r = 3.83$, $x_0 = 0.2$. An initial 10^6 iterations are discarded to ensure convergence. Sample sizes are 4050 points (left) and 4000 points (right). The importance of the sample size is clearly seen: the attractor is a period 3 orbit.

Sample sizes

Selecting a sample from an orbit involves two factors:

(i) The initial part of the orbit will, in most cases, be discarded. This is particularly important if the investigation is in connection with an attractor: almost certainly the chosen initial condition will not be on, or even near to, the attractor so an initial transient must be discarded.

(ii) The sample size must also be selected with care. If it suspected that the orbit is not periodic, several thousand points are recommended. In case there is a particular period n associated with the orbit, it is very important to choose a sample size which is a multiple of n. This consideration always overrides the use of a power of 2 — efficiency is never as important as drawing the correct conclusion!

The first point was already discussed in connection with figures 2.12 and 2.13, and requires no further comment. The importance of the second point is clearly seen in the two spectra shown in figure 2.14. Both are taken for the logistic map with $r = 3.83$, at which value it has a stable period 3 orbit. Both have discarded the first 10^6 iterations to make absolutely certain of convergence. The left hand picture leaves no doubt about the period 3 behaviour, with the only non-zero amplitudes being A_0 and $A_{1/3}$. The right hand picture is not so clear. The difference between the two is that 3 divides 4050, but not 4000. The point is that, if the sample size is not an exact multiple of 3, then the data cannot be fitted exactly using only the frequencies 0 and $1/3$.

The lesson is clear. If, as the result of Fourier analysis, exact periodic behaviour is suspected but not completely clear, then the question might be resolved by making sure that the sample size is divisible by that period. In the above example, the error is due to the fact that two of the points on the orbit are sampled 1333 times, the other 1334. Observe that $20 \log 1/1333 \approx -63$dB, which fits quite well the order of magnitude of the observed non-zero frequency components.

One final important comment. It is often a cause of confusion that the spectrum of a periodic orbit does not seem to include all of the expected frequencies. For example, in figure 2.14 (left) one might expect to find three spikes at frequencies 0, $1/3$ and $2/3$, to indicate period three. This cannot be; $2/3 > 1/2$ which is the maximum observable frequency in a discrete system. Similarly, for the period 7 orbit observed on page 111 of chapter 4 there are only four spikes, at the frequencies 0, $1/7$, $2/7$, $3/7$.

Exercises

2.29 Solve equation (2.21) for $x_0, \cdots, x_3$ in terms of a_0, $a_{1/4}$, $b_{1/4}$ and $a_{1/2}$ and verify that this agrees with (2.20). Repeat for the period 3 example of equation (2.22).

2.30 Give a quantitative explanation of the Fourier amplitudes of figure 2.13, by looking at the typical order of magnitude of the decaying oscillation using the ITERATE(1D) window of CHAOS FOR JAVA, and converting this to dB.

2.31 Use the FOURIER ANALYSIS window of CHAOS FOR JAVA to provide evidence that the TENT MAP at $t = 0.6$ has a strong period 2 component, but is not exactly periodic. Using the GRAPHICAL ANALYSIS and/or ITERATE(1D) windows, give a description of what is actually occurring. Repeat the investigation for $t = 0.55$.

2.32 Use the FOURIER ANALYSIS window of CHAOS FOR JAVA to determine what periodic or near periodic behaviour is exhibited by the LOGISTIC MAP for values of r just below, and just above, the critical value $1 + \sqrt{8} \approx 3.82842712475$. Catalogue the sequence of stable periodic orbits which you can find between this value of r and $r = 3.85$.

2.33 Use the FOURIER ANALYSIS window of CHAOS FOR JAVA to determine what periodic or near periodic behaviour is exhibited by the CUBIC #3 MAP (2.8) for values of p just below, and just above, the critical value $1 + \sqrt{8} \approx 3.82842712475$.

2.9 Lyapunov exponent of an orbit

I have shown that stability of periodic orbits of a map f is measured by the derivative f'. In general, if x_0^* is the initial point of an orbit, and if we start the system from a nearby point x_0 whose distance from x_0^* is δ_0, then after one iteration the distance between the two is approximated by

$$\delta_1 \approx |f'(x_0^*)|\delta_0 = M_0 \cdot \delta_0.$$

M_0 is the magnification factor for this step. At the next step

$$\delta_2 \approx |f'(x_1^*)|\delta_1 = M_1 \cdot \delta_1 \approx M_0 M_1 \cdot \delta_0,$$

where $M_1 = |f'(x_1^*)|$ is the magnification factor for the second iteration. Lyapunov exponents are a way to extend this to arbitrary orbits.

Periodic orbits

For a period n orbit, the total magnification factor over one cycle is the product

$$M_0 M_1 \cdots M_{n-1}.$$

Since this is an accumulation of magnification factors, it makes sense to consider the geometric average $M = (M_0 M_1 \cdots M_{n-1})^{1/n}$. For this purpose, note:

(i) Taking logarithms leads to the more common arithmetic average:

$$L = \ln M = \ln(M_0 M_1 \cdots M_{n-1})^{1/n} = \frac{1}{n} \left(\ln M_0 + \cdots + \ln M_{n-1} \right).$$

(ii) The condition for stability of a periodic orbit is that the average magnification factor should be less than 1, this is equivalent to

$$L < 0 \quad \text{(stable)}, \qquad L > 0 \quad \text{(unstable)}.$$

(iii) The average is easy to accumulate as the orbit is computed:

$$L = \frac{1}{n} \left(\ln |f'(x_0^*)| + \cdots + \ln |f'(x_{n-1}^*)| \right).$$

Arbitrary orbits

The crucial step is to extend the process of taking an average of logarithmic magnification factors to arbitrary orbits, as follows:

Definition 2.12 (Lyapunov exponent) *For a given initial point x_0, the Lyapunov exponent $L(x_0)$ of a map f is given by*

$$L(x_0) = \lim_{k \to \infty} \frac{1}{k} \sum_{i=0}^{k-1} \ln |f'(x_i)|,$$

provided the limit exists. In the case that any of the derivatives in the calculation is zero, we write $L(x_0) = -\infty$.

For an arbitrary orbit, the existence of the limit is an open question in general.

   If the orbit is periodic, then the average involves only the n points x_i^* on it; each contributes to the result according to the number of times m_i the orbit visits in the course of a large number of iterations. The Lyapunov exponent therefore has an alternative expression,

$$L(x_0^*) = \sum_{i=0}^{n-1} \frac{m_i}{k} \ln |f'(x_i^*)|.$$

Obviously the ratios m_i/k approach the limiting value $1/n$ for large k, giving,

$$L(x_i^*) = \frac{1}{n} \sum_{i=0}^{n-1} \ln |f'(x_i^*)| = \frac{1}{n} \ln |f_n'(x_i^*)|.$$

This makes it clear that the Lyapounov exponent of a periodic orbit is a property of the orbit as a whole; $f_n'(x_i^*)$ has a value independent of i. So the infinite limit does exist, at least for periodic orbits, stable or unstable.

Lyapunov exponents for basins of attraction

Suppose that we compute $L(x_0)$ for an eventually periodic orbit. This means that, after the first m iterations, we reach a point x_m which is actually on a periodic orbit. Splitting off the contribution from the first m points,

$$L(x_0) = \lim_{k \to \infty} \frac{1}{k} \left(\sum_{i=0}^{m-1} \ln |f'(x_i)| + \sum_{i=m}^{k-1} \ln |f'(x_i)| \right). \tag{2.26}$$

Clearly, in the limit of large k, the first term contributes nothing and we recover the Lyapunov exponent of the periodic orbit itself, $L(x_i^*)$.

   We can go a step further. Let x_0 be within the basin of attraction of a periodic orbit. Then the Lyapunov exponent will be exactly the same as that of the orbit itself. To show this, we must demonstrate that for any small number ϵ, no matter how small, the difference between $L(x_0)$ and

$L(x_0^*)$ is less than ϵ. Now the orbit is approaching the periodic attractor as k increases, so the differences between $\ln|f'(x_k)|$ and $\ln|f'(x_k^*)|$ are converging to zero. If we choose a number m in equation (2.26) large enough so that this difference is less than ϵ for all $k > m$, then the same consideration which we applied to the eventually periodic orbit shows that $L(x_0)$ is within ϵ of $L(x_i^*)$. The only effect of choosing a smaller ϵ is to require a larger m, but this is of no consequence with an infinite limit. This argument also shows that $L(x_0)$ is in fact defined for all orbits in the basin of attraction of a periodic orbit.

Tent map

For any orbit of the tent map which does not contain the point $x_{\max}$, where the derivative of f is not defined, we obviously have $L(x_0) = \ln 2t$. This is in accordance with the divergence of orbits for $t > 1/2$ and convergence for $t < 1/2$, already noted. In the case that $t = 1$, almost all orbits of the tent map do not attain the value $1/2$, in fact an uncountable number of them are irrational. It follows that $L(x_0) = \ln 2 \approx 0.693$ for almost all x_0. The tent map is almost unique in having a Lyapunov exponent which is easy to calculate theoretically.

Logistic map

Recall that the fixed point $x_1^* = (1 - 1/r)$ is stable in the parameter range $1 < r < 3$, and that the interval $B = (0, 1)$ is its basin of attraction. It follows that

$$L(x_0) = \ln|f'(x_1^*)| = \ln|2 - r|, \quad (0 < x_0 < 1), \quad (1 < r < 3). \quad (2.27)$$

Notice that $L \to 0$ at $r \to 1$ and $r \to 3$, $L \to -\infty$ as $r \to 2$. As for the fixed points, $L(x_0^*) = \ln|f'(x_0^*)| = \ln r$ for $0 \leq r \leq 4$, $L(x_1^*) = \ln|f'(x_1^*)| = \ln|2 - r|$ for $1 < r \leq 4$.

The 2-cycle is stable in the parameter range $3 < r < 1 + \sqrt{6}$. Using equation (2.16) we get

$$L(x_0) = \frac{1}{2}\ln|4 + 2r - r^2|, \quad (x_0 \neq x_0^*, x_1^*), \quad (3 < r < 1 + \sqrt{6}).$$

This time $L \to 0$ at $r \to 3$ and $r \to 1 + \sqrt{6}$, and $L \to -\infty$ as $r \to 1 + \sqrt{5} \approx 3.236$ (see exercise 2.16). For $r > 1 + \sqrt{6}$ there are two more points $x_{\pm}^*$ where the Lyapunov exponent has special values, $L(x_{\pm}^*) = 1/2\ln|4 + 2r - r^2|$, $1 + \sqrt{6} < r \leq 4$. Attempts to check these special values numerically will fail unless an algorithm is used which can find and track unstable orbits.

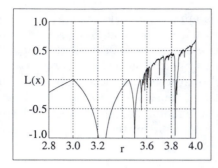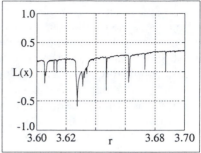

Figure 2.15: Lyapunov exponents for the logistic map, $x_0 = 0.499999$. The right hand figure is a close up of part of the left hand one. Sample size 10^3 points, initial 10^3 points discarded (left), both numbers were increased to 5×10^3 (right).

Numerical estimation

Numerical computations are made[32] by iterating the map to try to achieve convergence to any attracting set of states, after which the average value of $|\ln f'(x_i)|$ is computed over some sufficiently large sample.[33] Numerical results must be treated with caution. The use of a finite sample means that the exponent is only an estimate: once again we are exploring the infinite.

Windows of periodic behaviour are readily seen from graphs displayed in figure 2.15. However, there is also fractal structure, since there are an infinity of such windows.[34] Hints of this are seen in the pictures. Note the use of a larger sample size when constructing the closer view. The more complex the structure, and the finer the scale, the more calculation is required to see it.

Exercises

2.34 Consider the TENT #3 MAP of (2.19). Derive a formula for the Lyapunov exponent $L(x_0)$, and discuss the set of points x_0 for which it is defined.

2.35 The TENT #2 MAP, implemented in CHAOS FOR JAVA, uses a for-

---

[32] See appendix A.8 for documentation on the LYAPUNOV EXPONENTS window; A.6 for information about computing the exponent of an orbit using the ITERATE(1D) window.

[33] See page 49 for an earlier discussion of sample sizes in the context of Fourier analysis.

[34] Some consideration of this claim may be found in section 5.3.

mulae which incorporates some non-linearity

$$f(x) = \begin{cases} t\left[\frac{3}{2}x + x^2\right], & (x \leq 1/2), \\ t\left[\frac{3}{2}(1-x) + (1-x)^2\right] & (x \geq 1/2). \end{cases}$$

(i) Examine the Lyapunov exponent for this map using the LYAPUNOV EXPONENTS window of CHAOS FOR JAVA.

(ii) Derive a formula for $L(x_0)$, where x_0 is very close to 0.5, in the range $0 \leq t < \frac{1}{2}$, and also for $L(x_0)$ when $t = \frac{1}{2} + 0$, that is, $\lim_{t \to \frac{1}{2}+} L(x_0)$. Does this explain what you observe by numerical experimentation?

2.36 In this exercise we investigate some properties of the LOGISTIC MAP with $r = 4$, using CHAOS FOR JAVA.

(i) Use the GRAPHICAL ANALYSIS window of CHAOS FOR JAVA to find the values of $f'_n(x^*)$ for a few of the fixed points for $n = 1, 2, \cdots, 6$.

(ii) From these results, form a conjecture for a general formula for the derivative, and hence about the Lyapunov exponents of these unstable orbits.

(iii) Use the ITERATE(1D) window of CHAOS FOR JAVA to obtain numerical estimates of $L(x_0)$ for a couple of values and compare with the results you obtained for the periodic orbits.

2.37 Use the ITERATE(1D) window of CHAOS FOR JAVA to calculate $L(x_0)$ for the LOGISTIC MAP with $r = 4$ at a few initial points x_0, and verify that for large enough sample sizes, they appear to give the value $\ln 2$.

2.10 Chaotic orbits

Definition 2.13 (Chaotic orbits) *A chaotic orbit of a bounded system is one which is not periodic or eventually periodic, and which has positive Lyapunov exponent.*

A dynamical system will be said to be *chaotic* when it is in a regime with chaotic orbits.[35]   Actually showing that the Lyapunov exponent is positive, or even that it exists, may be a difficult problem for any particular system. Often numerical calculation is used as the main evidence, but it is important to have a theoretical analysis of some simple test cases. Note

---

[35]Some definitions of chaos include a requirement that there be a dense set of unstable periodic orbits. Here I follow the simpler path of just requiring chaotic orbits.

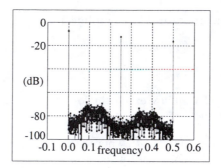

Figure 2.16: Fourier amplitudes for the logistic map, $r = 3.9615$, $x_0 = 0.4$. Sample size 2×10^3 points, initial 10^4 points discarded. There is a strong period 4 component, but the orbit is not periodic.

that the property of having a positive Lyapunov exponent implies that the orbit never falls within the basin of attraction of any periodic orbit. In case the orbit is periodic, or eventually periodic, it must be unstable.

Given a chaotic orbit starting from position x_0, then for any distance, no matter how small, there are starting points within this distance of x_0 for which the two orbits eventually separate from each other on a large scale.[36]

Numerical evidence for chaos

Fourier analysis can provide strong evidence of non-periodic behaviour. Given this, together with a positive numerically estimated Lyapunov exponent, one can be rather certain that a particular system is exhibiting chaos, even though a theoretical demonstration is not feasible.

As an example which is not completely trivial, consider the Fourier spectrum shown in figure 2.16, for the logistic map with $r = 3.9615$. The spectrum shows clear peaks at frequencies of $1/4$ and $1/2$, suggesting the possibility of a period 4 orbit. But the sample size, and the time allowed for the system to reach a stable situation, are both large, despite which there is a significant amount of what looks like noise. Nor is the noise caused by a bad choice of sample size: 2000 is divisible by 4. It is easy to estimate the Lyapunov exponent of this exact orbit using the ITERATE(1D) window of CHAOS FOR JAVA. Using the same initial value and sample size,

---

[36]The actual scale relates to the long-term accessible states of the system. For example, for the tent map with $t = 0.6$ the allowed states might be taken as the interval $[0, 1]$, but all orbits which start in $(0, 1)$ are drawn to an interval whose end points are $a \approx 0.48$, $b \approx 0.51$, which therefore contains an attractor (see exercise 2.44). For any initial separation, no matter how small, there are neighbouring initial states in this interval which lead to separations of the order of 0.03; this is the appropriate large scale.

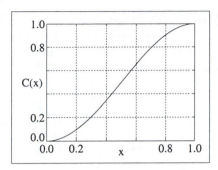

Figure 2.17: The function $C(x) = \sin^2 \frac{\pi x}{2}$.

the result is $L \approx 0.1261$, so the system is chaotic. I leave it to you to investigate precisely what is going on here.

Conjugacy of two maps

I already alluded to the difficulty of showing that Lyapunov exponents actually exist. One example for which it is easy to settle the question is the tent map with $t = 1$, for which $L(x_0) = \ln 2$ for almost all x_0. Exercises 2.36 and 2.37 indicate remarkable coincidences for Lyapunov exponents of the logistic map at $r = 4$, and also for values of f'_n at fixed points. All computed values of L are (numerically) equal to $\ln 2$, whilst at any fixed point x^* of f_n, $f'_n(x^*) = \pm 2^n$. These coincidences point to a very close connection between the two maps, which I now exhibit.

To simplify the discussion, denote the tent map with $t = 1$ by $T(x)$, and the logistic map with $r = 4$ by $R(x)$; introduce next the change of variables

$$y = C(x) = \sin^2 \frac{\pi x}{2}, \tag{2.28}$$

shown in figure 2.17. This is a one-to-one transformation of the interval $[0, 1]$ onto itself, giving a unique correspondence between values of x and y which lie in the interval. Consider the effect of applying $T(x)$ to a given x, that is,

$$x \ \rightarrow \ T(x) = \begin{cases} 2x, & (x \leq 1/2), \\ 2 - 2x, & (x \geq 1/2). \end{cases}$$

What happens to the corresponding y? If $x \leq 1/2$, then

$$\sin^2 \frac{\pi x}{2} \ \rightarrow \ \sin^2 \pi x = \left(2 \sin \frac{\pi x}{2} \cos \frac{\pi x}{2} \right)^2 = 4 \sin^2 \frac{\pi x}{2} \left(1 - \sin^2 \frac{\pi x}{2} \right),$$

that is,

$$y \ \rightarrow \ 4y(1 - y) = R(y).$$

Similarly, if $x \geq 1/2$, $\sin^2 \frac{\pi x}{2} \to \sin^2 \pi(1-x) = \sin^2 \pi x$, leading to the same result. So the evolution of x values under the tent map is equivalent to the evolution of corresponding y values under the logistic map.

Let's express this as an equation,

$$C(T(x)) = R(C(x)). \tag{2.29}$$

The left hand side says that we iterate x under T and then compute the corresponding new y value; the right hand side that we first find $y = C(x)$ and then iterate it under R. They are equivalent, and the formula is a *conjugation* of the two maps.

How about the second composition? Using the conjugation relation twice gives

$$C(T_2(x)) = C(T(T(x))) = R(C(T(x))) = R(R(C(x))) = R_2(C(x)),$$

which expresses the fact that the evolution of x under two iterations of the tent map is equivalent to the evolution of corresponding y under two iterations of the logistic map. Quite obviously we can apply this inductively, to get

$$C(T_n(x)) = R_n(C(x)). \tag{2.30}$$

Lyapunov exponents

We can use this to find derivatives, and hence Lyapunov exponents, for the logistic map at its fixed points. Differentiating the formula (2.30), each side of which is a function of a function, we get

$$C'(T_n(x)) \cdot T_n'(x) = R_n'(C(x)) \cdot C'(x). \tag{2.31}$$

In the case that we consider a period n orbit of the tent map starting from x_0^*, we have that $T_n(x_0^*) = x_0^*$, so the derivative of the C terms cancel and we get the remarkable fact that[37]

$$T_n'(x_0^*) = R_n'(y_0^*).$$

Since the Lyapunov exponent is obtained by taking the derivative and dividing by n (because of periodicity) it follows that for periodic orbits of the logistic map (with $r = 4$) it indeed has the same value as it does for the corresponding orbits of the tent map (with $t = 1$), namely $\ln 2$.

More generally, it follows that for any orbit of the logistic map starting from $y_0 = \sin^2 \frac{\pi x_0}{2}$,

$$L(y_0) = \ln 2 + \lim_{k \to \infty} \frac{1}{k} \left(\ln C'(x_k) - \ln C'(x_0) \right).$$

---

[37] If you skipped exercise 2.36, now is the time to do it.

It can be demonstrated that there are an (uncountably) infinite set of y_0 for which the correction term makes no contribution in the infinite limit, because of the factor $1/k$, although the proof is quite intricate.[38] The difficulty is that $C'(x_k)$ is very small whenever x_k is close to the ends of the interval, and the logarithm can assume large negative values in this case.

Exercises

2.38 Using the FOURIER ANALYSIS and ITERATE(1D) windows of CHAOS FOR JAVA, classify the long term behaviour of orbits of the SINE MAP, starting from $x_0 = 0.5$, for the following parameter values: $q = 0.86$, $q = 0.87$, $q = 0.88$, $q = 0.94$, $q = 0.945$, $q = 0.99827$. In each case where you find a stable periodic orbit, use the GRAPHICAL ANALYSIS window to check that the corresponding composition map has stable fixed points.

2.39 This exercise in concerned with the CUBIC #2 MAP at $r = 4.5$.

(i) Use the ITERATE(1D) window of CHAOS FOR JAVA to calculate $L(x_0)$, using sample sizes 10^6, $2 \cdot 10^6$, $5 \cdot 10^6$, 10^7, for at least four choices of initial value x_0. Are the results consistent with the hypothesis that the Lyapunov exponents converge to a common value, independent of x_0?

(ii) Use the GRAPHICAL ANALYSIS window of CHAOS FOR JAVA to locate the period 3 and period 4 orbits of the map. From the numerical data, compute the Lyapunov exponents of these orbits.

(iii) In light of the fact that the map has an infinite number of unstable periodic orbits at $r = 4.5$, how can you reconcile the numerical evidence found in these two experiments?

(iv) What result would you expect if this experiment were performed on the LOGISTIC MAP? (This should be a warning about putting too many eggs in one basket!)

2.40 We know that, in the case of the tent map and the logistic map, there is a simple formula for the derivative of f_n at a fixed point: $f_n'(x^*) = \pm 2^n$. Consider the one-dimensional maps available in the GRAPHICAL ANALYSIS window of CHAOS FOR JAVA, at the maximum allowed values of their parameter. Check that there is no such coincidence for the SINE MAP and TENT MAP. Can you find an interesting coincidence for any of the other pair of maps which are provided in CHAOS FOR JAVA?

---

[38]See chapter 3 of Alligood, Sauer and Yorke [3] for a detailed treatment.

2.41 Repeat exercise 2.37 for the CUBIC #3 MAP (2.8) with $p = 4$, and verify that for large enough sample sizes, they appear to give the value $\ln 3$ for the Lyapunov exponent.

2.42 If you have worked through examples 2.34, 2.40 and 2.41, it should be evident that the TENT #3 MAP (2.19) and the CUBIC #3 MAP (2.8) must be related at their maximum parameter values. Show that the transformation

$$y = \sin \frac{\pi x}{2},$$

gives the required conjugacy of the two.

2.11   Ergodic orbits

On page 39 I mentioned mixing for a unimodal map. This was a property of whole intervals under the evolution of the system, and as such is not easy to study experimentally.

Suppose we just take a single initial point, and observe its behaviour over a long time. For the logistic map with $r = 4$, the cobweb plot for 500 iterations shown in figure 2.18 displays a considerable degree of filling in. In fact, had I chosen to display 5000 iterations on this diagram then it would have been almost completely black to the resolution of the printing. You should examine this for yourself.

Definition 2.14 (Ergodic orbit) *An ergodic orbit has the property that every point in the set of accessible states is approached arbitrarily closely by some iteration x_k.*

More precisely, given an arbitrary $\delta > 0$, and an accessible state value $x = a$, there is at least one k such that

$$|x_k - a| < \delta.$$

Orbital density

A way to sample a single orbit over a long time is to calculate the statistics of where the iterations fall. That is, one divides the x-axis into small intervals, or *bins*, typically chosen to correspond to a single pixel at the available resolution, and records what fraction of the iterates of this single orbit falls into each bin.

More precisely, divide the interval $[0, 1]$ into a large number N of small subintervals I_k given by

$$I_k = [(k-1)/N, k/N), \qquad\qquad k = 1, \cdots, N.$$

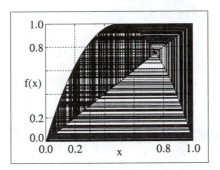

Figure 2.18: 500 iterations of the logistic map, $r = 4$.

Next, follow a single orbit of length m, and count the number of times m_k the orbit visits each I_k. Finally, define the fraction of the times the orbit visits each subinterval,

$$\mu_k = m_k/m.$$

If the process were random, we would interpret the function μ_k as an orbital probability distribution or orbital density, which is why it is normalised so that $\sum_{k=1}^{N} \mu_k = 1$.

Simple orbital densities

For the tent map with $t = 1$, it is not hard to guess[39] that the orbital density should be uniform on the interval $[0, 1]$. That is, for N equal bins,

$$\mu_k = 1/N.$$

I already discussed the equivalence of the tent map with the logistic map, given by the conjugacy transformation $y = \sin^2 \frac{\pi x}{2}$. The fraction of orbital visits of the tent map which are in the interval x to $x + \Delta x$ will be simply Δx. This fraction will fall in the interval y to $y + \Delta y$, where

$$\frac{\Delta y}{\Delta x} \approx \frac{dy}{dx} = \pi \sin \frac{\pi x}{2} \cos \frac{\pi x}{2} = \pi \sqrt{y(1 - y)}.$$

Consequently, we expect that the orbital density of the logistic map (with $r = 4$) should be given by the reciprocal of this simple expression

$$\rho(y) = \frac{1}{\pi \sqrt{y(1 - y)}}. \tag{2.32}$$

---

[39] Since a proper treatment of the general situation is well beyond the scope of the present book, I prefer just to use the obvious result at this point.

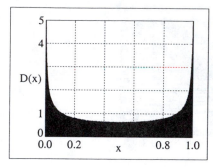 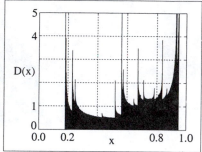

Figure 2.19: Orbital densities for the logistic map with $r = 4$ (left), $r = 3.8$ (right), initial value $x_0 = 0.2$. Sample size 10^7 points, initial 10^3 points discarded. The band edges in the second example mark points on the orbit (2.33).

Figure 2.19 (left) shows the result of sampling a single orbit of length 10^7 for the logistic map with $r = 4$. The result supports the postulated density (2.32). One sees immediately that there are two points at which the density becomes infinite; these are precisely the two values to which the critical (maximum) point $x_{\text{max}} = 1/2$ are mapped by f:

$$f(1/2) = 1, \qquad f(1) = 0.$$

Since the map has a quadratic maximum at x_{max}, images of points near x_{max} accumulate since they are much closer after iteration than before. This fact is also evident when dividing by f' to obtain equation (2.32). For this reason, an attempt to generate the density using $x_0 = 1/2$ is doomed to failure unless numerical error causes the calculation to shadow an orbit starting nearby rather than follow the exact one.

The general situation

Another orbital density for the logistic map , with $r = 3.8$, is shown in figure 2.19 (right). First note that the system is confined to an interval smaller than $[0, 1]$, the maximum is the maximum of the map, $f(0.5) = 0.95$, and the minimum is the image of this point under one iteration, $f(0.95) = 0.1805$. Within these limits there is a distribution of values, but now with an obvious complex structure, with many band edges instead of just the two observed when $r = 4$.

To understand the structure, consider the orbit generated by $x_0 = x_{\text{max}}$.

The first few points are

$$f(0.5) = 0.95, \quad f(0.95) = 0.1805, \quad f(0.1805) \approx 0.56209505,$$
$$f(0.56209505) \approx 0.93534798, \quad f(0.93534798) \approx 0.22979412, \qquad (2.33)$$
$$f(0.22979412) \approx 0.67255738, \quad f(0.67255738) \approx 0.83685101, \quad \cdots$$

and an inspection of the figure shows that these correspond to the most obvious band edges. Every point on the orbit generates an infinite singularity, caused by accumulation of iterates of the critical point $x_{\max}$; we expect that, in the infinite limit, such singularities will occur at a countable dense set of points as the orbit (2.33) fills the interval $[0.1805, 0.95]$. Furthermore, these singularities are generated by an unstable orbit, so the accumulation effect will be diluted at each iteration; this shows in the figure as a narrowing of the width of each successive edge.[40] The conclusion is that the density function $\rho(x)$ (should it exist!) will be particularly nasty at a dense countable set of points. This does not prevent its use as a *probability measure*, but it does put its investigation well beyond the scope of this book. For a theoretical introduction, see for example Ott [21].

Ergodic hypothesis

The question of ergodic orbits relates two distinct types of statistics which one might contemplate.

(i) In discussing mixing, I considered the evolution of all initial points lying in some interval. One method for performing statistical analysis is to assign a probability density to each subinterval, such as the function $\rho(x)$, and then compute average values with respect to this density. This kind of average is known in statistical mechanics as an *ensemble average*. It is clearly difficult to derive the necessary formulae.

(ii) One can replace the ensemble average with statistics performed on a single orbit over a long time period — the *time average*. Even this leaves difficult theoretical questions, but it does allow for simple numerical experimentation.

It is a much used assumption in equilibrium statistical mechanics that the two methods give equivalent results, an assumption known as the *ergodic hypothesis*. It would take us too far afield to follow this line of enquiry further.

---

[40]The argument for this is along the lines of the backward error analysis used in considering numerical shadowing (see page 41).

Exercises

2.43 Using the conjugacy found in exercise 2.42, together with a reasonable conjecture for the orbital density of the TENT #3 MAP (2.19) at $t = 1$, find the orbital density of the CUBIC #3 MAP (2.8) at $p = 4$. Show that it is exactly equivalent to the orbital density of the logistic map at $r = 4$, taking into account the different intervals on which the two are defined.

2.44 Recall exercise 2.31 for the TENT MAP. Using previous work plus other evidence you can assemble (such as orbital densities), make a case that the tent map has *chaotic attractors* (see page 68), even though it has no stable orbits.

2.45 If an (infinite) orbit is continuously distributed over an interval $[0, 1]$ according to some orbital density $\rho(x)$, then we might expect to compute its Lyapunov exponent as the average

$$L = \int_0^1 \ln |f'(x)| \, \rho(x) \, dx$$

(i) Evaluate this integral for the tent map at $t = 1$, assuming that $\rho(x) = 1$, and verify that it gives $L = \ln 2$.

(ii) Repeat the exercise for the logistic map at $r = 4$, using the orbital density of equation (2.32). [Hint: not surprisingly, the change of variable needed to do the integral is given by the conjugation (2.28).]

2.46 Use the ITERATE(1D) window of CHAOS FOR JAVA to examine the orbital density for the LOGISTIC MAP at $r = 4$ and CUBIC #2 MAP at $r = 4.5$, using a sample size of 10^7.

(i) What measurable differences can you find between the two.

(ii) Compare the computed Lyapunov exponents for the two maps. Do you think they are sufficiently different to support the claim that they really are different in the limit of an infinite orbit?

2.47 Use the ITERATE(1D) window of CHAOS FOR JAVA to examine the orbital density for the LOGISTIC MAP at $r = 3.8$, for large sample sizes. Try zooming in on some of the small peaks to see if their structure appears to be smooth, or if the numerics support the claim made in the text about the nasty nature of the density function.

Chapter 3

Bifurcations in one-dimensional systems

This chapter is concerned with some important aspects of bifurcations in simple one-dimensional systems. In its most general form, bifurcation theory is concerned with equilibrium solutions of nonlinear systems. In the present context the equilibrium solutions of interest are fixed points and periodic orbits, stable or unstable. Even this topic can be very technical for general non-linear discrete systems.

In chapter 2 we noted that a period 2 orbit of the logistic map first occurs at precisely the value $r = 3$ where a fixed point changes its behaviour from stability to instability. This is an example of a *bifurcation*, which involves a change in the structure of the set of periodic orbits of the map at some critical value of a parameter. The restriction to periodic orbits may appear to be rather limiting; but it turns out that they play a vital rôle in understanding chaos.

3.1 Bifurcation diagrams

The bifurcation at $r = 3$ is not the first structural change to occur for the logistic map. Earlier, two fixed points were found, given by the formulae (see page 22)

$$x_0^* = 0, \qquad x_1^* = 1 - 1/r.$$

Generally speaking, the behaviour of the system outside the interval $[0, 1]$ is not of great interest if r is in the range $0 \leq r \leq 4$, but it does have some significance for the stability properties of these two fixed points. Therefore, let's temporarily relax the condition to the weaker requirement that x is real, but continue to restrict the parameter range. As already noted, x_0^* is stable for $0 \leq r < 1$ and unstable for $1 < r \leq 4$. It is easy to see that x_1^* is unstable for $0 \leq r < 1$ and stable for $1 < r < 3$, the exact reverse of x_0^* in the vicinity of $r = 1$.

This behaviour is best appreciated using a diagram on which one plots

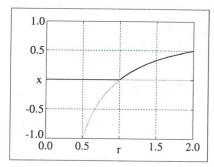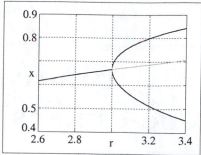

Figure 3.1: Two bifurcations of the logistic map. Transcritical at $r = 1$; two fixed points collide and exchange stability (left). Period doubling at $r = 3$; a period 2 orbit is born as a fixed point becomes unstable (right).

the fixed points, as functions of r, and also indicates their stability. Figure 3.1 shows two such diagrams, produced with the BIFURCATION DIAGRAMS window of CHAOS FOR JAVA;[1] the left hand one is the case under consideration. Stability is indicated by showing stable orbits as dark lines and unstable ones as light lines.[2] We see that, as the parameter is increased, the two fixed points collide, whereupon they exchange their stability. This type of bifurcation is known as *transcritical*; not the most common type of bifurcation in one-dimensional discrete systems.

We already know from page 31 that a period 2 orbit comes into being, stable for $3 < r < 1 + \sqrt{6}$ and unstable for $1 + \sqrt{6} < r \leq 4$. This bifurcation is shown on the right hand diagram, and it has the suggestive shape of a pitchfork. However, it is not the only important type of bifurcation with this appearance, and it should not be called a pitchfork bifurcation. One common technical classification is *flip bifurcation*, which draws attention to the fact that the iterates flip from side to side of x^*. I prefer to call it a *period doubling bifurcation*, although this is by no means universally accepted nomenclature.

Three points emerge from these diagrams:

(i) There is a structural change of the periodic orbits at a critical parameter value.

(ii) There is some kind of *conservation of stability*, related to the difference between the number of stable and unstable fixed points. In the case of the transcritical bifurcation, this number is zero before and after, for the period doubling bifurcation it is $+1$.

---

[1]See appendix A.3 for documentation on the BIFURCATION DIAGRAMS window.
[2]Blue and red are used in CHAOS FOR JAVA.

(iii) The first bifurcation saw a non-zero stable fixed point appear, the second bifurcation saw it replaced by two orbits, an unstable fixed point and a stable period 2 orbit. By the time $r = 4$ there are a dense set of unstable periodic orbits. Once again we are exploring the infinite.

These observations demonstrate the need for theoretical and computational tools, if order and understanding is going to emerge from the increasingly complex, and eventually chaotic, behaviour.

Definition 3.1 (Bifurcation) *A bifurcation is a change in the structure of the periodic orbits of a dynamical system as a system parameter varies continuously through a critical value.*

Exercises

3.1 Show that for the logistic map, regarded as a map of the real numbers rather than just the interval $[0, 1]$, the fixed point $x_1^* = (1 - 1/r)$ is stable for $1 < r < 3$ and unstable for $0 \leq r < 1$, $3 < r \leq 4$.

3.2 Consider the map[3]

$$f(x) = 1 - ax^2, \tag{3.1}$$

where the state variable x is restricted to the interval $I = [-1, 1]$.

(i) Show that f is a map of I into itself provided that $0 \leq a \leq 2$.

(ii) Show that the map has a single fixed point, which is stable for $0 \leq a < 3/4$, unstable for $a > 3/4$.

3.2 Final state diagrams

The bifurcation diagrams of figure 3.1 were produced by finding all solutions of the equations $\phi_n(x) = x - f_n(x) = 0$, as functions of a parameter, by a process of interval searching. The logistic map is about the most elementary example available for investigation; even for it f_n is a polynomial of degree 2^n, which can have as many as 2^n fixed points. The computational limit imposed by these facts indicates that one must complement such calculations by simple observation, using numerical iteration.

---

[3]This variant of the logistic map will assume importance in chapter 4.

Forward limit sets

Ideally, we would like to observe the limiting set of points to which the system is attracted. In practice one can only make computations of orbits which are numerical shadows of actual orbits, so it is important to be clear about the structure we are attempting to glimpse before proceeding.

Definition 3.2 (Forward limit set) *Let f be a map and x_k an orbit commencing from x_0. The forward limit set of the orbit is the set of points which the orbit approaches arbitrarily closely infinitely often.*

This definition is quite subtle, containing two references to the infinite.

(i) To return arbitrarily closely means that for any distance δ, no matter how small, and for any point ξ in the forward limit set, there are points on the orbit which satisfy

$$|x_k - \xi| < \delta. \tag{3.2}$$

(ii) Infinitely often means that there are always recurrences of this event: for any integer N, no matter how large, there remain values of $k > N$ for which equation (3.2) is again satisfied.

To understand the subtleties, first note that a stable fixed point of a map is itself the forward limit set of all orbits within its basin of attraction B. There are an uncountable number of points in B; with the exception of the fixed point itself, none of them are in the forward limit set. These observations apply also to periodic attractors, for which the forward limit set is the stable periodic orbit, and consists of a discrete set of n points. The way in which any given point in the limit set is approached is quite regular in this case, with every nth point on the orbit getting steadily closer to a corresponding limit point as the system evolves.

For chaotic orbits, the situation is far more complex, and the forward limit set can contain an uncountably infinite number of points. Such sets are usually called *chaotic attractors*. An example is the tent map with $t = 1$, which has chaotic orbits which visit any point in the interval $[0, 1]$ arbitrarily closely infinitely often. By conjugacy, so does the logistic map with $r = 4$. Another example was considered in exercise 2.44.

Numerical approximation

The problem for numerics is that the map should be iterated for an infinitely long time before any samples are used to approximate the forward limit set. In practice one first iterates the map a few hundred or thousand times, then takes a sample of a similar number of iterations. The sample itself is

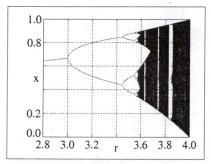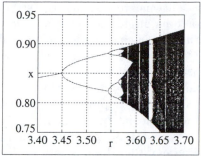

Figure 3.2: Final state diagrams of the logistic map. A global view for the parameter range $r = 2.8$ to $r = 4.0$ (left). Close up of the top branch of the period 2 orbit which appears at $r = 3.0$, showing remarkable self-similarity (right). Initial value $x_0 = 0.5$, sample size 10^3 points, initial 10^3 points discarded.

put into *bins* which are intervals whose size is the x (vertical) resolution represented by one pixel on the graphical device used to present the data. Obviously the resolution comes to the rescue when finding the limit sets of reasonably stable orbits, since it does not require too many iterations to converge within one pixel. Near to points of bifurcation, however, the rate of convergence can be as bad as we please. In fact, simple iteration can never replace more exact methods at such points, as you can easily discover by experimenting with the BIFURCATION DIAGRAMS window of CHAOS FOR JAVA.

The parameter range is traversed in increments whose size is the (horizontal) pixel resolution, and the process is repeated for all values of the parameter which are represented at this resolution. This gives a global picture of the final limit sets of the system. I follow the book by Peitgen, Jürgens and Saupe [24] in referring to such diagrams as *final state diagrams*. Even the simplest of these diagrams requires in the order of 500 iterations for each of 300 parameter values, a total of 150,000 iterations!

As an example, two final state diagrams for the logistic map, shown in figure 3.2, exhibit quite clearly the birth and death of the period 2 orbit already investigated. It also shows that the period doubling repeats itself, on an ever finer scale, up to the resolution of the picture. What it does not show is that periodic orbits do not really die, they simply become unstable. Eventually there are an infinite number of such unstable orbits in the background, creating chaos.

You should use the BIFURCATION DIAGRAMS window of CHAOS FOR JAVA to experiment with these bifurcation and final state diagrams for yourself, to check that period doubling does indeed continue in an infinite cascade, and to examine the structure of some unstable periodic orbits. Don't be afraid to spend a little time: final state diagrams are *fractal* structures in chaotic regions of the dynamical system, so one can never see all the detail, regardless of how closely one looks. Spend some time in the *period three window* at $r \approx 3.83$, and observe that each of the three legs exhibits a period doubling cascade.

In a later chapter I shall discuss properties of fractals. One thing to notice immediately are the many qualitative similarities between what one sees by repeatedly zooming in on interesting parts of a final state diagram. Because of their fractal nature, they become increasingly difficult to construct on finer and finer scale. One danger of placing too much reliance on them comes from the fact that unstable periodic orbits play an important rôle in understanding chaos, although simple numerical iteration will not find them. This is one of the reasons why theoretical investigation, even of simple models, is important to the understanding of non-linear dynamical systems.

Exercises

3.3 Recall exercise 2.12 which was concerned with the slow convergence of iterations of the logistic map at the bifurcation point $r = 3$. Use the BIFURCATION DIAGRAMS window of CHAOS FOR JAVA to examine iterations near to this critical value, comparing the exact position of the periodic orbits with the final state diagrams which can be produced with various choices of discard and sample sizes.

3.4 Use the BIFURCATION DIAGRAMS window of CHAOS FOR JAVA to examine the existence of periodic orbits for the TENT MAP. Specifically:

(i) By looking for orbits up to period 3, confirm that they exist only for $t > 0.8090\ldots$, and that this agrees with the theoretical value found in exercise 2.24.

(ii) How many orbits of period 1, 2, 4 are there for values of t just greater than $1/2$?

(iii) Examine final state diagrams in the vicinity of $t = 1/2$ and form a conjecture about the relationship between the holes in it, and the periodic orbits.

3.5 The CUBIC #3 MAP (2.8) has a bifurcation at $p = 3$, in which the period 2 orbit, born at $p = 2$, loses its stability. This exercise uses CHAOS FOR JAVA to investigate the phenomenon.

(i) Examine the bifurcation diagram and final state diagrams. Pay particular attention to the effect of choosing different initial conditions. How do your observations relate to exercise 2.20?

(ii) Use the FOURIER ANALYSIS window of CHAOS FOR JAVA to show that the bifurcation at $p = 3$ does not change the period of the stable orbits. Check orbits, for example, at $p = 2.9$ and $p = 3.1$.

(iii) Recall exercises 2.21 and 2.22. Repeat with $p = 3.1$, and try to determine, or at least describe, the basins of attraction which you observe in each case.

3.3 Period doubling mechanism

I have already investigated the genesis of a period 2 orbit of the logistic map using direct calculations involving f and f_2. Looking at bifurcation and final state diagrams in some detail, it is apparent that each stable period doubled orbit gives birth to a new stable period doubled orbit as it loses its own stability, and that there is an infinite cascade of orbits with periods $1 \rightarrow 2 \rightarrow 2^2 \rightarrow 2^3 \rightarrow \cdots$, ending in chaos. It is known as the *period doubling route to chaos*, and I want to throw some light on the mechanism, despite the complexity of the functions f_{2^n}.

The first period doubling

Let's examine the mechanism from a graphical point of view, as a preparation to using calculus to analyse the general situation. Figure 3.3 shows superposed graphs of f and f_2 for values of r a little below, and a little above, the critical value $r^* = 3$. The mechanism is very clear. As r increases through r^*, the derivative $f'(x_1^*)$, which determines the stability of the fixed point x_1^*, decreases through the critical value -1. The crucial observation is that f' passes through -1, not $+1$, which causes iterations to alternate from side to side, bringing about period doubling.

The derivative of the second composition at the critical point,

$$f_2'(x_1^*) = f'(x_1^*)^2,$$

simultaneously increases through the value $+1$. This reflects the fact that an unstable fixed point of f is also an unstable fixed point of f_2. The passage of $f_2'(x_1^*)$ through the critical value 1 has a profound effect on the graph of f_2. So long as $f_2'(x_1^*) < 1$, the graph only intersects the line $y = x$ at one point in the vicinity of x_1^*. But when $f_2'(x_1^*) > 1$, it intersects at three nearby points. By simple graphical reasoning we expect that $f_2'(x_\pm^*) < 1$

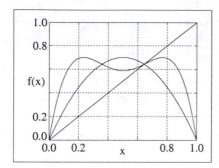 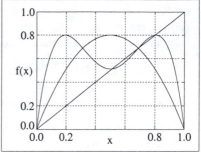

Figure 3.3: Fixed points of the logistic map f and composition f_2, parameter value $r = 2.8$ (left), $r = 3.2$ (right).

at the two new fixed points, at least while r is close to r^*. This produces a stable period 2 orbit, since the new fixed points of f_2 are not fixed points of f.

Recall that the period 2 orbit loses stability at $r = 1 + \sqrt{6} \approx 3.45$. It period doubles to a new stable period 4 orbit. The mechanism is seen in the graphs of f_2 and f_4 for $r = 3.4$ and $r = 3.5$ (figure 3.4). Evidently it is a duplication of what happened for f and f_2 at $r = 3$ except that now it is $f_2'(x_\pm^*)$ which passes through the critical value -1, while $f_4'(x_\pm^*)$ passes through $+1$, since

$$f_4'(x_\pm^*) = f_2'(x_\pm^*)^2.$$

Furthermore, period doubling seems to be moving much faster this time, considered as a function of r.

Approximation — Logistic Map

Let's begin our theoretical investigation of the first period doubling of the logistic map by setting r to the critical value $r^* = 3$, for which $x_1^* = 2/3$ and $f'(x_1^*) = -1$. The general form of $\phi_2(x) = x - f_2(x)$ is given by equation (2.13); when $r = r^*$, it may be further factored as $\phi_2(x) = x(3x - 2)^3$. Near to $x = x_1^*$ this leads to the approximation

$$\phi_2(x) \approx 18(x - x_1^*)^3, \qquad |x - x_1^*| \ll 1. \tag{3.3}$$

The period 2 orbit is born exactly where the fixed point loses its stability; (3.3) shows that the new orbit commences its life at exactly the same x values as well, which is important for understanding the bifurcation diagram, since everything will be a continuous function of r away from the critical point.

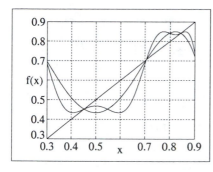 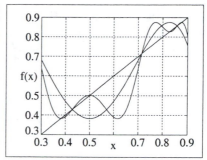

Figure 3.4: Fixed points of compositions f_2, f_4 of the logistic map, parameter value $r = 3.4$ (left), $r = 3.5$ (right).

Recall the formula (2.14) for the pair $x_\pm^*$. This was for arbitrary r; to investigate behaviour close to r^* it is useful to make the substitution $r = r^* + \Delta r$. With this done, the formula appears as

$$x_\pm^* = \frac{4 + \Delta r \pm \sqrt{(4 + \Delta r)\Delta r}}{6 + 2\Delta r}$$

If Δr is negative these solutions are not real. If Δr is positive but small, $\sqrt{(4 + \Delta r)\Delta r} \approx 2\sqrt{\Delta r}$, and since $\sqrt{\Delta r}$ is much bigger than Δr itself, it makes sense to approximate the formula to

$$x_\pm^* \approx x_1^* \pm \frac{1}{3}\sqrt{\Delta r}. \tag{3.4}$$

This is a sideways parabola, seen quite clearly in final state diagrams which were constructed earlier (figure 3.2).

Properties of derivatives

The behaviour of the logistic map at $r = 3$ comes from the fact that $\phi_2(x)$ is approximated by a cubic $C(x - x^*)^3$ near x^*. This is equivalent to the coincidence that, when $r = 3$,

$$\phi_2(x_1^*) = 0, \qquad \phi_2'(x_1^*) = 0, \qquad \phi_2''(x_1^*) = 0. \tag{3.5}$$

I do not want to restrict investigation solely to the logistic map, rather I shall investigate the general theory of a non-zero fixed point x^* of a smooth map f, which loses its stability at a parameter value r^* for which $f'(x^*) = -1$. Let's calculate the first two derivatives of ϕ_2, both as general formulae and evaluated at the fixed point itself. First, the general formula

$$f_2'(x) = f'(f(x)) \cdot f'(x),$$

which gives, using the fact that $f(x^*) = x^*$ and $f'(x^*) = -1$,

$$\phi_2'(x^*) = 1 - f_2'(x^*) = 1 - f'(x^*)^2 = 0.$$

Second

$$\begin{aligned} f_2''(x) &= \frac{d}{dx}\left[f'(f(x)) \cdot f'(x)\right] \\ &= f''(f(x)) \cdot f'(x)^2 + f'(f(x)) \cdot f''(x), \end{aligned} \tag{3.6}$$

which gives

$$\phi_2''(x^*) = -f_2''(x^*) = -f''(x^*)[f'(x^*)^2 + f'(x^*)] = 0.$$

So the coincidence (3.5) is quite general, depending only on the fact that loss of stability arises from the passage of $f'(x^*)$ through the value -1.

Approximation — general case

Recall that, in order to approximate a function $g(x)$ in the vicinity of a given point $x = a$, beyond a simple tangent line, the formula goes as follows:

$$g(x) \approx g(a) + g'(a)(x-a) + \frac{g''(a)}{2}(x-a)^2 + \frac{g'''(a)}{6}(x-a)^3 + \cdots \tag{3.7}$$

which is the *Taylor expansion*.[4] Normally one does not go to such high order in simple approximations. What makes it necessary here is the fact that, for the function ϕ_2 near the bifurcation point, a lesser order tells nothing at all.

In order to approximate the behaviour of ϕ_2 near to the critical parameter value r^*, write $r = r^* + \Delta r$, where $|\Delta r| \ll 1$. One subtlety which should be noted is that the expansion is about a point $x^*(r)$ which is itself a function of r, determined by the condition[5] $\phi(x^*) = 0$. The first two derivatives will no longer be zero when $r \neq r^*$, although they will be small if $|r - r^*|$ is small. To keep things simple, I introduce the simple approximations

$$f'(x^*) \approx -1 - A\Delta r, \tag{3.8}$$

and

$$\frac{\phi_2''(x^*)}{2} \approx B\Delta r, \qquad \frac{\phi_2'''(x^*)}{6} \approx C.$$

---

[4] If you take the first, second, and third derivatives of this formula, and substitute $x = a$ into each, you will see that this just extends the idea of matching the first derivative (slope of the tangent line) to matching the second and third derivatives.

[5] This approach is a little unusual in that it avoids the use of partial derivatives; this leads to approximations which are easy to analyse.

The approximation (3.8) for f' gives

$$\phi_2'(x^*) = 1 - f'(x^*)^2 \approx -2A\Delta r.$$

Substituting these values into the Taylor expansion of ϕ_2, the fixed points are approximated by the solutions of

$$\phi_2(x) \approx -2A\Delta r(x - x^*) + B\Delta r(x - x^*)^2 + C(x - x^*)^3 = 0, \qquad (3.9)$$

of which one is $x = x^*$. For the other pair the formula for the solution of a quadratic gives

$$\begin{aligned} x_\pm^* &= x^* + \frac{-B\Delta r \pm \sqrt{B^2\Delta r^2 + 8AC\Delta r}}{2C} \\ &\approx x^* \pm \sqrt{(2A/C)\Delta r}. \end{aligned} \qquad (3.10)$$

This generalises equation (3.4) for the logistic map to a large class of smooth functions.

Two kinds of bifurcation

Keep in mind that we are investigating the behaviour of f_2 in the situation that the fixed point x^* of f becomes unstable as the derivative $f'(x^*)$ decreases through the critical value -1. For simplicity I am assuming that x^* is stable for $\Delta r < 0$ and unstable for $\Delta r > 0$, although one can handle the other case in a similar way.

We see from (3.10) that everything hinges on the relative signs of A and C, which represents the behaviour of $\phi_2'(x^*)$ and $\phi_2'''(x^*)$ near to $r = r^*$. A describes the behaviour of $f'(x^*)$, here a decreasing function of r. Consequently

$$A > 0.$$

We cannot say whether C is positive or negative without specifying more about the map f. Let's put this question aside temporarily and investigate both possibilities for the sign of C.

A stable period doubled orbit

Positive C corresponds to a negative third derivative $f_2'''(x^*)$. In this case the new pair $x_\pm^*$ appears for $\Delta r > 0$. This is the first alternative in figure 3.5. First, we must check that the pair $x_\pm^*$ do form a period 2 orbit; using the simplest Taylor approximation for f (the tangent line)

$$f(x) \approx f(x^*) + f'(x^*)(x - x^*) \approx 2x^* - x.$$

Figure 3.5: The bifurcations resulting from decreasing $f'(x^*)$.

Substituting for $x_\pm^*$ from (3.10) gives the required result,

$$f(x_\pm^*) \approx f(x_\mp^*).$$

To settle the stability question, we must calculate the derivative $f_2' = 1 - \phi_2'$ at $x_\pm^*$. ϕ_2 is approximated by the cubic (3.9), whose zeros have already been found, so we may write it in the factored form

$$\phi_2(x) \approx C(x - x^*)(x - x_-^*)(x - x_+^*).$$

This is easy to differentiate using the product rule,

$$\phi_2'(x) \approx C[(x - x_-^*)(x - x_+^*) + (x - x^*)(x - x_+^*) + (x - x^*)(x - x_-^*)],$$

after which we may substitute each of the fixed points in turn. In doing so, remember that we already found in (3.10) that

$$x_+^* - x^* = x^* - x_-^* \approx \sqrt{(2A/C)\Delta r}$$

which gives

$$f_2'(x^*) = 1 + 2A\Delta r, \qquad f_2'(x_\pm^*) = 1 - 4A\Delta r. \tag{3.11}$$

There are two important conclusions to be drawn, remembering that A tells us the rate at which $f'(x^*)$ decreases through the critical value -1, as a function of r.

(i) The period doubled orbit $x_\pm^*$ is indeed stable with derivative $f_2'(x_\pm^*)$ which decreases from an initial value $+1$ at $r = r^*$.

(ii) The rate at which $f_2'(x_\pm^*)$ is initially decreasing is four times the rate at which $f'(x^*)$ was finally decreasing. The new orbit will itself become unstable when $f_2'(x_\pm^*)$ passes through the critical value -1: therefore the next period doubling should happen much faster than the previous one.

Death of an unstable period doubled orbit

Negative C corresponds to a positive third derivative $f_2'''(x^*)$. This is the second alternative in figure 3.5. In this case the real pair $x_\pm^*$ of solutions of equation (3.10) exists for $\Delta r < 0$ and disappear at $r = r^*$. Moreover, the period doubled orbit which exists for $\Delta r < 0$ is unstable. This is a kind of *reverse bifurcation*, in which a stable fixed point becomes unstable because it is joined by an unstable periodic orbit. Most of this behaviour will go unobserved in a simple numerical experiment, except for the mysterious disappearance of a stable orbit.

I have already presented all of the mathematical analysis required to demonstrate these assertions. In fact, the formulae obtained in the positive C case are still valid, what has changed is that Δr must be negative to get real values of $x_\pm^*$. In particular, we still have

$$f(x_\pm^*) \approx f(x_\mp^*)$$

and

$$f_2'(x^*) = 1 + 2A\Delta r, \qquad f_2'(x_\pm^*) = 1 - 4A\Delta r,$$

but, with negative Δr the interpretation is that the orbit $x_\pm^*$ is unstable. As for the bifurcation diagram, this unstable orbit (with two branches) joins the stable fixed point at $r = r^*$, after which the originally stable fixed point loses its stability.

Exercises

3.6 It was seen in exercise 2.7 that the fixed point x_+^* of the CUBIC #1 MAP (2.5) becomes unstable at $r \approx 3.16$. By obtaining an exact formula for $f'(x_+^*)$ as a function of r, show that bifurcation actually takes place at $r = 256/81$.

3.7 The SINE MAP was investigated in exercise 2.9 using the GRAPHICAL ANALYSIS window of CHAOS FOR JAVA. This exercise extends that work.

(i) Locate the value q^* of q at which x_1^* becomes unstable, to four decimal places. Use a bisection method: start by finding a pair of q values at which $f'(x_1^*) > -1$ and $f'(x_1^*) < -1$ (respectively), then examine an intermediate value to narrow the range in which the critical value -1 is attained. Continue in this way until q^* is determined to the required accuracy.

(ii) Extend the work done in exercise 2.9 by locating the positions of the fixed points of f_2, starting at $q = q^*$, and plotting this orbit also in the q-x plane, indicating where it is stable and where it is unstable.

3.8 Consider the map $f(x) = 1 - ax^2$, $-1 \leq x \leq 1$, which was the subject of exercise 3.2. Construct, and factor, the polynomial $\phi_2(x) = x - f_2(x)$, to show that there is a period 2 orbit for $a > 3/4$, and that it is stable for $3/4 < a < 5/4$, unstable for $5/4 < a < 2$. Sketch a bifurcation diagram to show the orbits thus found.

3.9 The equation of a standard parabola is $y = y_0 + a(x - x_0)^2$; it has its minimum value y_0 at $x = x_0$ (if $a > 0$, otherwise the maximum). Cast (3.4) into standard form, with r playing the rôle of y. Since it is usual to plot bifurcation diagrams with the parameter as the horizontal axis, this is a sideways parabola.

3.10 Equation (2.14) for the period 2 orbit of the logistic map comes from the zeros of the quadratic factor $(1 + r - rx - r^2x + r^2x^2)$ in $\phi_2(x) = x - f_2(x)$, found on page 31. Show that, under the substitution

$$x = 2/3 + \Delta x, \qquad r = 3 + \Delta r,$$

the expression becomes

$$-\Delta r + 9\Delta x^2 + \Delta r \Delta x - \frac{2}{9}\Delta r^2 - \frac{1}{3}\Delta r^2 \Delta x + 6\Delta r \Delta x^2 + \Delta r^2 \Delta x^2.$$

The first two terms give equation (3.4) above. If we include the other terms we certainly do not have a parabola. Examine the magnitude of each of these terms, as compared with the magnitude of Δr, to explicitly justify the approximation made in equation (3.4).

3.11 Repeat the analysis of the period doubling bifurcation in the case that $A < 0$, being careful to distinguish the behaviour for $C > 0$ from $C < 0$.

3.12 At the first period doubling of a unimodal map, I labelled the two points on the orbit $x_{\pm}^*$, to indicate their numerical ordering. Points on an orbit are more properly indicated by their sequential order, i.e. (x_0^*, x_1^*), for a period 2 orbit. Clearly this makes no difference for period 2 since the system alternates from x_0^* to x_1^* and back again. For a period 4 orbit $(x_0^*, \cdots, x_3^*)$, it is relevant to ask for the numerical order of the points once we specify which is the smallest. We are free to choose x_0^* as the smallest. Show that, as a consequence of the map being unimodal, the numerical ordering of the points $(x_0^*, \cdots, x_3^*)$ is uniquely determined, and find their order.

3.13 What is the value of A in equation (3.8) for the logistic map at its first period doubling?

3.14 Equation (2.16) gives $f_2'(x_\pm^*)$ for the period 2 orbit of the logistic map. Show that the rate at which $f_4'(x_i^*)$ is decreasing as a function of r, at the second period doubling, is ≈ 4.9 times the rate at which $f_2'(x_\pm^*)$ was decreasing at the first period doubling.

3.4 Period doubling cascades

I have been careful in the foregoing not to assume too much about the function f beyond a reasonable amount of differentiability. In fact we may replace f by any composition f_n, and f_2 by the corresponding doubled composition f_{2n}, at each step of the argument.

Let's apply this first to the cascade which emanates from the fixed point x_1^*. It becomes unstable and period doubles at some critical parameter value, provided that the third derivative f_2''' has the correct sign. At the birth of this new orbit, $f_2'(x_\pm^*) = 1$; immediately afterward it has decreased below this value. We expect that continued increase of the parameter will result in continued decrease in $f_2'(x_\pm^*)$, leading to loss of stability when it passes through the critical value -1.

At this point it is appropriate to pick ourselves up by the bootstraps. Setting f_2 into the place previously occupied by f, its second composition f_4 will take the place previously occupied by f_2. Since $f_2'(x_\pm^*) = -1$ for either point on the period 2 orbit, $f_4'(x_\pm^*) = +1$ and $f_4''(x_\pm^*) = 0$. Provided that the third derivative value $f_4'''(x_\pm^*)$ is negative, each of the two fixed points of f_2 undergoes a period doubling bifurcation, to produce four new stable fixed points $(x_0^*, \cdots, x_3^*)$ of f_4. They are not fixed points of either f or f_2, hence they form a stable period 4 orbit of f. The bootstrap process continues. At the critical point where $f_4'(x_i^*)$ reaches the critical value -1, f_8 acquires 8 new stable fixed points (as four pairs), which together form a stable period 8 orbit. And so on, in an infinite cascade.

And — there is more. Suppose that we commence with a stable period 3 orbit, that is, three connected stable fixed points of f_3 which are not fixed points of f. Their stability is determined by $f_3'(x_i^*)$. As the parameter value is increased, this may also pass through the critical value -1; if it does so, and again assuming something about the value of the third derivative $f_6'''(x_i^*)$, the composition map f_3 period doubles to give a stable period 6 orbit. Once started, this cascade will generally continue to chaos. In fact, it is the most common mechanism for the destruction of stable periodic orbits of any period. A period 3 case is shown in figure 3.6.

Schwarzian magic

Let's take stock. On the one hand, I have developed a simple and general theory which explains period doubling cascades, caused by successive

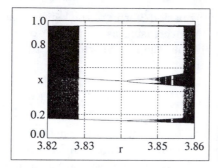 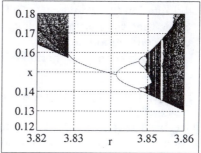

Figure 3.6: Period doubling in the period 3 window of the logistic map (left) and detail of the bottom branch (right). Initial value $x_0 = 0.5$, sample size 10^3 points, initial 10^3 points discarded.

derivatives, $f'_n, f'_{2n}, f'_{2^2 n}, \cdots$ passing through the critical value -1. On the other hand, it depends on knowing the sign of the third derivative of composition maps, evaluated at points x^* which it is impossible to determine in general. This is not a question to be avoided. Indeed it seems that we should expect a fair sprinkling of both positive and negative values of the third derivative, since we are working with ever more complicated and rapidly oscillating functions. Remember that the occurrence of even one positive value kills the cascade.

A little magic comes to the rescue. Let's look at the formula for $f'''_2(x)$

$$f'''_2(x) = \frac{d}{dx} \left[f''(f(x)) \cdot f'(x)^2 + f'(f(x)) \cdot f''(x) \right]$$
$$= f'''(f(x)) \cdot f'(x)^3 + 3f''(f(x)) \cdot f''(x) \cdot f'(x) + f'(f(x)) \cdot f'''(x).$$

It involves all three derivatives f', f'' and f''', but at $r = r^*$ we know that $f'(x^*) = \pm 1$ and $f''(x^*) = 0$, so the second derivatives make no contribution at x^*. That is,

$$f'''_2(x^*) = 2f'(x^*)f'''(x^*);$$

some memory of the third derivative survives the period doubling.

To exploit this fact, consider a rather complicated function $S[f]$ constructed using the following combination of the derivatives of f:

$$S[f] = 2f'f''' - 3f''^2. \tag{3.12}$$

First note:

(i) It has the property that, if we know the sign of $S[f]$ at a point where $f' = -1$ and $f'' = 0$, then we know the sign of f'''_2 at that point.

(ii) I have written $S[f]$ rather than S to indicate what function was used in its construction.

(iii) $S[f]$ is related to the *Schwarzian derivative* — in fact equation (3.12) must be divided by $2f'^2$ to get the usual definition.[6]

Now for the magic. Consider what happens under function composition. To avoid confusion, consider first the most general composition

$$h(x) = f(g(x)).$$

Then I claim that

$$S[h](x) = S[f](g(x)) \cdot g'(x)^4 + S[g](x) \cdot f'(g(x))^2. \tag{3.13}$$

This is a general formula, true for all x. Fortunately we don't care about the actual values, we simply want to know whether or not $S[h](x)$ is negative. The formula (3.13) tells us that $S[h](x)$ is calculated from $S[f](g(x))$ and $S[g](x)$ by multiplying each by a positive quantity then adding. This shows that if

$$S[f](x) < 0 \qquad \text{and} \qquad S[g](x) < 0,$$

then

$$S[h](x) < 0.$$

Period doubling of the logistic map

Let's apply this to the logistic map, $f(x) = rx(1 - x)$. First we need the derivatives:

$$f'(x) = r - 2rx, \qquad f''(x) = -2r, \qquad f'''(x) = 0.$$

Note, however, that in general $f_n'''(x) \neq 0$ for $n \geq 2$. Substituting into the defining formula for $S[f](x)$ gives the very simple result

$$S[f](x) = -12r^2.$$

This is negative for all x. Therefore we have shown that, for the logistic map,

$$S[f_n](x) < 0, \qquad (n = 1, 2, \cdots).$$

This really is a remarkable result. Just by checking a simple formula for f itself, we are able to tell that the third derivatives of the most horrendously complicated functions, evaluated at a set of points which we don't

---

[6] A detailed account of the rôle of the Schwarzian derivative in one-dimensional dynamics may be found in Devaney [10].

know how to find, are all negative. That is, we have explained the fact
that period doubling cascades are such a common mechanism by which a
smooth unimodal map sheds the stability of any periodic orbit which comes
into existence as a parameter is increased. The most obvious manifestation
of this is the initial period doubling cascade from the fixed point x_1^* to the
first occurrence of chaos. But there are an infinite number of other such
cascades just waiting to be observed.

Exercises

3.15 Use the GRAPHICAL ANALYSIS window of CHAOS FOR JAVA to show
that, for the LOGISTIC MAP, the observed bifurcation of the period
3 orbit at $r = 3.83$ to a period 6 orbit by $r = 3.845$ is through the
mechanism of period doubling operating on the composition map f_3.

3.16 In this exercise you will prove equation (3.13).

(i) By differentiating the elementary formula $h'(x) = f'(g(x)) \cdot g'(x)$,
show that

$$h''(x) = f''(g(x)) \cdot g'(x)^2 + f'(g(x)) \cdot g''(x).$$

(ii) By differentiating a second time, show further that

$$h'''(x) = f'''(g(x)) \cdot g'(x)^3$$
$$+ 3f''(g(x)) \cdot g''(x) \cdot g'(x) + f'(g(x)) \cdot g'''(x).$$

(iii) Substitute these results into the formula for $S[h]$ and make the
appropriate cancellations to arrive at equation (3.13).

3.17 Compute $S[f]$ for the SINE MAP (1.2). For what range of the parameter q is $S[f] < 0$ on the entire interval $[0, 1]$?

3.18 Calculate $S[f]$ for the CUBIC #3 MAP defined in equation (2.8). Show
that $S[f](x)$ is negative for all x when $p > 1$.

3.5   Feigenbaum's universal constants

A period doubling cascade proceeds at an ever more frenetic pace as the
parameter increases. In fact, an earlier calculation (page 76) suggested that
each step in the cascade should happen at least four times as fast as the
last. That is a geometric rate of convergence.

Define r_n as the value of r at the point where the nth period doubling
occurs. Let's adopt a *scaling hypothesis* that the sequence of values r_n

converges to a limiting value r_∞, and that convergence is geometric, that is,

$$r_n - r_\infty \approx A\delta^{-n}, \qquad n \to \infty. \tag{3.14}$$

Given accurate numerical values, it is not difficult to estimate δ and r_∞. Taking the difference of two adjacent equations,

$$(r_n - r_\infty) - (r_{n+1} - r_\infty) = r_n - r_{n+1} \approx A\delta^{-n}(1 - \delta^{-1}).$$

The ratio of two such relations gives

$$\frac{r_n - r_{n+1}}{r_{n+1} - r_{n+2}} \approx \delta.$$

To estimate r_∞ we again take a difference of two adjacent equations, multiplying one of them by δ, for which we already have a formula. This gives the equation

$$0 = (r_n - r_\infty) - \delta(r_{n+1} - r_\infty)$$

$$= (r_n - r_\infty) - \left(\frac{r_n - r_{n+1}}{r_{n+1} - r_{n+2}}\right)(r_{n+1} - r_\infty),$$

for r_∞, whose solution is

$$r_\infty \approx \frac{r_n r_{n+2} - r_{n+1}^2}{r_n - 2r_{n+1} + r_{n+2}}.$$

Scaling relations

Equation (3.14) is an example of a relation which gives important and general information about how a dynamical system behaves in an infinite or infinitesimal limit. Its precise meaning is that

$$\lim_{n \to \infty} \frac{r_n - r_\infty}{\delta^{-n}} = A,$$

which shows the different rôles of δ and A. Relations of this kind are an important feature of the theory of phase changes in statistical mechanics. In the context of chaos they are also important, giving laws which separate *universal constants* (here δ) which depend only on the general character of the system, from *amplitudes* (here A) which depend on the details.[7] Specifically, δ is the same for all period doubling cascades of a smooth unimodal map,[8] whereas A depends on the particular cascade. Scaling relations are used to extend the concept of dimension to strange attractors and other fractal objects, and in many other places.

---

[7] Here I have used a technical expression from the theory of critical phenomena; there is no connection with Fourier amplitudes.

[8] Well, most smooth maps! See footnote 9 on page 85.

Definition 3.3 (Scaling relation) *A scaling relation takes a form such as*

$$A_n \approx A_\infty \alpha^n, \qquad n \to \infty,$$

or

$$A(\epsilon) \approx A(0)\epsilon^{-d}, \qquad \epsilon \to 0.$$

The two forms of the definition are equivalent; making the substitution $n = -\ln \epsilon$ in the first ($\epsilon > 0$), so as to convert the limit $n \to \infty$ to $\epsilon \to 0$, the right hand side is transformed to the second form, since

$$\alpha^n = \exp(n \ln \alpha) = \exp(-\ln \epsilon \cdot \ln \alpha) = \epsilon^{-\ln \alpha}.$$

This shows also that the constant α is related to the exponent d by

$$d = \ln \alpha.$$

Logistic map

For the main period doubling sequence of the logistic map the first few r_n values are

$$r_1 = 3, \qquad\qquad r_2 = 3.4494897428, \quad r_3 = 3.5440903596,$$
$$r_4 = 3.5644072661, \quad r_5 = 3.5687594195, \quad r_6 = 3.5696916098, \quad \cdots$$

They were obtained using the GRAPHICAL ANALYSIS window of CHAOS FOR JAVA to locate, to ten decimal places, the values of r at which the derivative $f_n'(x_i^*)$ attains the critical value.

Since we need three adjoining values of r_n for each estimate, this gives the following sequence of numerical results:

$$(r_1, r_2, r_3) : \qquad \delta \approx 4.7514462, \qquad r_\infty \approx 3.5693075.$$
$$(r_2, r_3, r_4) : \qquad \delta \approx 4.6562512, \qquad r_\infty \approx 3.5699641.$$
$$(r_3, r_4, r_5) : \qquad \delta \approx 4.6682415, \qquad r_\infty \approx 3.5699458.$$
$$(r_4, r_5, r_6) : \qquad \delta \approx 4.6687414, \qquad r_\infty \approx 3.5699440.$$

The obvious convergence of these numbers is strong evidence to support the scaling hypothesis. As always in a good theory, that does not settle the question: rather it presents a challenge for understanding. It is clear that more accurate results, involving larger values of n, may only be obtained by very careful numerical analysis, since the calculations involve taking differences of numbers which are converging to a common value.

Similarly, one can examine how distances between points on period 2^n orbits scale with increasing n. A convenient way to choose a set of distances d_n for this purpose will be described shortly; it will be seen that they also scale geometrically, this time to zero,

$$d_n \approx B\alpha^{-n}, \qquad n \to \infty.$$

Theory and experiment both give the value

$$\alpha \approx 2.502908\ldots \tag{3.15}$$

The constants A, B depend on the actual map, but α and δ are *universal constants*, known as Feigenbaum's constants. They are the same for all period doubling cascades of a smooth unimodal map.[9] This remarkable fact was discovered by Mitchell Feigenbaum,[10] and originated as a conjecture based on numerical experiments performed with a hand calculator.[11]

Superstable orbits

Stability of a periodic orbit is determined by the derivative test; the smaller the magnitude $|f_n'(x_i^*)|$, the faster the rate of convergence. Parameter values for which the derivative is zero are of special note.

Normally stable orbits attract neighbouring orbits by a process of *linear convergence*. That is, the distance of an iteration from its final value decreases in a single step of f_n (n steps of f) according to the linear law

$$|x_{i+n} - x_i^*| \approx M|x_i - x_i^*|,$$

where M is less than 1 in magnitude. If $M = 0$, it can be shown that the convergence is quadratic, that is,[12]

$$|x_{i+n} - x_i^*| \approx K|x_i - x_i^*|^2,$$

for some constant K.

Definition 3.4 (Superstable) *A superstable period n orbit is one for which the derivative f_n' has the values $f_n'(x_i^*) = 0$.*

Recall the life of a period doubled orbit. It is born with derivative $f_n'(x^*) = +1$, and it dies (becomes unstable) when the derivative passes through the critical value -1. In between there must be a point at which it is superstable. Let's denote the values of r at which the period 2^n orbit is superstable by $\bar{r}_n$. The Lyapunov exponent has the value $-\infty$ wherever a derivative used in its computation becomes zero, so we can spot the superstable orbits by looking for sharp dips in numerical computations of the exponent, as seen in figures 3.7.

---

[9]More precisely, α and δ are the same for all smooth maps with a quadratic maximum, the usual case. In the general case they depend only on the order of the maximum.

[10]Mitchell J. Feigenbaum, "Quantitative universality for a class of nonlinear transformations", *Journal of Statistical Physics*, **19**, 25–52 (1978).

[11]The story is recounted in the Glieck's popular book [13], p177ff.

[12]The demonstration of this follows the line of argument given on page 20 but uses the next term in the Taylor series.

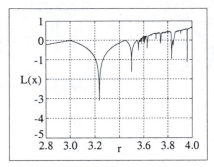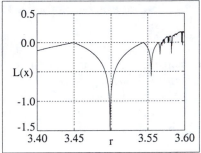

Figure 3.7: Lyapunov exponents of the logistic map, sharp dips indicate positions of superstable orbits. Initial value $x_0 = 0.5$, sample size 10^3 points, initial 10^3 points discarded.

In fact, we already know two superstable orbits for the logistic map: $\bar{r}_0 = 2$ and for $\bar{r}_1 = 1 + \sqrt{5}$ (see exercise 2.16). Numerical values for the first few $\bar{r}_n$ are

$$\bar{r}_0 = 2, \qquad \bar{r}_1 = 3.2360679775, \quad \bar{r}_2 = 3.4985616993,$$
$$\bar{r}_3 = 3.5546408628, \quad \bar{r}_4 = 3.5666673799, \quad \bar{r}_5 = 3.5692435316, \quad \cdots$$

Clearly the parameter values $\bar{r}_n$ should scale with the same universal Feigenbaum constant δ, according to the law

$$\bar{r}_n - r_\infty \approx \bar{A}\delta^{-n}, \qquad n \to \infty; \tag{3.16}$$

using the above data,

$$(\bar{r}_0, \bar{r}_1, \bar{r}_2): \quad \delta \approx 4.7089430, \qquad r_\infty \approx 3.5693349.$$
$$(\bar{r}_1, \bar{r}_2, \bar{r}_3): \quad \delta \approx 4.6807710, \qquad r_\infty \approx 3.5698766.$$
$$(\bar{r}_2, \bar{r}_3, \bar{r}_4): \quad \delta \approx 4.6629596, \qquad r_\infty \approx 3.5699507.$$
$$(\bar{r}_3, \bar{r}_4, \bar{r}_5): \quad \delta \approx 4.6684035, \qquad r_\infty \approx 3.5699458.$$

Scaling and self-similarity

Using the formula for the derivative in the condition for superstability,

$$f_n'(x_i) = \prod_{j=0}^{n-1} f'(x_{i+j}) = 0,$$

we see that, for a smooth unimodal map, an orbit is superstable if and only if $f'(x_k^*) = 0$ for some point x_k^* on it. That is, the maximum point $x_{\max}$ of f must belong to the orbit.

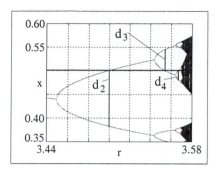

Figure 3.8: Final state diagram showing the definition of d_n as the distance between $x_{\max}$ and the $f_{2^{n-1}}(x_{\max})$.

Suppose we trace the branch of the bifurcation diagram which passes through the point $(\bar{r}_n, x_{\max})$ back to the point r_n at which this period 2^n orbit came in existence and then forward along the other branch. The two points are related by the composition $f_{2^{n-1}}$. Denote by d_n the distance between $x_{\max}$ and $f_{2^{n-1}}(x_{\max})$, that is,

$$f_{2^{n-1}}(x_{\max}) = x_{\max} + d_n, \qquad f_{2^{n-1}}(x_{\max} + d_n) = x_{\max}. \qquad (3.17)$$

Figure 3.8 shows the meaning of d_2, d_3 and d_4, on a portion of a bifurcation diagram for the logistic map. Corresponding to the values $\bar{r}_n$ already found for the logistic map, the d_n values, and the ratios d_n/d_{n+1}, are

$$
\begin{aligned}
d_1 &= 0.30901699, \\
d_2 &= 0.11640177, & d_1/d_2 &= 2.65475, \\
d_3 &= 0.04597521, & d_2/d_3 &= 2.53184, \\
d_4 &= 0.01832618, & d_3/d_4 &= 2.50872, \\
d_5 &= 0.00731843, & d_4/d_5 &= 2.50411,
\end{aligned}
$$

in good agreement with (3.15) for such a limited data set.

In section 3.10, I explain the rudiments of some powerful ideas which lead to theoretical explanation of Feigenbaum scaling and prediction of the value of the constants α and δ. For now, let's look at the function f_{2^n} for the logistic map with $r \approx r_\infty$. The graphs become extremely complicated with increasing n when viewed in the large. However, one can observe self-similarity in the functions f_{2^n} by expanding the horizontal and vertical scale by a factor of α for each increment of n. Figure 3.9 shows two examples for $r = 3.5699456$ ($\approx r_\infty$). The point to observe here is that the similarity involves scaling the graph and turning it upside down. Clearly this self-similarity is the source of the universal behaviour.

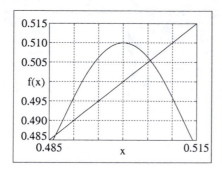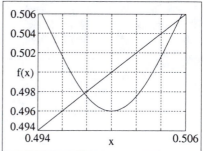

Figure 3.9: Logistic map, showing self-similarity of compositions, near $x = x_{\max}$, of f_{16} (left) and f_{32} (right), both for $r = 3.5699456 \approx r_\infty$; examination of the axes shows that the two appear to be related by the scaling factor $\alpha \approx 2.5$.

Exercises

3.19 Cast equation (3.14) in the first form of the definition 3.3; that is, give the definition of A_n, A_∞ and α of the latter in terms of r_n, r_∞, A and δ of the former.

3.20 Find the values of the first six r_n for the SINE MAP (1.2), to eight decimal places, using bisection and the GRAPHICAL ANALYSIS window of CHAOS FOR JAVA as in exercise 3.7. Use your data to estimate the Feigenbaum constant δ for this cascade.

3.21 This exercise is concerned with the CUBIC #2 MAP of exercise 2.3.

(i) Using the LYAPUNOV EXPONENTS window of CHAOS FOR JAVA, locate the values $\bar{r}_0, \cdots, \bar{r}_4$ for the superstable orbits of period $2^0, \cdots, 2^4$, to three decimal places. You will need to use quite large numbers in the computation, for example discard the first 1000 iterations and use sample sizes of 1000.

(ii) By examining composition maps using the GRAPHICAL ANALYSIS window of CHAOS FOR JAVA, and applying the bisection method to locate superstable fixed points (zero derivative), obtain values of $\bar{r}_n$ to 8 decimal places. Note also the corresponding d_n values.

(iii) Use your values of $\bar{r}_n$ to estimate the Feigenbaum universal constant δ, and the critical value r_∞ at which the period doubling cascade ends.

(iv) Use your values of d_n to estimate the Feigenbaum constant α.

3.22 Use the FOURIER ANALYSIS window of CHAOS FOR JAVA to examine the spectra of the CUBIC #2 MAP at the superstable points found in the previous exercise. By making careful measurement, show that the average amplitude of each successive set of period-doubled frequency components is about 8dB below the previous frequency components. Can you suggest an explanation for this figure?

3.6 Tangent bifurcations

Periodic windows are a common and obvious feature of final state diagrams, for example the period 4 window of the logistic map shown in figure 3.10. The chaotic behaviour at $r = 3.96$ suddenly switches to a stable period 4 orbit, which takes the period doubling route back to chaos.

The mechanism which gives birth to this period 4 orbit is seen quite clearly in figures 3.10 and 3.11. On the right of the former is a complete graph of f_4, with $r = 3.96$. There are four points where the graph seems to be touching the line $y = x$. The other two graphs (figures 3.11) show the situation for $r = 3.959$ and $r = 3.961$, near the largest of these points, $x \approx 0.99$.[13]

It's quite clear what is happening. For $r = 3.96$ the function has three minima and one maximum which do not quite meet the line, and there are only eight fixed points of f_4, all unstable. With a slight increase in r, the four peaks push through the line, creating a further eight fixed points. Initially four are stable, four unstable, so the collision gives birth to a pair of period 4 orbits, one stable and one unstable. At the critical value r^* when the collision takes place, the line $y = x$ is tangent to the graph. For this reason, this kind of bifurcation is known as a *tangent bifurcation*.

At first sight it looks like a coincidence that all four points are simultaneously tangent to the line $y = x$. However this is a simple consequence of the composition of maps; since the fixed points are new, they must lie on period 4 orbits. For a point of tangency with the line $y = x$ we need the further condition

$$f_4'(x_i^*) = 1.$$

But this derivative is a property of the orbit since it is calculated as the product $f_4'(x_i^*) = \prod_{k=0}^{3} f'(x_{i+k}^*)$ taken over the period. Therefore tangency of one point implies tangency of all.

Approximate description of the bifurcation

Let's concentrate on approximating the function $\phi_n(x) = x - f_n(x)$ near to a tangent point. (In the example shown, $n = 4$.) If the parameter r is

---

[13]I chose this one because it's not easy to be sure about it without zooming in.

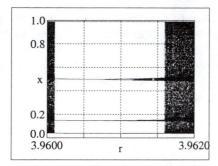 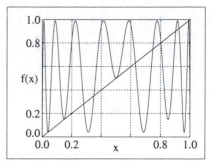

Figure 3.10: Tangent bifurcation of the logistic map. Final state diagram, initial value $x_0 = 0.499999$, sample size 10^3 points, initial 10^3 points discarded (left). Graph of f_4, $r = 3.96$ (right).

exactly at the critical value r^*, and if $x = x^*$ is a point of tangency, then we have $\phi_n(x^*) = 0$ and $\phi_n'(x^*) = 0$, which informs us that the simplest approximation is the parabola

$$\phi_n(x) \approx \frac{\phi_n''(x^*)}{2}(x - x^*)^2.$$

This differs fundamentally from the period doubling case where the condition $f_n'(x^*) = -1$ implied that $f_{2n}''(x^*) = 0$, leading to a third order approximation. Here there is no implied restriction on the value of either f_n'' or f_{2n}'' at x^*, which is why the tangent bifurcation is the most usual case.[14]

Note that ϕ_n has a minimum at $x = x^*$ if $\phi_n''(x^*) > 0$, or a maximum if $\phi_n''(x^*) < 0$. As with period doubling, I shall investigate nearby values of r, by setting $r = r^* + \Delta r$. The simplest approximation to ϕ_n is still a parabola, but it will either cut the x-axis at a pair of fixed points, or it will miss it altogether. It is natural, therefore, to use the approximation

$$\phi_n(x) \approx \phi_n(x^*) + \frac{\phi_n''(x^*)}{2}(x - x^*)^2. \tag{3.18}$$

$\phi_n(x^*)$ is zero when $r = r^*$, so we use linear approximation to describe its nearby dependence on r, $\phi_n(x^*) \approx A\Delta r$. We are not particularly interested in the actual value of the derivative $\phi_n''(x^*)$ either, and replace it by a second constant $K = \phi_n''(x^*)/2$. This gives the approximate fixed point equation as

$$A\Delta r + K(x - x^*)^2 = 0, \tag{3.19}$$

a sideways parabola.

---

[14]Some other cases are treated in section 3.9.

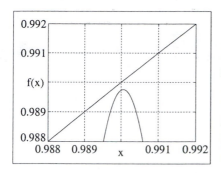
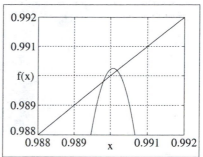

Figure 3.11: Detail of graphs of f_4 for the logistic map, $r = 3.959$ (left), $r = 3.961$ (right) showing tangent bifurcation mechanism.

If A and K have the same sign, then there is no solution of (3.19) for $r < r^*$, while for $r > r^*$ the solution is

$$x_{\pm}^* \approx x^* \pm \sqrt{(A\Delta r)/K}.$$

The reverse situation, that A and K have opposite sign, causing a periodic orbit to suddenly lose its stability by joining up with an unstable orbit of the same period, does not occur for the logistic map. It is known as a *reverse tangent bifurcation*.

Figure 3.12 shows a detail of the period 3 tangent bifurcation of the logistic map. Periodic orbits up to period 3 have been added to the final state diagram; as in previous figures the unstable branch is a light line. It is clear that the theoretical analysis gives a proper account.

Period 3 for the logistic map

For the period 3 tangent bifurcation of the logistic map, the critical value r^* can be found exactly. To do this we must find some special property of the 8th order polynomial $\phi_3(x) = x - f_3(x)$. The two fixed points of f are also fixed points of f_3, which tells us two of the zeros of ϕ_3,

$$\phi_3(x) = x(1 - r + rx)P_6(x),$$

where $P_6(x)$ is sixth order in x. But, using a computer algebra package to find P_6 reveals that it has 21 distinct terms, and that it can't be factored in any simple way for arbitrary r. However, using the same package after substituting $r = 1 + \sqrt{8}$, P_6 does factor as the exact square of a cubic, so it has three double roots in this case. This is exactly the period 3 tangent bifurcation at the critical value r^*, giving

$$r^* = 1 + \sqrt{8}.$$

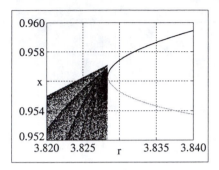

Figure 3.12: Tangent bifurcation of logistic map. Final state diagram, initial value $x_0 = 0.499999$, sample size 2×10^3 points, initial 2×10^3 points discarded. One branch of the associated period 3 orbit also shown; stable (dark) unstable (light).

Exercises

3.23 Use elementary algebra and calculus to show that the CUBIC #1 MAP has a tangent bifurcation at $r = 64/27$. (See also exercise 2.6.)

3.24 The period 3 orbits of the logistic map are the fixed points of f_3 which are not fixed points of f, which implies that the function ϕ_3/ϕ_1 is a sixth order polynomial. Use a computer algebra package to construct this polynomial, and after substituting the value $r = 1 + \sqrt{8}$ (as an exact value), to show that it is the exact square of a cubic polynomial at this value of r. Use the facilities for numerical solution to find the corresponding critical values x_i^*.

3.7 Intermittent behaviour

There is an interesting phenomenon associated with tangent bifurcations, which manifests itself as *intermittent* behaviour of the system. It is quite easily observed for the logistic map just before the period 3 tangent bifurcation. For this purpose, it is helpful that we know the precise critical value $r^* = 1 + \sqrt{8}$ for this bifurcation.

Figure 3.13 shows two pictures, in which the iterations are joined so as to show the action of the third composition map. That is, $x_0, x_3, x_6, \cdots$ are joined by straight lines, similarly for $x_1, x_4, x_7, \cdots$ and $x_2, x_5, x_8, \cdots$. Looking at 1000 iterations you can see that there are long stretches when it appears that the orbit is almost stable period 3, called *laminar regions*, interspersed by *chaotic bursts*. Observe also that the length of the laminar regions is bigger for $r = 3.8284$, which is closer to $1 + \sqrt{8}$, than for $r =$

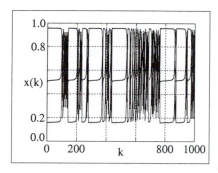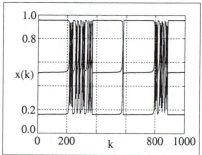

Figure 3.13: Intermittent behaviour of logistic map just before the tangent bifurcation. Parameter values, $r = 3.8283$ (left), $r = 3.8284$ (right), initial value $x_0 = 0.5$, every third point joined to show laminar regions.

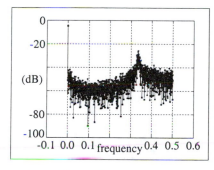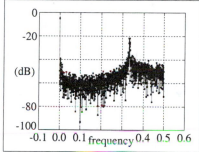

Figure 3.14: Fourier spectra for the iterations of previous figure. A peak is developing at frequency $1/3$. Initial value $x_0 = 0.5$, sample size 3×10^3 points, initial 10^4 points discarded.

3.8283. The influence of these laminar regions, which prefigure the period 3 orbit, is seen quite clearly in the accompanying Fourier spectra shown in figure 3.14. A sharp peak is developing at frequency $1/3$.

A scaling relation

I shall investigate what is going on in the laminar region by considering the cobweb plot. Evidently we must examine the behaviour of the third composition map f_3 just below the critical value of r. Looking at figure 3.15, it is clear that the long stretches of almost periodic behaviour are caused by the iterates getting trapped in the narrow channel near the minimum of $\phi_3(x)$.

Let's model the situation using the approximation derived earlier in

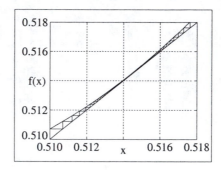

Figure 3.15: Cobweb plot near to tangent bifurcation of the logistic map. Approximately 180 iterations of f are required to make the passage. ($r = 3.8284$, $x_0 = 0.51$.)

equation (3.19), which gives

$$\phi_3(x) \approx A\Delta r + K(x - a)^2.$$

It is clear that the progress made in a single iteration is $\Delta x_k = (x_{k+1} - x_k) = \phi_3(x_k)$. Since the number of iterations required to get through the channel is large, we can think of the rate of progress as if the iteration count k is a continuous quantity, just as we think of large numbers of insects in a population model.[15]

This gives

$$\frac{dx}{dk} \approx A\Delta r + K(x - a)^2.$$

Taking the reciprocal,

$$\frac{dk}{dx} \approx \frac{1}{A\Delta r + K(x - a)^2},$$

from which we can obtain an estimate of the number of iterations to progress from $x = a - \Delta x$ to $x = a + \Delta x$, as

$$k(a + \Delta x) - k(a - \Delta x) \approx \int_{a-\Delta x}^{a+\Delta x} \frac{dx}{A\Delta r + K(x - a)^2}.$$

When Δr is small compared with Δx, which is the present case, we might as well replace $\pm\Delta x$ by $\pm\infty$, after which our estimate of the total number L of iterations required to navigate the bottleneck becomes

$$L \approx \int_{-\infty}^{\infty} \frac{dx}{A\Delta r + K(x - a)^2} = \frac{\pi}{\sqrt{AK\Delta r}}. \tag{3.20}$$

---

[15]See exercise 2.12 for a similar treatment of slowly varying iterations.

This is a standard integral, but I omit the details because the only thing which matters is the dependence on Δr, which can be found without actually evaluating the integral. So we have the scaling relation between the length of a typical laminar region, L, and the distance from the critical parameter value, Δr:

$$L \approx M(\Delta r)^{-1/2}.$$

The relation is readily observed in numerical experiments.

Exercises

3.25 The CUBIC #3 MAP is in a period 3 window at $p = 3.7$. Using the GRAPHICAL ANALYSIS window of CHAOS FOR JAVA demonstrate that there is a tangent bifurcation just before this p value, and locate the critical p value to at least 5 decimal places using the FOURIER ANALYSIS window. Discard a large number of iterations before taking the samples so as to allow for convergence to any periodic orbit.

3.26 The most prominent periodic window of the CUBIC #3 MAP is of period 4.

(i) Using the same techniques as in the previous exercise, locate the critical value of p to at least 6 decimal places.

(ii) Compare your results with the critical r value for the period 3 window of the logistic map. This suggests the conjecture that $p^* = 1 + \sqrt{8}$ for this bifurcation of the CUBIC #3 MAP.

(iii) In a similar way to exercise 3.24, the period 4 orbits of the CUBIC #3 MAP are the roots of the polynomial ϕ_4/ϕ_2, but since f_4 is of degree 81, f_2 of degree 9, their quotient is a polynomial of degree 72. Use a computer algebra package to show that this polynomial has an eighth order even polynomial as an exact factor, and that, for $p = 1 + \sqrt{8}$, this factor is the square of a fourth order polynomial. This justifies the conjecture about the critical p value for this tangent bifurcation.

(iv) Using the facilities for numerical solution (notice that the fourth order polynomial is a quadratic in x^2), find the critical x values at this bifurcation, and check that they are in agreement with what you observe in the BIFURCATION DIAGRAMS window of CHAOS FOR JAVA.

3.27 Consider the integral (3.20). Introduce the new integration variable ξ via

$$x = a + \sqrt{A\Delta r/K}\,\xi.$$

Show that this reduces it to the given form in its dependence on A, K and Δr, because the new integral is independent of all three.

3.28 Consider the CUBIC #1 MAP at $r = 64/27 - \epsilon$, where ϵ is positive but small. Using the ITERATE(1D) window of CHAOS FOR JAVA, investigate the number of iterations N, starting from $x_0 = 0.6$, required to get through the channel, by measuring the number N of iterations required to reach, e.g., $x_N = 0.3$. The graph of N versus $\epsilon^{-1/2}$ should approximate a straight line according to the scaling law. Collect data for a number of different values of ϵ between 10^{-4} and 10^{-8} and construct such a graph to check the relation in practice.

3.29 The previous exercise is made simple by the fact that the system is not chaotic, so that the length of a laminar region is a well determined quantity. Repeat the experiment for the period 3 window of the LOGISTIC MAP, setting $r = 1 + \sqrt{8} - \epsilon$ for different small values of ϵ. If you choose to join every third iterate in the ITERATE(1D) window of CHAOS FOR JAVA, the laminar regions will be easy to see and measure, because they keep recurring after periods of chaos. However, it will be necessary to get an average length for the laminar regions by counting a reasonably large number of them for each value of ϵ. Collect the necessary data and graph N versus $\epsilon^{-1/2}$ as before.

3.8   Unstable orbits and crises

One of the common features of final state diagrams is the fact that a chaotic attractor may change its size discontinuously, or even appear or disappear suddenly, at a critical value of a parameter. Such an occurrence is an example of a *crisis*. A tangent bifurcation may precipitate a crisis, as for example the sudden disappearance of chaos with the emergence of a periodic window, but this is not the only form a tangent bifurcation can take. In fact, a simple example of tangent bifurcation not associated with a crisis was investigated in exercises 3.23 and 3.28.

In terms of the earlier strict definition 3.1, crises do not qualify as bifurcations, since there does not need to be a change in the structure of the periodic orbits. However, crises are intimately connected with unstable periodic orbits, and it is appropriate to deal with the phenomenon here.

An exterior crisis

An exterior crisis is typified by the sudden disappearance of a chaotic attractor due to the fact that the system gains access to a second attractor at some critical parameter value. The feature which distinguishes the crisis as *exterior* is that the new attractor is outside the original set of final states.

As a simple example, I show in figure 3.16 a final state diagram for the CUBIC #1 MAP (2.5), superposed with a bifurcation diagram showing the

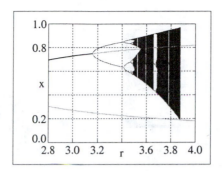

Figure 3.16: Exterior crisis of the CUBIC #1 MAP. Final state diagram, initial value $x_0 = 0.666667$, sample size 10^3 points, initial 10^3 points discarded. The fixed points are also shown; stable (dark) unstable (light).

fixed points and their stability. For the final states, the first 1000 iterations have been discarded, the next 1000 displayed, using the initial condition $x_0 = 0.666667$.

At a critical value, the chaotic attractor simply disappears. To understand this, note that the map has a second attractor in the interval $[0, 1]$, namely the trivial fixed point $x_0^* = 0$, which is stable for all r. In addition, there are two non-zero fixed points $(x_\pm^*)$ for $r > 64/27$. x_-^* is unstable[16] for $r > 64/27$, x_+^* is stable for $64/27 < r < 256/81$ and unstable for $r > 256/81$. Both are unstable in the parameter range of chaotic behaviour; both are shown in the figure. The mechanism for the crisis is clearly seen; collision of the unstable orbit x_-^* with the chaotic attractor.

It is easy enough to check that x_-^* is unstable due to the fact that $f'(x_-^*) > 1$. This means that iterations which start nearby are repelled without switching sides; consequently, if they are on the smaller side they are attracted to x_0^*. We can also calculate the largest interval which can be filled by a chaotic attractor. The maximum is the maximum value of the function, $f(2/3) = r/4$, the minimum is the image of this point under a single iteration,

$$x_{\min} = f(x_{\max}) = \frac{27r^3(4 - r)}{64}.$$

The crisis occurs when the bottom of this band collides with x_-^* i.e., $x_{\min} = x_-^*$. From exercise 2.6, the formula for x_-^* is

$$x_-^* = \frac{9r - \sqrt{81r^2 - 192r}}{18r},$$

---

[16]These facts were the subject of exercises 2.6 and 3.6.

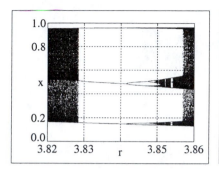 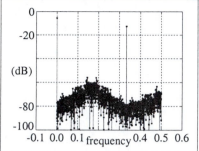

Figure 3.17: Interior crisis of the logistic map. Final state diagram, initial value $x_0 = 0.5$, sample size 500 points, initial 500 points discarded (left). Fourier amplitudes, $r = 3.853$, $x_0 = 0.5$, sample size 3×10^3 points, initial 10^4 points discarded (right).

and on solving (numerically) for the point of collision, the critical values for the crisis are found to be

$$r^* \approx 3.877519248, \qquad x^* \approx 0.1882753825. \tag{3.21}$$

These are in accordance with the displayed figures.

An interior crisis

An example of an interior crisis of the logistic map is shown in the left hand picture of figure 3.17. At the value $r \approx 3.8568$, the system switches from chaos with a strong period 3 component, in which the three bands are visited in regular order, to chaos in a much wider band. The periodic order within this three-band attractor has its origin in the fact that it is at the end of the period 3 window, and is evident from the Fourier spectra, an example of which is also shown. There is a strong peak at frequency $1/3$.

These pictures suggest that the final limit set suddenly jumps from three disjoint intervals to a larger single interval which contains them. Once again the crisis is precipitated by the collision of a chaotic attractor with an unstable orbit. However, it is an *interior* crisis because the former attractor is a subset of the latter, so the effect is a sudden jump in size. The mechanism is seen quite clearly if we use the BIFURCATION DIAGRAMS window of CHAOS FOR JAVA to superpose periodic orbits (unstable as well as stable) on the final state diagram and then zoom in to one of the bands. In principle one can solve for the critical value r^* as in the previous example, by noting that each of the bands is contained between a local maximum x_i^{max} of f_3, and the corresponding minima to which these are mapped under one iteration of f_3: $x_i^{min} = f_3(x_i^{max})$. Equating any one of these with the

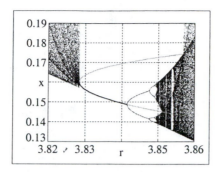

Figure 3.18: Mechanism of an interior crisis — detail from figure 3.17 showing the period 3 orbit, stable (dark) and unstable (light).

position of the corresponding unstable period 3 orbit will give r^*. Clearly this is a non-trivial, although relatively straightforward, task for a computer package. In any case, the critical value can be read off to some considerable accuracy by careful use of the BIFURCATION DIAGRAMS window of CHAOS FOR JAVA.

Exercises

3.30 Using the BIFURCATION DIAGRAMS window of CHAOS FOR JAVA, verify that the critical values given in (3.21) accord with computation, at least in the first five decimal places. You will have to experiment with quite large discard and iteration numbers to get an unambiguous result.

3.31 Show that the logistic map experiences an exterior crisis if the parameter is allowed to exceed the value $r = 4$. To what attractor does the system switch?

3.32 Use the BIFURCATION DIAGRAMS window of CHAOS FOR JAVA to find the critical value between $r = 3.855$ and $r = 3.86$ at which an interior crisis takes place for the LOGISTIC MAP map, to six decimal places.

3.33 Use the FOURIER ANALYSIS window of CHAOS FOR JAVA to investigate the Fourier spectra of the LOGISTIC MAP just after the interior crisis at $r \approx 3.855$. Compare with the behaviour of the Fourier spectra just before the period 3 tangent bifurcation. Give an explanation for the similarities by examining the properties of the function f_3.

3.34 As intimated in the previous question, there is a form of intermittency occurring just after the interior crisis. In this case the laminar regions are periods during which the orbit, though chaotic, visits each band in a strictly period 3 order. Use the ITERATE(1D) window of CHAOS FOR JAVA, as in exercise 3.29, to investigate this.

3.35 Examine the final state diagram of the CUBIC #2 MAP using the BIFURCATION DIAGRAMS window of CHAOS FOR JAVA. Commence by zooming out as far as possible.

(i) Try positive as well as negative initial conditions and observe the behaviour.

(ii) It is evident that there are two crises. Explain the mechanism for each, and classify the type of each.

(iii) Using the results of exercise 2.18, find the exact r value for the second crisis, and check numerically for the consistency of your formula.

3.9   Transcritical and pitchfork bifurcations

I have treated period doubling and tangent bifurcations in considerable detail since each is encountered repeatedly as a typical smooth unimodal map is followed through its complete parameter range. This section presents a brief account of two other types of bifurcation which, although not so common, have been encountered in earlier parts of the book. They therefore deserve an explanation.

Let's first recall the essentials of the theory. There is a critical parameter value r^*, and an associated critical state value x^*, at which a structural change takes place to a periodic orbit, due to the fact that

$$f_n'(x^*) = \pm 1.$$

The investigation proceeds by approximating the function

$$\phi_n(x) = x - f_n(x),$$

for values of r and x close to r^* and x^*, then using elementary algebra.

The case that $f_n'(x^*) = -1$, although technically quite intricate, has a compensating simplification, namely that a single condition implies no less than two coincidences (see equation (3.5)),

$$\phi_{2n}'(x^*) = 0, \qquad \phi_{2n}''(x^*) = 0.$$

The second condition is crucial, implying that the simplest approximation is a cubic. This fixes the type of bifurcation on the basis of a single condition involving only the first derivative.[17]

The case that $f'_n(x^*) = +1$ allows for more variation, and it is essential to understand that the particular behaviour depends on coincidences regarding certain derivatives being zero at the critical point. The simplest case is that there are no coincidences, leading to the tangent bifurcation. That is, at $r = r^*$ the function f_n exactly touches the line $y = x$, but on either side of this value it either cuts the line twice or not at all. This is expressed in equation (3.19) where $\phi_n(x^*)$ is approximated by $A\Delta r$, because it is simply not possible to choose a real function x^* of r to satisfy the equation $\phi_n(x^*) = 0$ as r passes through r^*. In fact, x^* is the point at which the function ϕ_n attains is minimum (or maximum).

Transcritical bifurcation

The foregoing sets the stage. I want to consider the implications of the coincidence that there is a fixed point $x^*(r)$ of f_n, in a range of parameter values r which includes a critical point r^* at which

$$f'_n(x^*; r^*) = 1, \qquad \phi'_n(x^*; r^*) = 0. \qquad (3.22)$$

For $r \neq r^*$, the first derivative $\phi'_n(x^*)$ will no longer be zero, so I replace it by the linear approximation $A\Delta r$. Assuming no further coincidences, the second derivative $\phi''_n(x^*) \neq 0$, and the Taylor approximation (3.7) assumes the form

$$\phi_n(x) \approx A\Delta r\Delta x + B\Delta x^2, \qquad B = \frac{\phi''_n(x^*)}{2}. \qquad (3.23)$$

Regardless of the value of B, one solution of the fixed point equation $\phi_n(x) = 0$ is $x = x^*$, a simple restatement of the assumption made to define x^*. For the other solution x^*_1

$$x^*_1 \approx x^* + \Delta x = x^* - \frac{A\Delta r}{B}.$$

Recalling that $\phi_n(x) = x - f_n(x)$, we have $f'_n = 1 - \phi'_n$, and on the two branches of the bifurcation

$$f'_n(x^*) \approx 1 - A\Delta r, \qquad f'_n(x^*_1) \approx 1 + A\Delta r.$$

This displays quite clearly the transfer of stability from one fixed point to the other as r passes through its critical value.

---

[17] In the unusual circumstance that the third derivative is also zero, there is extra complication. The general theory of behaviour near to a point where $\phi(x^*) = \phi'(x^*) = \cdots \phi^{(n-1)}(x^*) = 0$, $\phi^{(n)}(x^*) \neq 0$ is the subject of *Catastrophe theory*. The case $n = 3$ is relatively simple; it can be shown that the behaviour is controlled by essentially a single parameter in this case, no matter how many parameters occur in the definition of f. For $n > 3$ complications mount rapidly. For an elementary introduction, see Saunders [29].

Pitchfork bifurcation

Unlikely as it might seem, it is not uncommon to have the further coincidence that $\phi_n''(x^*) = 0$. Then we must take the approximation (3.23) to one more term, writing

$$\phi_n(x) \approx A\Delta r \Delta x + C\Delta x^3, \qquad C = \frac{\phi_n'''(x^*)}{6}. \qquad (3.24)$$

This is exactly like the equation (3.9) investigated in the case of period doubling. This time, however, the only function under consideration is f_n, and the new orbits have the same period as the one which changes its stability. The mathematical analysis found on pages 75 – 77 is nevertheless unchanged, and the two possibilities for a bifurcation diagram are still those of figure 3.5. The essential difference is that each arm of the bifurcation diagram is a separate period n orbit, so a pitchfork bifurcation gives rise to two coexisting stable orbits and two competing basins of attraction.

I conclude with a simple example for the CUBIC #3 MAP (2.8). In exercise 2.17 it was found that the fixed point $x_0^* = 0$ period doubles at $p = 2$ to produce a symmetric period 2 orbit, consisting of the pair

$$x_\pm^* = \pm\sqrt{(p-2)/p}, \qquad (p \geq 2).$$

Further, the following derivatives were found in the exercises: $f'(x_\pm^*) = 2p - 5$, $f_2'(x_\pm^*) = (2p-5)^2$. These are for arbitrary parameter p; the bifurcation point is at $p^* = 3$, where

$$f'(x_\pm^*) = 1, \qquad f_2'(x_\pm^*) = 1, \qquad f_2''(x_\pm^*) = 0.$$

The reason that the second derivative is zero is that the original orbit is symmetric. To see this, recall the formula (3.6) for the second derivative of a composition: $f_2''(x) = f''(f(x)) \cdot f'(x)^2 + f'(f(x)) \cdot f''(x)$. Applying this at the bifurcation point, and using the fact that f'' is an antisymmetric function like f itself, we find

$$f_2''(x_\pm^*) = f''(-x_\pm^*) + f''(x_\pm^*) = 0.$$

So symmetry, which is responsible for ensuring that the first derivative $f_2'(x^*)$ cannot be negative, also implies that the second derivative $f_2''(x^*)$ is zero. A pitchfork bifurcation produces two new attractors to replace the single orbit which became unstable, so it is generally associated with *symmetry breaking*.

Exercises

3.36 The SINE MAP (1.2) undergoes a bifurcation at $q = 1/\pi$, with the appearance of a non-zero fixed point. Show that this is a pitchfork bifurcation, and explain what symmetry is broken.

3.37 The CUBIC #2 MAP (1.2) undergoes a bifurcation at $r = \sqrt{3}$, with the appearance of a non-zero fixed point. Classify the type of bifurcation.

3.38 In exercise 2.20, some properties of symmetric periodic orbits of the CUBIC #3 MAP were explored. In particular a symmetric periodic orbit is of even length, allowing us to write $f_n(x) = f_{n/2}(f_{n/2}(x))$.

(i) Show that this implies, at a point of bifurcation of a period n orbit, that $f_n'(x_i^*) = +1$, and also that $f_n''(x_i^*) = 0$ if $f_{n/2}'(x_i^*) = +1$.

(ii) Describe the two scenarios which might be expected for the route to chaos starting from a new periodic window.

3.39 This is a follow up to the previous exercise on the CUBIC #3 MAP.

(i) Use the BIFURCATION DIAGRAMS window of CHAOS FOR JAVA to examine the period 4 window again which begins at $p \approx 3.82$, and explain your observations in light of the previous exercise.

(ii) Examine the period 3 window which begins at $p \approx 3.7$. Explain the fact that there is just the normal period doubling route in this case.

3.10 Theory of Feigenbaum scaling

The hypothesis of Feigenbaum scaling is obviously well supported by numerical evidence, including the universal nature of the constants α and δ. This section is devoted to an elementary introduction to the theory.

The fixed point equation

To proceed, it is convenient to use the value d_n defined in (3.17) to set the scale and to move the origin to $x = x_{\max}$, i.e. to substitute $x = x_{\max} + d_n \xi$ and define

$$g_n(\xi) = \frac{1}{d_n}[f_{2^{n-1}}(x_{\max} + d_n \xi) - x_{\max}].$$

The functions $g_n(\xi)$ map an interval of length $\approx 2/d_n$ into itself, moreover they should be related, for different n, by self-similarity and scaling. In general, the theory of this uses the method of the *renormalisation group* — a concept originally developed in statistical mechanics,[18] and for which the originator was awarded the Nobel prize. The vital point is that the functions $g_n(\xi)$ are essentially the same except that the length scale changes

---

[18] Connections between the concepts and methods of chaos and equilibrium statistical mechanics are discussed in some advanced books such as Schuster [30].

by a factor α each time n is increased by 1. This behaviour was already noted on page 88. One therefore expects $g_n(\xi)$ to satisfy the following functional equation:

$$g_{n+1}(\xi) \approx -\alpha g_n(g_n(-\xi/\alpha)), \tag{3.25}$$

One also expects that the solution of this equation in the limit of large n will give the Feigenbaum constants α and δ.

Assuming that there is a limiting function, $g_n(\xi) \to g(\xi)$, drop the subscript and begin by considering the equation in this limit

$$g(\xi) = -\alpha g(g(-\xi/\alpha)). \tag{3.26}$$

This is known as the *fixed point equation*, the solution g is Feigenbaum's *universal function*. It is easy to see that if $g(\xi)$ is a solution then so is $\mu g(\xi/\mu)$ where μ is an arbitrary scale factor. That is, the theory will give the relation between different scales, not their absolute values. Thus at $\xi = 0$ one can fix the scale arbitrarily. It is convenient to take $g(0) = 1$; substituting $\xi = 0$ into (3.26) shows that $g(1) = -1/\alpha$. In addition, the equation should be solved for an even function, since g is supposed to represent the universal behaviour of a function which is locally a parabola.

Solution of the fixed point equation

The fixed point equation cannot be solved exactly by any known function. But it can be solved approximately, to within a 4th order error, by a quadratic:[19]

$$g(\xi) \approx 1 - 1.366\xi^2 + \mathcal{O}(\xi^4),$$
$$\alpha \approx 2.732. \tag{3.27}$$

To get this solution, first set $g(\xi) = 1 + b\xi^2$. Then

$$\alpha g(g(\xi/\alpha)) = \alpha(1 + b) + 2(b\xi)^2/\alpha + \mathcal{O}(\xi^4).$$

Equating the coefficients gives $1 = -\alpha(1 + b)$ from the constant term and $b = -\alpha/2$ from the ξ^2 term. Eliminating b gives a quadratic equation for α:

$$\alpha^2 - 2\alpha - 2 = 0,$$

with the positive solution $\alpha = 1 + \sqrt{3} = 2.732\ldots$. This value is within 10% of Feigenbaum's value — not bad for such a simple approximation!

One can substitute a longer series into the fixed point equation and evaluate the coefficients numerically after truncating to the desired order.

---

[19]The notation $\mathcal{O}(\xi^4)$ indicates that terms of this power and higher are to be discarded at every step of the working.

This is extremely difficult in practice, even using a computer algebra package, because the equations are nonlinear. The result of such a calculation is that[20]

$$g(\xi) = 1 - 1.527632997\xi^2 + 0.1048151943\xi^4 + 0.02670567349\xi^6$$
$$- 0.003527413864\xi^8 + 0.00008158191343\xi^{10}$$
$$+ 0.00002536842339\xi^{12} - 0.000002687772769\xi^{14} + \cdots \tag{3.28}$$
$$\alpha = 2.502907876\ldots$$

Since this is the observed value of α, the idea of using a scaling hypothesis and investigating its consequences is clearly worth while.

Parameter dependence

Recall that the fundamental equation (3.25) came from looking at the self-similar behaviour of superstable orbits. The self-similarity is between functions $f_{2^n}(x)$ and $f_{2^{n-1}}$. So, in the fixed point equation $g(\xi) = -\alpha g(g(\xi/\alpha))$, the g on the left-hand side comes from $f_{2^n}(x)$, and on the right-hand side from $f_{2^{n-1}}(x)$. Similarly, one must pay attention to the relation between the values of $\bar{r}$ which apply to the two sides of the equation. A proper treatment is beyond what I wish to cover here.[21]

Briefly one assumes that g is a function of two variables, and then uses a linear approximation for its dependence on $\bar{r}$ near to the fixed point r_∞. That is,

$$g(r_\infty - \bar{r}_n, \xi) \approx g(\xi) + (r_\infty - \bar{r}_n)h(\xi),$$

where it is assumed that the fixed point function $g(\xi)$ is already known. After some quite technical arguments, the determination of $h(x)$ and δ reduces to the solution of a nonlinear eigenvalue problem:

$$- \alpha\big[h(g(\xi/\alpha)) + g'(g(\xi/\alpha))h(\xi/\alpha)\big] = \delta h(\xi). \tag{3.29}$$

This has an infinite number of eigenvalues and eigenfunctions. Because of the nonlinearity it is a most difficult problem. The largest eigenvalue is the one which corresponds[22] to δ as $n \to \infty$. Using the fact that $g(0) = 1$ and dividing by the factor $h(0)$ gives

$$\delta = -\alpha\big[h(1)/h(0) + g'(1)\big].$$

To find $g'(1)$, differentiate the fixed point equation twice with respect to ξ and then set $\xi = 0$, which gives $g'(1) = -\alpha$. Thus

$$\delta = \alpha\big[\alpha - h(1)/h(0)\big]. \tag{3.30}$$

---

[20] Mitchell J. Feigenbaum, "The universal metric properties of nonlinear transformations", *Journal of Statistical Physics*, **21**, 669–706 (1979).

[21] An exposition may be found, for example, in Rasband [27], or Schuster [30].

[22] It can be shown that there is only one eigenvalue > 1, i.e., *relevant* to the problem.

Since the fixed point equation (3.25) for g and α can only be solved numerically to obtain the coefficients of its Taylor expansion, the new equation (3.29) also requires numerical analysis. One can make a crude estimate by replacing $h(\xi)$ by a constant. This gives $\delta = \alpha^2 - \alpha \approx 3.8$, which is not too good. The source of the error is in setting $h(1)/h(0) = 1$. The correct value of $\delta = 4.669202\ldots$ can be obtained by proper analysis of the eigenvalue problem.

Exercises

3.40 (You should use a computer algebra package for this exercise.) Substitute the fourth order polynomial

$$g(\xi) \approx 1 + a\xi^2 + b\xi^4,$$

into equation (3.26), expand and discard all terms of higher order than ξ^4. Show that, on solving the ensuing equations for a, b and α, the result is

$$g(\xi) = 1.0 - 1.52224\xi^2 + 0.127613\xi^4 + \mathcal{O}(\xi^6),$$
$$\alpha = 2.53403.$$

3.41 Obtain an approximate solution of (3.29) for δ and $h(\xi)$ by the substitution

$$h(\xi) \approx 1 + b\xi^2,$$

using the quadratic approximations to α and $g(\xi)$ found in the text. The quadratic approximation for g and α is not particularly accurate. What difference does it make it you use the results of the previous exercise instead?

Chapter 4

Two-dimensional systems

It is time to initiate study of dynamical systems in more than one dimension. The appropriate generalisation of definitions 2.1 and 2.2 are

Definition 4.1 (Two-dimensional system) *A pair of equations of the form*

$$x_{k+1} = f(x_k, y_k; \mu), \qquad y_{k+1} = g(x_k, y_k; \mu), \qquad (4.1)$$

is called a discrete two-dimensional dynamical system, whose state variable is the vector (x_k, y_k)*. The coefficient(s)* μ *are the control parameter(s).*

In the one-dimensional case it is usually convenient to restrict attention to maps of an interval; for typical two-dimensional systems this is rarely so and we simply assume that x_k, y_k are real numbers and regard (4.1) as a map from the two-dimensional (real) plane to itself. This plane is often called the *state space*, and the pair of functions (f, g) are components of a *vector valued* function.[1] Similarly, we have

Definition 4.2 (Orbit) *The sequence of points* (x_k, y_k)*,* $k = 0, 1, \cdots$ *generated by the system (4.1) is called an orbit of the system, while the point* (x_0, y_0) *from which it commences is the initial state.*

Evidently every orbit is uniquely specified by the initial state (x_0, y_0).

4.1 The Hénon map

The classic example is the two-dimensional Hénon map

$$f(x, y) = 1 - ax^2 + y,$$
$$g(x, y) = bx, \qquad (4.2)$$

---

[1]An important special class of two-dimensional dynamical systems is obtained by treating the vector components as real and imaginary parts of a complex variable: $z = x + iy$, $\phi(z) = f(x, y) + ig(x, y)$. This is useful only if the resulting function ϕ is analytic; a very restrictive condition which I do not define here. Note, however, that many of the well known fractals, such as the Mandelbrot and Julia sets, come from such systems.

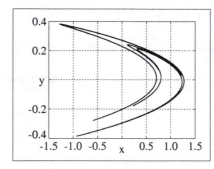 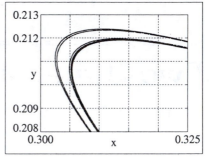

Figure 4.1: The Hénon attractor, $a = 1.4$, $b = 0.3$. Initial state $(0.5, 0.5)$, sample size 10^6 points, initial 10^3 points discarded.

in which a and b are parameters. The map was introduced by M. Hénon in 1976 as a model which exhibits much of the interesting dynamical behaviour of more complicated systems, but using simple algebraic functions.[2] It can be regarded as an extension of the logistic map to two dimensions, produced by applying a linear feedback loop. The present section is a survey of some of the important and complex features to be found in the Hénon system.

The Attractor

Hénon concentrated much attention on the parameter values $a = 1.4$, $b = 0.3$. Let's start there, using the ITERATE(2D) window of CHAOS FOR JAVA.[3] It is interesting to examine the set of points in the x-y plane which are visited by a single long orbit of the map; two such pictures are shown in figure 4.1.

Such figures are numerical approximations to a forward limit set, a concept introduced on page 68. That is to say, the theoretical construct we are attempting to visualise is the set of points which are visited arbitrarily closely, infinitely often, by the orbit. In interpreting these pictures, it is important to remember that exact construction is not possible by straightforward numerical iteration: computation gives a finite approximation whose validity must be tested by experiment.[4] The right hand picture is a detail of part of the left hand one. There is a hint of the infinitely complex, fractal, structure of a *strange attractor*[5] in just these two diagrams. A few min-

---

[2] Note that this pair (f, g) are not the real and imaginary parts of an analytic function.

[3] See appendix A.7 for documentation on the ITERATE(2D) window, which include basins of attraction and Lyapunov exponents.

[4] Remember also a previous discussion (page 41ff.) of the numerical problems associated with investigating unstable orbits. The orbit shown is quite strange in that, even on the attractor, motion is always essentially unstable!

[5] Attractors with fractal properties were called strange attractors by D. Ruelle and F.

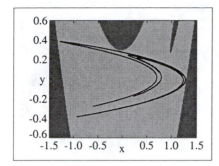
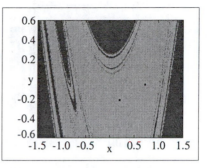

Figure 4.2: Basins of attraction (light grey) of the Hénon map. $a = 1.4$, $b = 0.3$, strange attractor (left), $a = 1.4$, $b = -0.3$, period 2 attractor (right). Dark grey areas are the basins of infinity.

utes experimentation with CHAOS FOR JAVA will convince you that here is something unexpectedly rich, albeit of simple origin. You will also find that the cost of seeing ever more detail, by zooming in, is a rapidly increasing amount of computation which becomes a barrier to further observation.

The orbits in figure 4.2 started from $(x_0, y_0) = (1/2, 1/2)$, although the first 1000 iterations are not actually displayed. This is intended to provide convergence to the attractor, to within the pixel resolution. Of course, the strange attractor contains an infinite number of points which can only be represented by a finite number of pixels, which is the reason for seeking more detail as in the right hand view of figure 4.1. Such *fractal* properties will be considered further in the next chapter.

Definition 4.3 (Attractor) *A forward limit set with the property that all orbits which start sufficiently close to it converge to points in it, will be called an attractor.*

This extends an earlier definition of an attracting periodic orbit. In the simple periodic case, the forward limit set consists of the orbit itself: just n points, where n is the period. Recalling that the definition in use is asymptotic stability, it is easy to see that such a stable orbit is an attractor. The strange attractor of the Hénon map contains an uncountably infinite number of points, so what is meant by convergence for it is that, for any chosen distance δ, no matter how small, after some number N (which will depend on the initial state (x_0, y_0) as well as on δ) every iteration (x_k, y_k) of the orbit starting from (x_0, y_0) is within distance δ of some point of the attractor.

Takens in an article "On the nature of turbulence", *Communications in Mathematical Physics*, **20**, 167 – 192 (1971).

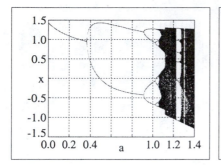 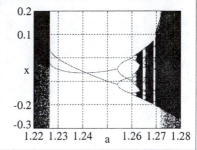

Figure 4.3: Final state diagrams for the Hénon map. Initial state
$(0.5, 0.5)$, sample size 500 points, initial 500 points discarded (left);
both numbers increased to 5000 in the close-up (right).

Basins of attraction

Regardless of whether the attractor is periodic or strange, its basin of attraction may be infinitely complex, even fractal. First, the definition:

Definition 4.4 (Basin of attraction) *The set of initial conditions whose
orbits converge to a given attractor constitute its basin of attraction.*

Once a numerical orbit has been computed, it is not difficult to compute
a numerical approximation to its basin of attraction, although it is a com-
putationally intensive task. The reason the basin is not the entire plane is
that, for most initial points which are at a large distance from the origin,
the term ax^2 in (4.2) acts to increase that distance without bound; the
point at infinity is therefore also an attractor, corresponding to the system
running completely out of range. Two pictures are shown in figure 4.2; in
each the *basin of infinity* is the dark grey area, while the bounded attractor
is shown sitting in a light area which is its basin.[6]

The basins are generated as follows: the coordinates represented by
each pixel in the plot area are used, in turn, to generate an orbit, which is
followed to see if it converges to an attractor or to infinity. It is entirely
possible that the simple process thus described may not ever converge,
particularly if there are initial values which are not in the basin of either
the computed orbit or of infinity. For this reason, a limit is set for the
number of iterations which are performed, for each pixel, before the search
is abandoned for it. Such point are displayed as belonging to the basin
of an unknown attractor; increasing the limit may change the numerical
result so that experimentation may be necessary in some cases, particularly

---

[6]In CHAOS FOR JAVA orbits and their basins are indicated by colours.

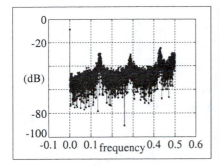 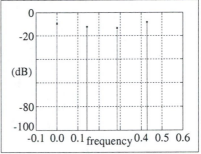

Figure 4.4: Fourier spectra for the Hénon map. $a = 1.226$, $b = 0.3$ (left), $a = 1.227$, $b = 0.3$ (right). Initial state $(0.5, 0.5)$, sample size 7×10^3 points, initial 10^6 points discarded.

where basins are fractal.[7] The first figure (left) corresponds to the strange attractor already viewed, for which $a = 1.4$, $b = 0.3$. The orbit itself is infinitely complex, but the boundary of its basin of attraction appears relatively simple, consisting of only a few smooth curves in the area shown. The second figure (right) is for $a = 1.4$, $b = -0.3$. We see that the orbit now is quite simple, in fact stable period 2. However, the basin boundary has become complex, with an infinite amount of detail in a finite region.[8]

Bifurcations

The second equation of the Hénon system shows that successive y values are a constant multiple of the previous x values. So the dynamical information is completely contained in the sequence x_k alone, even though it is far richer than for a one-dimensional map. This implies that it is useful to investigate the sequences x_k using tools already developed for the one-dimensional case, although the definition of Lyapunov exponent will require some fundamental changes.

Figure 4.3 shows two final state diagrams which display quite clearly period doubling cascades to chaos and tangent bifurcation. The most prominent periodic window has period 7, unlike the logistic map where period 3 has this distinction. The two branches of the period 7 orbit shown in the right hand picture appear to cross; actually they have different y values at the point where the x values coincide, so they do not. This is explored in exercise 4.3 below. But the general features are exactly as in one dimension,

---

[7]For details of how to set this parameter, see appendix A.7. In all of the displayed figures it is set to the default value of 10^3.

[8]The first basin boundary also consists of an infinite number of curves, but they are not evident since they accumulate at infinity.

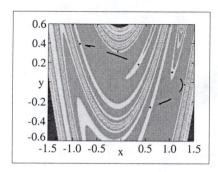

Figure 4.5: Coexisting attractors of the Hénon map, $a = 1.07$, $b = 0.3$. The strange attractor is produced using an initial state $(0.5, 0.5)$, the period six orbit from the initial state $(-0.8, -0.4)$. The intertwined basins have an obvious complex structure.

including the fact that periodic windows normally end in a period doubling cascade to chaos.

As further proof that the right hand figure in 4.3 does indeed show a tangent bifurcation from chaos to a periodic attractor, two Fourier spectra are shown in figure 4.4, taken just below and above the critical value of a. They provide strong evidence of aperiodic behaviour which suddenly switches to a stable period 7 orbit. The peaks which prefigure the stable orbit are clearly visible; I have chosen 7000 as sample size because of the importance of its divisibility by the period.

Coexisting Attractors

Setting $a = 1.07$ and $b = 0.3$, it is easy to discover that there are two bounded attractors, one periodic, the other a strange attractor. They are shown in figure 4.5. Each orbit has its basin of attraction, and infinity is a third attractor. It is interesting to examine these basins, indicated using shades of grey. It is evident that the basins of the two bounded attractors are intertwined in an extremely complex way; in fact they furnish yet another example of a fractal arising from a simple dynamical system.

Exercises

4.1 Use the Iterate(2D) window of Chaos for Java to examine orbits of the Hénon map at $a = 1.07$, $b = 0.3$.

(i) There are two coexisting attractors. Display them in a common window by using initial values $(0.5, 0.5)$ for one and $(-0.8, -0.4)$ for the other.

(ii) Using the same initial values, compute the Fourier spectra for each.

(iii) What conclusions can you draw about the periodicity of each attractor?

(iv) Repeat with $a = 1.073$, 1.075 and 1.077. (You may have to adjust the initial state so as to track the desired attractor.) What kind of bifurcation sequence do you see?

4.2 Using the BIFURCATION DIAGRAMS window of CHAOS FOR JAVA, estimate to 4 decimal places the value of a at which the orbits in figure 4.3 cross; then use ITERATE(2D) window to list the seven points (x_i^*, y_i^*) on the orbit and to show that they really are distinct in state space.

4.3 Another well-studied two-dimensional map is the Lozi map, originally introduced in 1978 as a simplification of the HÉNON MAP; it is defined by

$$x_{n+1} = 1 - a|x_n| + y_n, \qquad y_{n+1} = bx_n. \qquad (4.3)$$

Using CHAOS FOR JAVA, classify the periodicity of its attracting orbits, and examine the basins of attraction, for $a = 0.5$, 1.0 and 1.5, all with $b = 0.3$.

4.2 Fixed points

As in the one-dimensional case, fixed points play a fundamental rôle in the theory of higher-dimensional systems, and have a similar definition:

Definition 4.5 (Fixed point) *Any pair* (x^*, y^*) *for which*

$$f(x^*, y^*) = x^*, \qquad g(x^*, y^*) = y^*, \qquad (4.4)$$

is called a fixed point of the two-dimensional dynamical system.

The important point to note is that the pair of formulae (4.4) are a single condition; (f, g) is a vector-valued function defined on states (x, y) which are vectors.

Similarly, compositions of the map are defined by formulae which are easy to write down, but difficult to deal with:

$$f_2(x, y) = f(f(x, y), g(x, y)), \qquad g_2(x, y) = g(f(x, y), g(x, y)),$$

and, in general (see definition 2.9)

$$f_n(x, y) = f_{n-1}(f(x, y), g(x, y)), \qquad g_n(x, y) = g_{n-1}(f(x, y), g(x, y)).$$

As on page 34, a *periodic orbit* is a cycle of n fixed points of the n-fold composition, each of which is not a fixed point of an m-fold composition for any $m < n$; evidently there are few situations where one can hope to derive useable formulae for such orbits.

Fixed points of the Hénon map

The functions f and g are specified in (4.2) by single formulae valid for all states (x, y), consequently fixed points of the Hénon map are given as solutions of the simultaneous equations

$$x^* = 1 - ax^{*2} + y^*, \qquad y^* = bx^*. \qquad (4.5)$$

Eliminating y^*, we get a quadratic equation for x^*, from which there are two solutions $(x_\pm^*, y_\pm^*)$ given by

$$x_\pm^* = \frac{-(1 - b) \pm \sqrt{(1 - b)^2 + 4a}}{2a}, \qquad y_\pm^* = bx_\pm^*. \qquad (4.6)$$

Provided that $a > 0$, they satisfy $x_+^* > 0$, $x_-^* < 0$ (exercise 4.4).

Let's consider the parameter b to be fixed and investigate the dependence of the fixed points on a. Obviously they exist only for $(1-b)^2 + 4a \geq 0$, or

$$a \geq a_0 = -\frac{1}{4}(1 - b)^2.$$

The birth of a pair of fixed points at a critical parameter value is typical of a tangent bifurcation. Therefore we expect that one is stable, the other unstable. As with one-dimensional maps, the question of stability may be settled using derivatives, but the mathematics is more subtle.

When a is small and $|b| \leq 1$, we have the approximation

$$\sqrt{(1 - b)^2 + 4a} = (1 - b)\sqrt{1 + 4a/(1 - b)^2}$$
$$\approx (1 - b) + 2a/(1 - b),$$

from which we find that

$$x_+^* \approx \frac{1}{1 - b}, \qquad y_+^* \approx b\frac{1}{1 - b},$$
$$x_-^* \approx -\frac{1 - b}{a}, \qquad y_-^* \approx -b\frac{1 - b}{a}. \qquad (4.7)$$

It follows that the fixed point (x_-^*, y_-^*) does not move continuously, in state space, as a passes through the value zero. For this reason,[9] I shall restrict attention to $a \geq 0$.

Iteration for $a = 0$

The fixed point (x_+^*, y_+^*) is stable for sufficiently small a, meaning that nearby points are attracted to it under iteration of the map. It is instructive

---

[9]This problem can be circumvented by changing the scale of the x coordinate via the substitution $x \to ax$, but I prefer to keep to Hénon's original notation.

to consider the case that $a = 0$, for which the map is actually linear. Let the initial point be

$$x_0 = x_+^* + \xi_0 = \frac{1}{1-b} + \xi_0,$$

$$y_0 = y_+^* + \eta_0 = \frac{b}{1-b} + \eta_0,$$

so that (ξ_0, η_0) measures the state relative to the fixed point. Our interest is in the sequence $(\xi_k, \eta_k) = (x_k - x_+^*, y_k - y_+^*)$. Simple calculation gives

$$x_1 = x_+^* + \xi_1 = \frac{1}{1-b} + \eta_0 = x_+^* + \eta_0,$$

$$y_1 = y_+^* + \eta_1 = \frac{b}{1-b} + b\xi_0 = y_+^* + b\xi_0,$$

followed by

$$x_2 = x_+^* + \xi_2 = \frac{1}{1-b} + b\xi_0 = x_+^* + b\xi_0,$$

$$y_2 = y_+^* + \eta_2 = \frac{b}{1-b} + b\eta_0 = y_+^* + b\eta_0.$$

After two steps, we see that the distance from the fixed point has decreased by the factor b. The sign of b determines which side it is on. Under further iteration, we have

$$x_{2k} = x_+^* + b^k \xi_0,$$

$$y_{2k} = y_+^* + b^k \eta_0,$$

so the fixed point is an attractor if $|b| < 1$. However, it is important to note that the approach is not uniform at each step. In fact, if we choose $\xi_0 = 0$, so that the initial point is vertically in line with the fixed point, then after one iteration it is horizontally in line and just as far away. It is this possibility of a constantly changing direction of approach which necessitates the development of more general theoretical methods.

Exercises

4.4 Show that the solutions of equation (4.6) satisfy

$$x_+^* > 0, \qquad x_-^* < 0,$$

for all $a > 0$, $|b| < 1$. (First note that $0 < 1 - b < 2$.)

4.5 Show that, for all $|b| < 1$ and $a > 0$, the second fixed point of the Hénon map satisfies $ax_-^* < -1$.

4.6 Find the fixed points of the Lozi map for arbitrary a, b, provided $|b| < 1$. In particular, show that:

(i) If $a + b > 1$, there are two fixed points $(x_\pm^*, y_\pm^*)$, with $x_+^* > 0$, $x_-^* < 0$.

(ii) If $b - 1 < a < 1 - b$, there is one fixed point (x_+^*, y_+^*), with $x_+^* > 0$.

4.7 To find a period 2 orbit of the Hénon map requires the solution of the simultaneous equations

$$x_1^* = 1 - ax_0^{*2} + y_0^*, \qquad y_1^* = bx_0^*,$$
$$x_0^* = 1 - ax_1^{*2} + y_1^*, \qquad y_0^* = bx_1^*,$$

from which y_0^* and y_1^* are readily eliminated, after which x_1^* may also be eliminated; in this way a fourth order equation may be found for x_0^*. Obtain this equation, and using the fact that a quadratic factor is known from equation (4.5), obtain a quadratic equation for the two new fixed points of the second composition map. Show that the solutions of this quadratic are real only for $a \geq \frac{3}{4}(1 - b)^2$.

4.8 If $b > 0$ and $a = 1 - b$, the Lozi map has a period 2 orbit given by

$$(x_0^*, y_0^*) = \left(\frac{1}{1 - b}, 0\right), \qquad (x_1^*, y_1^*) = \left(0, \frac{b}{1 - b}\right).$$

(i) Find the period 2 orbit of the Lozi map in the parameter range $1 - b \leq a \leq 1 + b$.

(ii) Investigate the corresponding situation for $b < 0$.

4.3   Area contraction

In order to give the ensuing discussion wider applicability, I shall consider the *generalised Hénon map* defined as

$$f(x, y) = h(x) + y,$$
$$g(x, y) = bx. \qquad\qquad (|b| < 1) \qquad\qquad (4.8)$$

The more general form still retains the essential feature that non-linearity enters through a single one variable function $h(x)$. For the standard Hénon map, $h(x) = 1 - ax^2$, for the Lozi map, $h(x) = 1 - a|x|$.

Now let's consider the transformation of a small square region, with corners at

$$(x, y + \delta) \qquad (x + \delta, y + \delta)$$
$$(x, y) \qquad\qquad (x + \delta, y)$$

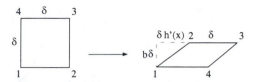

Figure 4.6: Transformation of small square ($h'(x) > 0$, $b > 0$).

which I have laid out so as to indicate their relative positions in the plane, and let[10]

$$x' = f(x, y) = 1 + h(x) + y,$$
$$y' = g(x, y) = bx,$$

be the image of the bottom left corner under one iteration of the map. Assume for the time being that $b > 0$; in this case we shall see that it is also the bottom left corner of the image.

The top left corner $(x, y + \delta)$ maps to

$$x'' = f(x, y + \delta) = h(x) + y + \delta = x' + \delta,$$
$$y'' = g(x, y + \delta) = bx = y'.$$

This has the same vertical coordinate as the image of the bottom left corner, but for the horizontal coordinate we have $x'' > x'$, so it is the bottom right corner of the image. Now for the image of the bottom right corner, we use the approximation $h(x + \delta) \approx h(x) + \delta h'(x)$, to get

$$x''' = f(x + \delta, y) = h(x + \delta) + y$$
$$\approx h(x) + \delta h'(x) + y = x' + \delta h'(x),$$
$$y''' = g(x + \delta, y) = b(x + \delta) = y' + b\delta.$$

so this becomes the top left corner of the image. Finally, for the fourth corner,

$$x'''' = f(x + \delta, y + \delta) = h(x + \delta) + y + \delta$$
$$\approx h(x) + \delta h'(x) + y + \delta = x' + \delta h'(x) + \delta,$$
$$y'''' = g(x + \delta, y + \delta) = b(x + \delta) = y' + b\delta.$$

so it is mapped to the top right corner of the image.

Examination of these formulae shows that the image of the square is a parallelogram,[11] with bottom of length δ. The perpendicular distance be-

---

[10]Throughout this calculation, x, x', y, y', etc., denote different values of the state variables, whereas h' is the derivative of the function h. The distinction should be clear from the context.

[11]Because of the restriction to a generalised Hénon map, the top and bottom are precisely straight lines; the sides, which are curved, may be made as near to straight as desired by taking δ sufficiently small. This is the meaning of linear approximation.

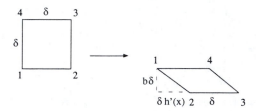

Figure 4.7: Transformation of small square ($h'(x) > 0$, $b < 0$).

tween bottom and top is $b\delta$, so the new area if $b\delta^2$. Furthermore the corners of the image have their orientation reversed compared to the original.

The case $b < 0$ involves exactly the same equations, however there is no reversal of orientation in this case, while the area is transformed to $|b|\delta^2$. In both cases there is a 90° rotation, and for positive b a reversal of orientation as well. All these factors contribute to the richness of the dynamics.

The important conclusion is that, for the generalised Hénon map, the area of any simple small region of the x-y plane is multiplied, at each iteration, by the factor $|b|$. Since we are only concerned with the case that $|b| < 1$, this is an area contraction. Two-dimensional maps which have the area contracting property are said to be *dissipative*.

Exercises

4.9 Investigate precisely what happens to a small square if $h'(x) < 0$, both for $b > 0$ and $b < 0$. Pay particular attention to the orientation.

4.10 Invert equations (4.8) for the generalised Hénon map, that is, if

$$x' = h(x) + y, \qquad y' = bx,$$

find the equations expressing (x, y) as functions of (x', y'). Show also that the inverse map[12] is area expanding, with factor $1/b$.

4.11 Holmes suggested the following cubic version of the Hénon system[13]

$$x_{k+1} = dx_k - x_k^3 - b_H y_k, \qquad y_{k+1} = x_k.$$

(i) Show that the rescaling $-b_H y \to y$ exhibits it as a generalised Hénon map

$$x_{k+1} = dx_k - x_k^3 + y_k, \qquad y_{k+1} = bx_k, \tag{4.9}$$

---

[12]Non-invertibility is necessary for chaos in one-dimensional maps; evidently this is not so in higher dimension.

[13]See footnote 14 on page 11 for the reference; note that I have interchanged the variables x and y compared with the original.

with $h(x) = dx - x^3$ and $b = -b_H$ (which is why I appended the subscript H to Holmes' b).

(ii) Find the fixed points of the map; in particular show that there is a transition from a single fixed point to three fixed points when d increases through the critical value $d = 1 + b_H = 1 - b$, with the two new fixed points given by

$$x^* = \sqrt{d + b - 1}, \qquad (d > 1 - b).$$

4.12 Holmes constructed the cubic map of the previous exercise to be completely antisymmetric under simultaneous inversion of x and y,

$$f(-x, -y) = -f(x, y), \qquad g(-x, -y) = -g(x, y),$$

where the notation is taken from equation (4.1).

(i) Show that this implies that orbits may be as in exercise 2.20.

(ii) Follow the method of exercise 2.15 to show that the map has a symmetric period 2 orbit given by

$$x^*_\pm = \pm\sqrt{1 - b + d}, \qquad y^*_\pm = bx^*_\pm, \qquad (d > b - 1).$$

4.4 Stability of fixed points

A stable fixed point is one which is an attractor in the terms of definition 4.3. The problem is that this employs the *Euclidean distance* between pairs of points (x, y), (x', y'):

$$d = \sqrt{(x - x')^2 + (y - y')^2},$$

which is non-linear even when the quantities $(x - x')$, $(y - y')$ are themselves small. In this section I develop the theory required for investigating stability using linear algebra.

The eigenvalue problem

To commence, let's consider the following general question: suppose that a point (x, y) maps to the point $(x', y') = (f(x, y), g(x, y))$, not necessarily close to it, what then is the linear approximation for the motion of a nearby point $(x + \xi, y + \eta)$? For the generalised Hénon map,

$$
\begin{aligned}
x + \xi &\to h(x + \xi) + (y + \eta) \\
&\approx x' + h'(x)\xi + \eta = x' + \xi', \\
y + \eta &\to b(x + \xi) \\
&= y' + b\xi = y' + \eta'.
\end{aligned}
\tag{4.10}
$$

Our interest is in the relative position (ξ', η') of the two new points, which is linear in (ξ, η). Expressed in matrix form, equation (4.10) may be written as

$$
\begin{pmatrix} \xi' \\ \eta' \end{pmatrix} = \begin{pmatrix} h'(x) & 1 \\ b & 0 \end{pmatrix} \begin{pmatrix} \xi \\ \eta \end{pmatrix}.
\tag{4.11}
$$

In general, the matrix operation (4.11) acts to change both length and direction; the vectors (ξ, η) and (ξ', η') differ in both properties. There may be, however, independent directions with the property that vectors in those directions only change their length. Finding them is an eigenvalue problem, which I shall treat here using elementary mathematics. If the direction is not changed, then the vector (ξ', η') must be a multiple of (ξ, η). Denoting the multiplying factor by λ, everything will be determined from the solutions (if any) of the *eigenvalue equation*

$$
\begin{pmatrix} h'(x) & 1 \\ b & 0 \end{pmatrix} \begin{pmatrix} \xi \\ \eta \end{pmatrix} = \lambda \begin{pmatrix} \xi \\ \eta \end{pmatrix}.
\tag{4.12}
$$

Written out as a pair of homogeneous simultaneous equations, this is

$$
(h'(x) - \lambda)\xi + \eta = 0, \qquad b\xi - \lambda\eta = 0.
\tag{4.13}
$$

Eliminating ξ, η gives the *characteristic equation* which must be satisfied by λ,

$$
\lambda^2 - \lambda h'(x) - b = 0;
\tag{4.14}
$$

this will determine, in general, two distinct *eigenvalues*, $\lambda_\pm$. Once the eigenvalues are determined, the corresponding *eigenvectors* may be obtained by substituting into either of equations (4.13). This gives only the ratio $\xi : \eta$, which is consistent with the fact that the vectors (ξ, η) only determine directions.

Properties of the eigenvalues and eigenvectors

First, some properties of the zeros of (4.14). Writing

$$
\lambda^2 - \lambda h'(x) - b = (\lambda - \lambda_+)(\lambda - \lambda_-),
$$

it is immediate that

$$\lambda_+ + \lambda_- = h'(x), \qquad \lambda_+\lambda_- = -b. \tag{4.15}$$

The second relation implies the area reduction previously investigated,[14] but there is another consequence of great importance: in the dissipative case ($|b| < 1$) only one of the eigenvalues can have magnitude greater than unity.

Now let's write a formula for the eigenvalues:

$$\lambda_\pm = \frac{h'(x) \pm \sqrt{h'(x)^2 + 4b}}{2}. \tag{4.16}$$

There are three distinct possibilities:

(i) The eigenvalues are real but unequal. In this case it follows from equation (4.13) that the corresponding eigenvectors are not in the same direction, so they may be used to define coordinate axes.

(ii) The eigenvalues are complex. Then the formula (4.16) shows that they are complex conjugate, and satisfy

$$\overline{\lambda}_+ = \lambda_-, \qquad |\lambda_\pm| = \sqrt{|b|},$$

where $\overline{\lambda}$ denotes the complex conjugate. From (4.13) it follows that the eigenvectors must also be complex, so they can only be used to construct a coordinate system after further work.

(iii) The eigenvalues are real and equal. This occurs as a transitional case between the previous two, when matters conspire so that $h'(x)^2 + 4b = 0$. Since $h'(x)^2$ is positive, this requires that b is negative, giving $\lambda_\pm = h'(x)/2 = \pm\sqrt{-b}$. Either way $|\lambda_\pm| < 1$.

The Hénon map for $a = 0$, $b > 0$

The stability of the fixed point (x_+^*, y_+^*) given in equation (4.7), for $a = 0$, $b > 0$, is readily demonstrated using the eigenvalue method. In fact, using the fact that $h' = 0$ if $a = 0$, the eigenvalues and corresponding eigenvectors are given by

$$\lambda_+ = b^{1/2}, \qquad (1, b^{1/2}),$$

and

$$\lambda_- = -b^{1/2}, \qquad (1, -b^{1/2}).$$

---

[14]Using the eigenvectors to define the edges of a sufficiently small parallelogram, it is mapped to another with sides parallel to the original, and lengths scaled by the eigenvalues whose product is $-b$. However, this argument needs modification if the eigenvalues are complex.

An arbitrary orbit may be expressed in terms of these two, since for any initial displacement (ξ_0, η_0) from the fixed point (x_+^*, y_+^*),

$$(\xi_0, \eta_0) = \frac{\xi_0 + b^{-1/2}\eta_0}{2}(1, b^{1/2}) + \frac{\xi_0 - b^{-1/2}\eta_0}{2}(1, -b^{1/2}).$$

Using the defining properties of the eigenvectors this may be turned into a general formula for subsequent displacements:

$$(\xi_k, \eta_k) = b^{k/2}\frac{\xi_0 + b^{-1/2}\eta_0}{2}(1, b^{1/2}) + (-1)^k b^{k/2}\frac{\xi_0 - b^{-1/2}\eta_0}{2}(1, -b^{1/2}),$$

which demonstrates convergence to the fixed point. Because the second term contains the alternating sign factor $(-1)^k$, this convergence may not be equally apparent at each step, a fact already noted.

Loss of stability for the Hénon map

For $a > 0$, $b > 0$, we have $h'(x_+^*) = -2ax_+^*$, from which

$$\lambda_{\pm}(a) = -ax_+^* \pm \sqrt{(ax_+^*)^2 + b}. \qquad (4.17)$$

Both eigenvalues are real since $b > 0$. We want to investigate the solutions of this equation, $\lambda_{\pm}(a)$, as a function of a, to find out for what value the fixed point loses its stability, and by what mechanism. Before delving into details, recall equations (4.15). Substituting the present values,

$$\lambda_+(a) + \lambda_-(a) = -2ax_+^*, \qquad \lambda_+(a)\lambda_-(a) = -b. \qquad (4.18)$$

Now x_+^* is a function of a, moreover $x_+^* \geq 0$. Therefore $\lambda_+(a)$ is positive, since $\sqrt{(ax_+^*)^2 + b} > ax_+^*$; also $\lambda_+(a) \leq b^{1/2}$, since $\sqrt{(ax_+^*)^2 + b} < ax_+^* + b^{1/2}$ (try squaring both sides), and $\lambda_-(a)$ is negative. Summarising, as functions of a,

$$0 < \lambda_+(a) < b^{1/2}, \qquad \lambda_-(a) < 0.$$

This means that the fixed point cannot become unstable through the direction connected with λ_+; rather it must be because λ_- passes through the critical value -1. Moreover, iterates whose position relative to (x_+^*, y_+^*) is in the direction connected with λ_- oscillate from side to side. At the critical value of a for which $\lambda_- = -1$, a period doubling bifurcation occurs.

Let's find the critical value, a_1, for this first period doubling. Substituting $\lambda_+ = b$, $\lambda_- = -1$ into the condition (4.18) gives

$$b - 1 = -2ax_+^*;$$

substituting further the formula (4.6) for x_+^* leads to the required equation for the critical value of a,

$$-(1 - b) = (1 - b) - \sqrt{(1 - b)^2 + 4a},$$

the solution of which is

$$a_1 = \frac{3}{4}(1 - b)^2. \tag{4.19}$$

From exercise 4.7, this result might have been anticipated. If $b = 0.3$, it yields $a_1 = 0.3675$.

The period doubling cascade

At $a = a_1$, double iteration of (4.12) gives the linear approximation

$$(\xi_0, \eta_0) \rightarrow \lambda(\xi_0, \eta_0) \rightarrow \lambda^2(\xi_0, \eta_0).$$

So the contraction/expansion factors for the second composition map are[15]

$$\lambda_+^{(2)} = \lambda_+^2 = b^2, \qquad \lambda_-^{(2)} = \lambda_-^2 = 1, \qquad a = a_1.$$

This is exactly parallel to the result for one-dimensional maps undergoing period doubling, for which $f'(x^*) = -1$, $f_2'(x^*) = f'(x^*)^2 = 1$ at $r = r^*$. The new period doubled orbit is a fixed point of the second composition map $(f_2(x, y), g_2(x, y))$ (see page 114) which is not a fixed point of $(f(x, y), g(x, y))$; initially (when $a = a_1$), $\lambda_-^{(2)} = 1$, $\lambda_+^{(2)} = b^2$, however as a is increased, we expect a further period doubling to occur, caused by $\lambda_-^{(2)}$ passing through the value -1.

How can this happen? Apart from the obvious complication of having to deal with functions of two variables, and the associated eigenvalue problems, there is a fundamental problem. In the one-dimensional case, the value of $f_2'(x^*)$ decreases continuously from positive to negative values, passing through a superstable orbit, where $f_2'(x^*) = 0$, on the way; this was particularly convenient for the study of Feigenbaum scaling. For the generalised Hénon map we have shown that there is a constant area reduction by the factor $|b|$ per iteration, from which it follows that neither of the eigenvalues $\lambda_\pm^{(2)}$ can ever be zero; there are no superstable orbits. Nevertheless, for any reasonable function $h(x)$ we expect that the eigenvalues will vary continuously as a is changed, exactly as in the one-dimensional case.

This paradox has a resolution: the pair $\lambda_\pm^{(2)}$ first vary continuously from their initial values $(1, b^2)$, to the common value (b, b), while remaining

---

[15]The notation $\lambda^{(2)}$ is a reminder that these eigenvalues are associated with the second composition map.

real, then move as a complex conjugate pair of magnitude $|b|$ until they
meet again at the common value $(-b, -b)$, after which they move as real
eigenvalues to $(-1, -b^2)$ to produce the next period doubling.

In case $b = 0.3$, the critical value is $a_2 = 0.9125$, and one can see this
quite clearly from the numerical computation of bifurcation diagrams and
Lyapunov exponents (see figure 4.9). This is the beginning of a period-
doubling cascade to chaos. Denote by a_n the value at which the nth period
doubling occurs; the first few values are ($b = 0.3$)

$$a_1 = .3675, \qquad a_2 = .9125, \qquad a_3 \approx 1.0258,$$
$$a_4 \approx 1.0511, \qquad a_5 \approx 1.0566, \qquad \cdots$$

More accurate values can be obtained by careful numerical experimentation,
but it is not as easy as in the one-dimensional case. The values converge
geometrically according to the general scheme with Feigenbaum constant
$\delta \approx 4.669$ and $a_\infty \approx 1.05805$.

Exercises

4.13 The above treatment of the stability of the fixed point (x_+^*, y_+^*) of the
Hénon map was restricted to $b > 0$.

(i) Show that, if $b < 0$, then for small but positive values of a the
eigenvalues (4.17) are complex.

(ii) Determine that the condition for the eigenvalues to be real and equal
is that a satisfy the relation

$$a^2 + 2ab + b(1 - b + b^2) = 0.$$

(iii) Hence show that the eigenvalues are complex for

$$0 \le a < -b + (1 - b)\sqrt{-b},$$

and that they are real and less than unity in magnitude for

$$-b + (1 - b)\sqrt{-b} < a < \frac{3}{4}(1 - b)^2.$$

4.14 Fixed points of the Lozi map were found in exercise 4.6. Use the
eigenvalue method to show that the point (x_+^*, y_+^*) is linearly stable
for $a < 1 - b$; show also that the other fixed point (x_-^*, y_-^*) is always
unstable.

4.15 Because the Lozi map is piecewise linear, it is possible to make a global analysis of stability in some cases. Experiments with the ITERATE(2D) window of CHAOS FOR JAVA show strong evidence for the conjecture that (x_+^*, y_+^*) is the only attracting point when $-1 + b < a < 1 - b$. Prove that this is so; that is, prove that iteration from any initial point always converges to (x_+^*, y_+^*). (Hint: you will need to treat the cases $b > 0$, $b < 0$ separately.)

4.16 Holmes' cubic map was introduced in exercise 4.11.

(i) Show that the fixed point $(0,0)$ is an attractor for $d < 1 - b$ and that it is unstable for $d > 1 - b$. Use equation (4.16) to show that the mechanism by which this bifurcation takes place is that the eigenvalue of largest magnitude passes through $+1$.

(ii) Show that the pair of fixed points born at $d = 1 - b$ are initially stable, but that they become unstable at $d = 2(1 - b)$, because the eigenvalue of largest magnitude passes through -1.

4.17 In the notation of equation (4.12), a small displacement (ξ, η) from an initial point (x, y) is mapped, under linear approximation, to

$$\begin{pmatrix} \xi' \\ \eta' \end{pmatrix} = \begin{pmatrix} h'(x) & 1 \\ b & 0 \end{pmatrix} \begin{pmatrix} \xi \\ \eta \end{pmatrix}.$$

Obviously this equation can be used iteratively. The matrix which appears is a particular example of a *Jacobian matrix*, which in general is a matrix of partial derivatives. In particular, for the displacement under two iterations, $(\xi, \eta) \to (\xi', \eta') \to (\xi'', \eta'')$, the Jacobian matrix is the product

$$\begin{pmatrix} h'(x') & 1 \\ b & 0 \end{pmatrix} \begin{pmatrix} h'(x) & 1 \\ b & 0 \end{pmatrix}.$$

(i) Calculate the product in both orders, and show that the result is not the same (matrix products are not commutative).

(ii) It was shown in section 4.3 that the area reduction factor per iteration is b; this is simply the determinant of either matrix appearing in the product. Using a property of determinants of matrix products, show that this factor is the determinant of the product Jacobian matrix.

4.18 A period 2 orbit of the Hénon map was found in exercise 4.7; the linear approximation for iteration of the second composition was considered in the previous exercise.

(i) Calculate the product Jacobian matrix for the period 2 orbit by matrix multiplication.

(ii) Check that the determinant is b^2.

(iii) Show that the trace (sum of the diagonal entries) is given by $4 + 4b^2 - 6b - 4a$.

(iv) For a two-dimensional matrix, the sum of the eigenvalues is given by the trace, the product by the determinant (this is the essential content of equation (4.18)). Use this fact to deduce that the period 2 orbit loses stability because the eigenvalues attain the values -1 and $-b^2$, and that this happens when

$$a = \frac{5}{4} - \frac{3}{2}b + \frac{5}{4}b^2.$$

4.19 A period 2 orbit of the Lozi map was found in exercise 4.8 for $1 - b < a < 1 + b$.

(i) Calculate the product Jacobian matrix for this orbit by matrix multiplication, as in the previous exercise.

(ii) Investigate the stability of this orbit as a function of a.

4.20 Investigate the stability of the period 2 orbit of Holmes' cubic map, which was found in exercise 4.12.

4.21 To find all period 2 orbits of Holmes' cubic map requires solution of the simultaneous equations

$$x_1^* = dx_0^* - x_0^{*3} + y_0^*, \qquad y_1^* = bx_0^*,$$
$$x_0^* = dx_1^* - x_1^{*3} + y_1^*, \qquad y_0^* = bx_1^*.$$

Reduction to a single equation for x_0^*, as in exercise 4.7, results in a 9th order polynomial, of which five roots are already known from exercises 4.11 and 4.12. This leaves a 4th order factor which is in fact a quadratic in x_0^{*2}. Use a computer algebra package to find this factor, followed by the formula for solution of a quadratic to find the new orbits. Show that the bifurcation occurs at the critical value $d = 2(1 - b)$ of exercise 4.16, and that the new branches emanate from those fixed points.

4.5 Lyapunov exponents

For one-dimensional maps the Lyapunov exponent is defined by tracking the image of an interval of negligible length (section 2.9). The geometry of that situation is simple, using linear approximation a small interval maps to another. For two-dimensional maps we know that expansion and contraction is non-uniform; for this reason it is necessary to track a small ellipse. I shall show that, to linear approximation, the image of a small ellipse is another, although the lengths of the axes and their orientation are changed. Two elementary methods are available to demonstrate this fact; elementary calculation (used here) and linear algebra (see exercises).

Formula for an ellipse

In cartesian coordinates, the general equation for points $(x + \xi, y + \eta)$ on an ellipse centred at (x, y) is

$$A\xi^2 + 2B\xi\eta + C\eta^2 = 1, \qquad AC - B^2 > 0. \tag{4.20}$$

The first equation defines a *conic section*, the second is the requirement that it be an ellipse, rather than a parabola or hyperbola. Furthermore, the quantity $AC - B^2$ which appears in (4.20) is inversely proportional to the area of the ellipse squared.

To demonstrate this claim, let's commence with the equation of an ellipse of semi-major axis $\delta^{\max}$ and semi-minor axis $\delta^{\min}$, oriented along the x and y-axes respectively, namely

$$\left(\frac{\xi}{\delta^{\max}}\right)^2 + \left(\frac{\eta}{\delta^{\min}}\right)^2 = 1. \tag{4.21}$$

In general, the ellipse will be rotated through an angle α with respect to the axes used to describe the dynamical system (see figure 4.8). Such a rotation requires the substitutions

$$\xi \to \xi \cos\alpha - \eta \sin\alpha, \qquad \eta \to \xi \sin\alpha + \eta \cos\alpha.$$

Making these substitutions and regrouping leads immediately to the required form, and shows that

$$AC - B^2 = \left(\frac{1}{\delta^{\max}\delta^{\min}}\right)^2. \tag{4.22}$$

The quantity $AC - B^2$ is therefore an *algebraic invariant*. Verification is left as an exercise.

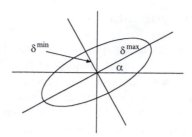

Figure 4.8: Rotation of an ellipse by an angle α.

Transformation of an ellipse

Consider the set of points on a small ellipse centred at (x, y). Under one iteration the centre of the ellipse maps to (x', y'), and the relative coordinates of points on the ellipse map according to equation (4.10). We want to check that the new relative coordinates ξ', η', again satisfy the equations of an ellipse. Let's start by recalling equation (4.10), rearranged so as to make ξ, η the subject of the formulae:

$$\xi = \eta'/b, \qquad \eta = \xi' - h'(x)\eta'/b.$$

Substituting into the first of equations (4.20) gives the formula

$$\begin{aligned}
1 &= A\big(\eta'/b\big)^2 + 2B\big(\eta'/b\big)\big(\xi' - h'(x)\eta'/b\big) + C\big(\xi' - h'(x)\eta'/b\big)^2, \\
&= A'\xi'^2 + 2B'\xi'\eta' + C'\eta'^2,
\end{aligned}$$

where

$$\begin{aligned}
A' &= C, \\
C' &= \big(B - Ch'(x)\big)/b^2, \\
B' &= \big(A + Ch'(x)^2 - 2Bh'(x)\big)/b.
\end{aligned}$$

This already shows that the image of the original ellipse is a conic section; it remains to check the condition required for it to be an ellipse (second of of equations (4.20)). An elementary calculation gives

$$A'C' - B'^2 = (AC - B^2)/b^2,$$

due to cancellation of several terms. So the image is an ellipse as claimed. From the known meaning of the invariant $AC - B^2$, we also get an independent check on area contraction,

$$\delta'^{\max}\delta'^{\min} = |b|\,\delta^{\max}\delta^{\min}, \tag{4.23}$$

which reflects the fact that the area of an ellipse is $\pi\delta^{\max}\delta^{\min}$.

Definition of the exponents

The foregoing enables us to define a pair of Lyapunov exponents for a two-dimensional map as follows:

Definition 4.6 (Lyapunov exponents of two-dimensional map) *For a given initial point (x_0, y_0), the Lyapunov exponents $L_1(x_0, y_0)$, $L_2(x_0, y_0)$ of a map are given by the formulae*

$$L_1(x_0, y_0) = \lim_{k \to \infty} \frac{1}{k} \left(\lim_{\delta_0 \to 0} \ln |\delta_k^{\max}/\delta_0| \right),$$

$$L_2(x_0, y_0) = \lim_{k \to \infty} \frac{1}{k} \left(\lim_{\delta_0 \to 0} \ln |\delta_k^{\min}/\delta_0| \right),$$

provided the limits exists. Here δ_0 is the radius of an initial circle about (x_0, y_0) and the limit $\delta_0 \to 0$ is taken first to ensure that we only deal with a small ellipse at every stage of the computation.

For a generalised Hénon map, we already know that there is an area contraction by the factor $|b|$ at each iteration. That is, after k iterations, we know that

$$\delta_k^{\max} \delta_k^{\min} = |b|^k \delta_0^2.$$

Taking logarithms, this informs us that

$$L_1(x_0, y_0) + L_2(x_0, y_0) = \ln |b|.$$

As already noted (page 123), this implies that Lyapunov exponents of these two-dimensional maps can never take the value $-\infty$; there are no superstable orbits.

Lyapunov exponents computed for the Hénon map are shown in figure 4.9. One clearly sees the fact that their sum is $\ln |b|$, also the flat portions between one period doubling and the next, the reason for which was discussed already on page 123. The left-hand figure also shows the fact that $L_1 = L_2 = \frac{1}{2} \ln |b|$ when $a = 0$, already discovered by direct calculation. The right-hand figure explores the parameter range where the period 7 tangent bifurcation, and subsequent period doubling cascade, takes place.

With the extension of Lyapunov exponents to two dimensions, the previous definition 2.13 of chaotic orbits may also be extended as follows:

Definition 4.7 (Chaotic orbits of two-dimensional map) *A chaotic orbit of a bounded two-dimensional system is one which is not periodic or eventually periodic, and which has at least one positive Lyapunov exponent.*

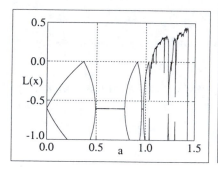 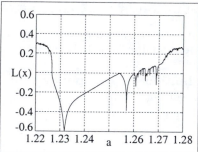

Figure 4.9: Lyapunov exponents for the Hénon map, $b = 0.3$, values of a as displayed. Initial state $(0.5, 0.5)$ in both cases. Sample size 10^3 points, initial 10^4 points discarded (left). The period 7 window, sample size increased to 10^4 points (right).

Recall that a dynamical system is said to be chaotic when it is in a regime with chaotic orbits. Computation of Lyapunov exponents and Fourier spectra for the Hénon map are compelling evidence that it exhibits chaotic behaviour, interspersed with periodic windows, exactly as for one-dimensional maps.

Exercises

4.22 Recall exercise 4.13. Using the LYAPUNOV EXPONENTS window of CHAOS FOR JAVA, check that the Lyapunov exponents of the HÉNON MAP map, for $b = -0.3, -0.6$, have the constant value $-1/2 \ln |b|$ for the range of values of a found therein, after which L_1 climbs to the value zero at $a = a_1 = 3/4(1 - b)^2$.

4.23 By making the substitutions

$$\xi \to \xi \cos \alpha - \eta \sin \alpha, \qquad \eta \to \xi \sin \alpha + \eta \cos \alpha,$$

into the special form for an ellipse (4.21), obtain the general form (4.20).

4.24 Obtain formaulae for the constants A, B, C, of (4.20) in terms of the geometrical quantities so as to verify equation (4.23).

4.25 An alternative (and more usual) derivation of the fact that small ellipses map to small ellipses uses matrix algebra. This exercise explores some properties needed for this.

Let $A = \begin{pmatrix} a & b \\ b & c \end{pmatrix}$ be a real symmetric matrix. It is said to be *positive definite* if

$$(\xi \quad \eta) \begin{pmatrix} a & b \\ b & c \end{pmatrix} \begin{pmatrix} \xi \\ \eta \end{pmatrix} > 0,$$

for all real vectors (ξ, η). It is a standard result of linear algebra that the eigenvalues of a real symmetric matrix are real and that such a matrix is positive definite if and only if all the eigenvalues are positive. Show that, in the present case, this reduces to the conditions $a > 0$, $c > 0$ and $ac - b^2 > 0$. The last condition involves the determinant: $\det A > 0$.

4.26 Another standard equation for an ellipse oriented along the x-y axes is $a\xi^2 + c\eta^2 = 1$ with $a > 0$, $c > 0$; the semi major and semi-minor axes have length $1/\sqrt{a}$, $1/\sqrt{c}$. This may be written

$$(\xi \quad \eta) \begin{pmatrix} a & 0 \\ 0 & c \end{pmatrix} \begin{pmatrix} \xi \\ \eta \end{pmatrix} = 1.$$

Show that, under the rotation of exercise 4.23, this is transformed to

$$(\xi' \quad \eta') \begin{pmatrix} a' & b' \\ b' & c' \end{pmatrix} \begin{pmatrix} \xi' \\ \eta' \end{pmatrix} = 1,$$

show also, by direct computation, that the new matrix is positive definite.

4.27 Recall the Jacobian matrix investigated in exercise 4.17. Consider the set of points lying on the general ellipse

$$(\xi \quad \eta) \begin{pmatrix} a & b \\ b & c \end{pmatrix} \begin{pmatrix} \xi \\ \eta \end{pmatrix} = 1,$$

The image of this ellipse is the set of points satisfying the equation

$$(\xi' \quad \eta') \begin{pmatrix} a' & b' \\ b' & c' \end{pmatrix} \begin{pmatrix} \xi' \\ \eta' \end{pmatrix} = 1,$$

where the new matrix $\begin{pmatrix} a' & b' \\ b' & c' \end{pmatrix}$ is obtained from the original by matrix multiplications involving the Jacobian.

(i) Show that, if A is a real symmetric positive definite matrix, and if J is any invertible matrix, then $A' = J^t A J$ is also real symmetric positive definite. (^{t} denotes the matrix transpose.)

(ii) Obtain the formula relating $\begin{pmatrix} a & b \\ b & c \end{pmatrix}$ to $\begin{pmatrix} a' & b' \\ b' & c' \end{pmatrix}$ in terms of the Jacobian matrix, and show that the result (i) applies.

(iii) Show that this implies that the image of an ellipse is an ellipse.[16]

4.28 Recall exercise 4.1 in which coexisting attractors of the HÉNON MAP were investigated for $a = 1.07$, 1.073, 1.075, 1.077, all with $b = 0.3$. There is a facility in ITERATE(2D) window of CHAOS FOR JAVA to compute the Lyapunov exponents of individual orbits. Use it, together with the FOURIER ANALYSIS window, to classify the nature of the observed orbits.

4.29 Use the ITERATE(2D) window of CHAOS FOR JAVA to examine the orbits, and basins of attraction, of the LOZI MAP map with $a = 1.4$, $b = 0.3$. Classify the orbit, being careful to explain its strong period 2 tendency.

4.6   Basin boundaries

On looking at pictures of attractors and their basins, it is natural to ask what determines the boundaries between basins. An immediate clue may be found in figure 4.10, which is for the Hénon map, but which illustrates a general feature, the discovery of which goes back to the work of Poincaré. The left hand picture shows the stable period 1 orbit at $a = 0.3$, $b = 0.3$, together with its basin of attraction and the two fixed points of the map. The latter are shown as crosses, the black[17] cross is the stable fixed point (x_+^*, y_+^*) and is the forward limit set of the orbit, the light cross is the unstable point (x_-^*, y_-^*). The right hand picture is similar, except that now $a = 1.4$, at which value both fixed points are unstable, the orbit chaotic. The common feature is that the point (x_-^*, y_-^*) sits on the basin boundary in both cases.

The unstable fixed point

The treatment of the contraction/expansion factors $\lambda_\pm$ in section 4.4 does not depend on the formula for the values of $x_\pm^*$. Therefore, for the other fixed point (x_-^*, y_-^*), equation (4.16) gives the eigenvalue pair

$$\lambda_\pm = |ax_-^*| \pm \sqrt{|ax_-^*|^2 + b},$$

---

[16]This approach to ellipses can be extended to ellipsoids of higher dimension, permitting the definition of Lyapunov exponents for systems of arbitrary dimension n.
[17]As always, colour is used in CHAOS FOR JAVA.

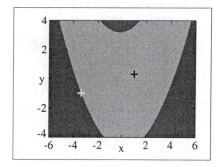 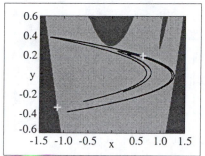

Figure 4.10: Two basins for the Hénon map, showing also fixed points. $a = 0.3$, $b = 0.3$ (left), $a = 1.4$, $b = 0.3$ (right). Stable fixed point is dark cross, unstable is light cross.

where I have used the fact that $x_-^* < 0$ (exercise 4.4); from that exercise it also follows that

$$\lambda_+(a) > 1,$$

after which the relation $\lambda_+\lambda_- = -b$ gives

$$-b < \lambda_-(a) < 0, \qquad (b > 0),$$
$$0 < \lambda_-(a) < |b|, \qquad (b < 0).$$

The point (x_-^*, y_-^*) is therefore unstable for all values of a, b, since there is always one direction along which iterates are repelled. The repulsion is uniform, there is no alternation from side to side; the other direction is one of attraction. This kind of unstable fixed point, with one stable and one unstable direction, is known as a hyperbolic point or saddle point.

Definition 4.8 (Hyperbolic fixed point) *A hyperbolic fixed point of a dissipative two-dimensional map is a point for which the expansion/contraction factors satisfy*

$$|\lambda_1| > 1, \qquad |\lambda_2| < 1.$$

The fixed point (x_-^*, y_-^*) is always hyperbolic, the other point (x_+^*, y_+^*), becomes hyperbolic at the period doubling for $a = a_1$.

Stable or unstable?

The rôle of the hyperbolic point (x_-^*, y_-^*) is quite profound. What happens to those points which are exactly on the boundary of the basin, under iteration of the system? The answer is that they remain on the boundary, for otherwise they are inside one of the basins rather than on the boundary

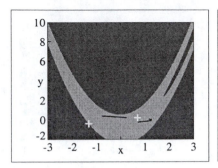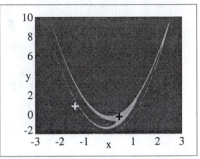

Figure 4.11: Basin boundaries and fixed points of the Hénon map.
$a = 1.1$, $b = 0.3$ (left), $a = 1.7$, $b = -0.6$ (right).

between the two. One of these points is (x^*_-, y^*_-) itself, a fixed point. There are no other fixed points on the boundary, yet boundary points must remain on the boundary under iteration. The conclusion is that this hyperbolic point is in fact an attractor for points exactly on the boundary! This is because the direction of instability is involved in taking iterations away from the boundary, implying that the stable direction is along the boundary itself. It is important also to note that $\lambda_+ > 1$, otherwise iterations would switch from one side of the boundary to the other no matter how close, in contradiction of the definition of a boundary.

Although it is not possible to track points along the boundary by simple numerical iteration, the boundary is clearly seen in figure 4.11, also the difference between positive and negative values of b (alternatively of λ_-).

(i) On the left, $b > 0$, $\lambda_- < 0$. The boundary has more than one piece; indeed there is every reason to suspect that there are an infinite number of pieces which go off to infinity. Moreover, points on the boundary must oscillate from side to side of the hyperbolic point as they approach it. This is also the mechanism whereby points on other sections of the boundary can switch from one to another as they are drawn in.

(ii) On the right, $b < 0$, $\lambda_- > 0$. Now the boundary is fractal.[18] Being infinite, the boundary must be infinitely complicated, because it is unchanged by the stretching and folding action of the map. Since iterates do not switch from side to side, it must therefore be infinitely convoluted within a finite region. Further examples of fractal boundaries are explored in the next section.

---

[18]The static figure is insufficient to form this conjecture, you should spend some time exploring for yourself using the ITERATE(2D) window of CHAOS FOR JAVA.

Stable and unstable manifolds

The systems under consideration are discrete, so individual orbits do not move continuously along curves in the x-y plane. Nevertheless, we have clear evidence that there are continuous plane curves associated with particular aspects of the dynamics. I have argued (but certainly not proved) that basin boundaries are curves with the special property that all iterations which originate exactly on the curve stay on it, even though individual orbits only visit a discrete set of points. Since the curve in question is associated with the stable eigenvalue of the hyperbolic point through which it passes, it is called a *stable manifold*.

The same hyperbolic point has an unstable eigenvalue with an associated *unstable manifold*. Recall that generalised Hénon maps are invertible (exercise 4.10), so we may run the iterations backward, at least in theory. Using this fact, the unstable manifold may be defined as the stable manifold for backward iteration. These manifolds are easy to describe, hard to find by actual computation, and extremely difficult to investigate using pure theory; this brings us to the edge of what can be attempted in an elementary introduction such as this. For more information see, for example, Alligood, Sauer and Yorke [3] or Ott [21], which are at a more advanced level.

Exercises

4.30 The fixed points of the Lozi map were found in exercise 4.6, the point (x_-^*, y_-^*) is on the basin boundary. Since the map is piecewise linear, linear approximation near the fixed point is valid up to some finite distance. Even more, the complete manifold consists of an infinite number of straight line segments, as may be seen using CHAOS FOR JAVA.

(i) Find the equation of that portion of the stable manifold which is a straight line segment through (x^*, y^*), that is, find the equation of a line with the property that iterates which are on it stay on it, getting closer at each iteration.

(ii) Find the limits beyond which this line is no longer part of the stable manifold (due to the fact that the meaning of $a|x|$ differs according as x is positive or negative).

(iii) Find the corresponding portion of the unstable manifold which is a straight line segment passing through (x_-^*, y_-^*).

(iv) Find the equation for that portion of the stable manifold for which $x > 0$, and which joins the part found in (i) at $x = 0$.

4.31 There is no facility in the ITERATE(2D) window of CHAOS FOR JAVA for finding fixed points of compositions of a two-dimensional map. Recall the coexisting attractors of the HÉNON MAP investigated in exercises 4.1 and 4.28; one of the orbits has period 6.

(i) Use the ITERATE(2D) window to observe the stable period 6 orbits for decreasing values of a, starting from $a = 1.07$; in particular observe the approach of one of these points to the basin boundary (on which the companion unstable orbit must reside).

(ii) Try to estimate the value of a at which the tangent bifurcation occurs.

(iii) Strengthen your observations using the FOURIER ANALYSIS window.

4.32 Continuing with the previous example, investigate (using all the tools available) what kind of transitions the two attractors make just beyond the value $a = 1.08$.

4.33 I mentioned the possibility of *backward iteration* in the preceding section. Consider the inverse map (exercise 4.10); show that any fixed point of this system, or of any composition of this system, is either totally unstable (the eigenvalues which determine stability are both greater the unity in magnitude) or hyperbolic.

4.7 Return Maps

The concept of a *return map* was discussed briefly on page 15; such a diagram for the Lorenz equations shown in figure 2.2 as a way to get a simplified picture of a particular aspect of the dynamics. For one-dimensional systems there is no need to look at numerically generated return maps, since the function f and its compositions may be graphed exactly, moreover it is convenient to view a cobweb plot. This was done, for example, in section 3.7, where the intermittent behaviour which prefigures a tangent bifurcation was investigated (page 94 ff.). Exercise 4.31 above shows that the situation is not so straightforward for two-dimensional systems.

In general, a return map is constructed by plotting pairs (x_k, x_{k+d}), for some sequence x_k of an interesting state variable of a dynamical system. The integer d is the *delay*, in the case of figure 2.2, $d = 1$. This is commonly called a *first return map*, similarly for $d = 2$ we have the *second return map*, corresponding to the second composition, etc.

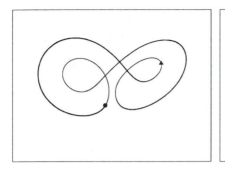
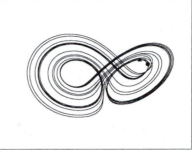

Figure 4.12: Orbits of the Lorenz equation, $r = 166.07$. A laminar region, total time 40 units, apparently periodic behaviour (left). The next 10 time units, showing a chaotic burst (right).

Tangent bifurcation of the Lorenz system

As a prelude, which requires no knowledge of the theory of differential equations,[19] let's see how useful return maps can be for explaining a phenomenon associated with the Lorenz equations (1.1). Figure 4.12 shows orbits of the Lorenz equations with the parameter r set to 166.07. There are comparatively long periods for which the solution appears to be periodic, but these are spasmodically broken by shorter chaotic bursts. This is obviously the intermittent behaviour associated with a tangent bifurcation, but it is hard to draw firm conclusions just by viewing orbits.

Return maps come to the rescue, two typical ones are shown in figure 4.13.[20] Apart from the obvious strong correlation of successive points, which is responsible for the near one-dimensionality of the plotted points, the first return map also exhibits something of the complexity of the behaviour. Compared with the case $r = 28$, it has developed a pronounced hook, giving the map an additional feature which can lead to bifurcations; the sharp peak, associated with chaotic motion, is still present, but the smooth minimum leads to period doubling and tangent bifurcations,[21] which is the new feature.

The second return map (right) is appropriate for examining the particular tangent bifurcation under observation, because of the obvious period 2 nature of the associated orbits.[22] The passage of points through a nar-

---

[19]Technically, I am investigating a two-dimensional map of the Poincaré surface of section whose definition was given in equation (2.4). Three-dimensional orbits are viewed using the ODE ORBITS window of CHAOS FOR JAVA.

[20]See appendix A.11 for documentation on the RETURN MAPS window.

[21]The fact that the unimodal part is associated with a minimum leads, in the present case, to reverse period doubling and reverse tangent bifurcations.

[22]Whether this orbit is labelled period 2 or period 4 is not immediately apparent,

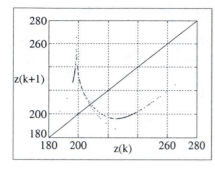 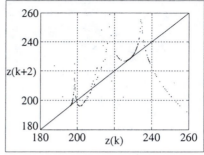

Figure 4.13: Maximum in z return map, Lorenz equations, $r = 166.07$. Sample size 2×10^3 points, initial 10 points discarded. First return (left). Second return, clear evidence of proximity to a period 2 tangent bifurcation (right).

row channel is clearly seen; zooming in on either of the two assists with observation.

Tangent bifurcation of the Hénon system

For the generalised Hénon map, the linear relationship between x_k and y_{k+1} implies that a first return simply displays iterations in the plane, with the y coordinate scaled; this is not expected to provide new information.[23] However, return maps are a powerful tool for investigating tangent bifurcations of such systems. I illustrate this in connection with the most prominent (period 7) window of the bifurcation diagram displayed in figure 4.3; the window commences somewhere between $a = 1.226$ and $a = 1.227$. The data in figure 4.14 is for $a = 1.2265$, at which value the system is clearly still in the intermittent, chaotic, phase. This is evidenced also from Fourier analysis, and from the fact that the Lyapunov exponents are $L_1 \approx 0.1274$, $L_2 \approx -1.331$ (estimates using a sample of 10^6 points). The return map with $d = 7$ provides clear evidence of what is happening, it can also be used, with relatively little effort, to narrow down the critical value to $1.22662 < a^* < 1.22663$.

Exercises

4.34 Show that, for a generalised Hénon system, the first return map is simply a display of iterations in the form $(y_k/b, x_k)$. What is the situa-

---

period 2 is consistent with the rôle of 2 as the delay.

[23]The more general situation, that the sequence x_k comes from a dynamical system in two or more dimensions, is related to the question of *reconstruction* of motion from partial data, a subject which is not addressed in this book.

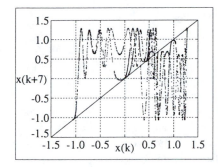 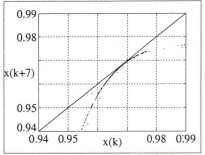

Figure 4.14: Seventh return maps for the Hénon system with $a = 1.2265$, $b = 0.3$. Sample size 10^4 points, first 100 points discarded. Global view (left), Detail of close approach (right).

tion if y_k values are used instead of x_k to construct the plot?

4.35 Investigate the birth of the period 6 orbit, examined already in exercise 4.31. Compared with the period 7 window looked at above, there is an obvious extra difficulty; if a is set to a value just less than the critical value, the system will not be intermittent because there is an existing attractor.[24] It will only be possible to see the passage through the bottleneck once per experiment, even that requires careful choice of initial conditions. With these warnings, use the RETURN MAPS window of CHAOS FOR JAVA to determine the critical value a^* for this bifurcation, to four or five decimal places. (Experiment with the initial value $(-0.7, -0.35)$.)

4.36 Use the RETURN MAPS window of CHAOS FOR JAVA to determine, to four decimal places, the critical value $r^* \approx 166$ for the reverse tangent bifurcation of the Lorenz equations.

4.37 Use the ODE ORBITS window of CHAOS FOR JAVA to observe the intermittent behaviour just after the reverse tangent bifurcation whose critical value was found in the previous exercise.

4.38 Use the RETURN MAPS and ODE ORBITS windows of CHAOS FOR JAVA to examine the first and second period doublings of the Rössler equations (2.6), the first of which happens in the interval $2.8 < \mu < 2.85$.

---

[24]This is reminiscent of exercise 3.28; there the second attractor was a stable fixed point, the system one-dimensional, here the second attractor is chaotic.

4.8   Linear feedback and control

A unimodal one-dimensional map f will typically have some range of parameter for which there is a non-zero stable fixed point. For example, for
the logistic map in the range $1 < r < 3$, all orbits which commence within
the interval $0 < x < 1$ converge to the fixed point $x_1^* = 1 - 1/r$.

Suppose we wish to extend that stable behaviour to larger parameter
values by incorporating a *feedback loop*. Just beyond the critical value
r^*, iterations of f will tend to alternate as they converge to the stable 2-
cycle. This tendency is measured by the values of $x_k - x_{k-1}$, and we can
feed back a multiple of these differences as a form of linear stabilisation
or destabilisation. The result is the discrete dynamical system $x_{k+1} =
f(x_k) - b(x_k - x_{k-1})$, which I shall call a controlled map. It is more usefully
viewed as a generalised Hénon map

$$x_{k+1} = f(x_k) - bx_k + y_k,$$
$$y_{k+1} = bx_k; \tag{4.24}$$

this makes the two-dimensional structure explicit. Stabilisation corresponds
to negative b, in which case the feedback term $-b(x_k - x_{k-1})$ corrects the
tendency to oscillate about the fixed point. That is, if $x_k > x_{k-1}$, we expect
$f(x_k)$ to be below the desired value which calls for positive correction.

In the case that f is the logistic map, this gives the CONTROLLED
LOGISTIC MAP of CHAOS FOR JAVA,

$$x_{k+1} = rx_k(1 - x_k) - bx_k + y_k,$$
$$y_{k+1} = bx_k. \tag{4.25}$$

The function $h(x) = rx(1 - x) - bx$ is a downward parabola, just like the
standard Hénon map; the relation between them requires the parameter
change

$$a = \frac{(r - b)(r + b - 2)}{4}, \tag{4.26}$$

together with linear transformation of x and y. The necessary calculations
are the subject of exercise 4.39.

Fixed points

It is possible to re-use the known results for the Hénon map, but it is more
enlightening to re-cast them into the present notation. The calculations
are sketched out here, details are left to the exercises. Since $y^* = bx^*$, the
fixed point equations (4.4) reduce to the single condition

$$x^* = f(x^*) - bx^* + y^* = f(x^*),$$

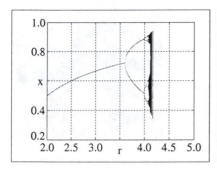
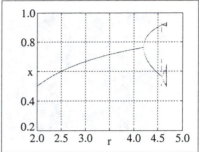

Figure 4.15: Final state diagrams, CONTROLLED LOGISTIC MAP. $b = -0.3$ (left), $b = -0.6$ (right). Initial state $(0.8, -0.4)$, sample size 10^3 points, initial 10^3 points discarded.

so the fixed points are not affected by the feedback. This is to be expected, since the purpose of feedback is to hold the original one-dimensional system at its fixed points.

The stability of these points is of vital interest. Here I restrict the analysis to the case that f is the logistic map, of which the fixed points x_0^*, x_1^* are known from equation (2.10). I also assume throughout this section that[25] $r > 1$ and $b < 0$, and write $|b|$ in place of $-b$. For either of the fixed points, the eigenvalues are determined from the characteristic equation

$$\lambda^2 - \lambda(f'(x^*) + |b|) + |b| = 0, \qquad (4.27)$$

from which follows

$$\lambda_+ + \lambda_- = f'(x^*) + |b|, \qquad \lambda_+\lambda_- = |b|.$$

The point (x_1^*, y_1^*) is stable for values of $1 < r < r_1$, where r_1 is the value at which period doubling occurs. Following the method of section 4.4, this is determined by the fact that $\lambda_+ + \lambda_- = -1 + b$; substituting $f'(x_1^*) = 2 - r$, gives

$$r_1 = 3 + 2|b|. \qquad (4.28)$$

This shows the effect of control in extending stability beyond the original period doubling at $r_1 = 3$; it also shows that the maximum possible extension is to $r_1 = 5$, and that period doubling is still the mechanism of the first bifurcation. The final state diagrams shown in figure 4.15 for two values of b quite clearly exhibit the stabilisation.

---

[25]There is a transcritical bifurcation at $r = 1$, this is explored in the exercises.

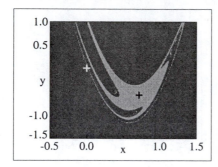 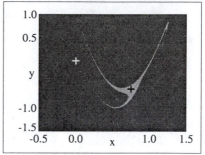

Figure 4.16: Erosion of basin boundaries due to increase of feedback. $r = 3.5$, $b = -0.8$ (left), $r = 4.0$, $b = -0.8$ (right).

The cost of control

Let's begin with stability analysis of the other fixed point $(x_0^*, y_0^*) = (0, 0)$. Equation (4.27) still holds, in fact it is simplified by the fact that $f'(0) = r$. The explicit formula for the eigenvalues is

$$\lambda_\pm = \frac{r + |b| \pm \sqrt{(r + |b|)^2 - 4|b|}}{2},$$

which are real, positive and distinct for $r > 1$. In fact, it is easy to see that

$$0 < \lambda_- < |b|, \qquad 1 < \lambda_+,$$

for all $r > 1$, so (x_0^*, y_0^*) is a hyperbolic point and we expect it to determine the basin boundary. One point to notice is that $\lambda_- > 0$; this is the essential fact which results in the boundary being fractal, as discussed on page 134 for the Hénon map, which we know to be equivalent to the controlled logistic map. It is easy to see folds developing in the stable manifold (basin boundary) by observing it, first for r just a little larger than 1, then increasing r in small steps. As a consequence most of the territory between the two fixed points is not safe.

An extreme example is shown in figure 4.16. Here the feedback has been increased to 80%. Setting $r = 3.5$, the desired stable operating point is still present (left) and the basin boundary is fractal. Similarly with $r = 4.0$, however the basin is much reduced in size (right). Figure 4.17 explores what causes this reduction. First, setting $r = 3.7$, well inside the range for stability, we see a coexisting period 3 attractor; its (fractal) basin has taken over much of the former basin of the fixed point (left). The period 3 orbit experiences a crisis between $r = 3.7$ and $r = 4.0$, whereupon its basin joins the basin of infinity. Setting $r = 4.5$, still within the stability limit, shows

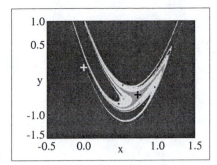 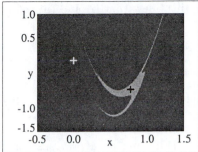

Figure 4.17: Fractal invasion of basin boundaries. $a = 3.7$, $b = -0.8$, coexisting periodic attractors, periods 1 and 3 (left). $a = 4.5$, $b = -0.8$, single fixed point, badly eroded safe basin (right).

that control continues to be effective, but that the *safe basin of attraction* is not looking particularly safe (right).

The phenomenon of a sudden rapid decrease of the safe basin, with increase in an operating parameter, has been called the *Dover cliff phenomenon* by one writer.[26] A good place to commence further reading on the control of chaos is the collection of articles in Ref. [22]; it is, of course, an area of importance and ongoing research.

Exercises

4.39 This exercise is about the relationship between the controlled logistic map and the Hénon map. To keep the distinction clear, use the symbols ξ, η for the latter, writing

$$\xi' = 1 - a\xi^2 + \eta, \qquad \eta' = b\xi. \tag{4.29}$$

The essential step is to find a substitution

$$x = \alpha + \beta\xi, \qquad y = \gamma + \delta\eta,$$

which transforms (4.24) to the standard form (4.29); this determines the relationship between the parameters.

(i) Make the given substitutions in equations (4.24), and show that the conditions $\gamma = b\alpha$, $\delta = \beta$ are necessary to put the second equation into the form $\eta' = b\xi$.

(ii) Using these results, show that the condition for the coefficient of ξ (in the first equation) to be zero is $\alpha = (r - b)/2r$.

---

[26] J. M. T. Thompson, "Chaos and fractal basin boundaries in engineering", [20], p201.

(iii) Show that (i) and (ii) reduce the first equation to

$$\xi' = \frac{(r+b-2)(r-b)}{4r\beta} - r\beta\xi^2 + \eta$$

and hence deduce (4.26).

(iv) Using these results in equation (4.28), recover the fact that the critical a for the first period doubling of the Hénon map is $a_1 = \frac{3}{4}(1-b)^2$.

4.40 Following on a previous exercise, consider the controlled tent map. Show that it is equivalent to a generalisation of the Lozi map, with

$$h(x) = \begin{cases} 1 - a_+ x, & x \geq 0, \\ 1 + a_- x, & x \leq 0, \end{cases}$$

and find the relationship between the original parameter t of the TENT MAP and the parameters $a_\pm$.

4.41 Show that the controlled logistic map exhibits a transcritical bifurcation at $r = 1$; that is, show that (x_0^*, y_0^*) is stable for $0 < r < 1$, hyperbolic for $r > 1$ whereas (x_1^*, y_1^*) is hyperbolic for $0 < r < 1$, stable for $1 < r < r_1$.

4.42 Confirm the analysis of (4.28) for the period doubling of the fixed point (x_1^*, y_1^*) of the controlled logistic map.

4.43 Use the RETURN MAPS window of CHAOS FOR JAVA to investigate the period 3 tangent bifurcation of the CONTROLLED LOGISTIC MAP which is responsible for the second basin in figure 4.17 (left).

4.44 Holmes' cubic map, introduced in exercise 4.11, is clearly a cubic map with linear feedback. The purpose of this exercise is to show that it corresponds to the CUBIC #2 MAP of equation (2.7), to find the relationship between the parameters, and to investigate the effect of the feedback.

(i) By making the rescaling $x \to \alpha x$, $y \to \alpha y$, show that $f(x) = h(x) + bx$ may brought to the form

$$f(x) = (d + b)x(1 - x^2),$$

where α is real provided that $(d + b) > 0$, which is consistent with the interesting range of parameter values. It follows that $r = \sqrt{3}(d + b)$, giving the CONTROLLED CUBIC MAP of CHAOS FOR JAVA,

$$\begin{aligned} x_{k+1} &= rx_k(1 - x_k^2)/\sqrt{3} - bx_k + y_k, \\ y_{k+1} &= bx_k. \end{aligned} \tag{4.30}$$

(ii) Use this to show that the effect of negative feedback on the CONTROLLED CUBIC MAP is to extend the range of stability of the period 1 orbits to the parameter range

$$\sqrt{3} < r < \sqrt{3}\,(2 - b).$$

Note that the pitchfork bifurcation (investigated in exercise 3.37) is not affected by feedback.

4.45 Holmes found a strange attractor of his cubic map for $b = -0.2$, $d = 2.77$. Investigate this attractor, for the equivalent CONTROLLED CUBIC MAP, using the tools available in CHAOS FOR JAVA; in particular estimate the capacity and Lyapunov dimensions.

4.46 Investigate the bifurcation sequence of the CONTROLLED CUBIC MAP, as a function of r, with the parameter b fixed at $b = -0.2$. Pay attention to the first (symmetry breaking) bifurcation, to its effect on the basins of attraction, and to the crisis whereby Holmes' attractor is born. Suggested initial values are $(0.6, -0.6)$ and $(-0.6, 0.6)$.

4.9   Producing the strange attractor

Let's consider the mechanism which produces strange attractors. The first thing to notice is that there actually is an attractor, that is, a set of points in the plane to which all iterations are inexorably drawn as the system evolves. This follows from two facts.

First it is possible to show, either by exact analysis, or by careful computation, that there is a *trapping region*, which has the property that it is mapped inside itself under one iteration. This is important, since it is not possible to find simple formulae for the basin boundaries, but it is possible to find reasonably simple trapping regions in some interesting cases.[27]

Second, the trapping region as a whole is mapped, at every iteration, to a region whose area is reduced by the factor $|b| < 1$. So it must continually contract toward a limiting set of zero area. The attractor itself is defined as an infinite limit obtained by considering the intersection of all these sets. This is a delicate mathematical operation, to which I devote some attention in the next chapter.

The horseshoe — bringer of chaos

To understand the shape of the Hénon attractor, and the origin of the chaotic behaviour, consider what happens to a rectangle (not small) extending from $x = x_1 < 0$ to $x = x_2 > 0$ in the horizontal direction and

---

[27]Details of such a region may be found in Peitgen, Jürgens and Saupe [24], p664.

Figure 4.18: Mapping a large rectangle.

from $y = y_1 < 0$ to $y = y_2 > 0$ in the vertical. Expressed in terms of a parameter t, the bottom of the rectangle is the horizontal line

$$x = t, \qquad y = y_1, \qquad x_1 \le t \le x_2.$$

After one iteration, it is mapped to part of a sideways parabola with coordinates (x', y') given by

$$x' = 1 + y_1 - at^2, \qquad y' = bt, \qquad x_1 \le t \le x_2.$$

This parabola extends from $x = 1 + y_1 - ax_1^2$ to $x = 1 + y_1$ and back again to $x = 1 + y_1 - ax_2^2$. Similarly for the top, which only differs in having the constant value y_1 replaced by y_2. The two parabolas are separated by a horizontal distance equal to the height of the original rectangle. As for the sides of the rectangle, they map to horizontal straight lines (u is the parameter)

$$x' = 1 - a + u, \qquad y' = \pm bx_{1,2}, \qquad y_1 \le u \le y_2,$$

at the top and bottom of the image.

Thus the original rectangle has been deformed into a shape resembling a horseshoe by a process of stretching and bending. If it also has the property that the image completely crosses the original region twice, then it is known as a *horseshoe map*. It can be shown that such a map, together with a trapping region, produces chaotic orbits and a strange attractor.[28]

The action of the iteration is to continually apply this stretching and bending action, but always respecting the vertical scale. As for individual orbits, they can only have points in common if one of them joins the other; that is, if the starting point of one of them is actually on the other orbit. Since orbits consist of a simple sequence (x_k, y_k), which is a countable set of points, whereas the set of all points in the basin is uncountable, what we observe in an actual calculation is a set of points merely indicative of the actual attractor.

---

[28] See, for example, Refs. [3] or [21], for treatments of this topic.

Chapter 5

Fractals

In the course of the last 90 or so pages, *fractals* have been mentioned from time to time; indeed it is becoming apparent that[1]

> ... Chaos is the delicate dance of dynamics on fractals ...

This makes it all the more curious that nowhere have I attempted to explain the meaning of the word! This short chapter[2] will attempt to rectify the omission, even though no precise definition will be given. Indeed, Alligood, Sauer and Yorke [3] write

> ... Scientists know a fractal when they see one, but there is no universally accepted definition ...

The word itself was coined by Mandelbrot [17], the root is from the Latin *fractus* (broken). Mandelbrot's definition is that the *Hausdorff dimension*[3] should exceed the *geometric dimension*, which usually implies a fraction; there is however no requirement for this. I follow Falconer [11] by referring to an object as fractal if it exhibits the following properties:

(i) It has fine structure, meaning that there is always more detail to be seen at arbitrarily small scales.

(ii) It is too irregular to be described using traditional geometry, in particular it is not simply a finite collection of smooth geometrical objects.

(iii) It has some form of exact or approximate self-similarity.

(iv) The fractal dimension is not the natural geometric dimension.[4]

Falconer also points out that fractals are often defined in simple ways; the present book is in fact restricted to precisely such objects, being concerned with the deterministic evolution of non-linear dynamical systems.

---

[1] An appealing description given by a colleague, Bruce Henry, in a public lecture.

[2] For a thorough, yet elementary, introduction to the subject I can do no better than recommend the well known book by Peitgen, Jürgens and Saupe [24].

[3] To keep the mathematics at an elementary level, I do not use Hausdorff dimension.

[4] I define three different fractal dimensions in this chapter; no attempt is made to make the concept of geometric dimension (more exactly, *topological dimension*) precise, although there are clear intuitive ideas which suffice for the present discussion.

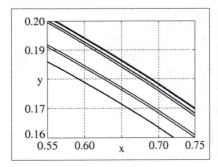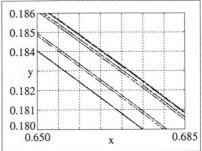

Figure 5.1: Self-similarity of the Hénon attractor. The right-hand picture is a detail of the left one; itself a detail from figure 4.1. The repetition of structure at increasingly fine scales is apparent.

5.1   The Hénon attractor

Let's revisit the Hénon attractor originally shown in figure 4.1; some magnified detail is shown above. You will have to look at the axes to work out that they really differ from each other, since there is no noticeable distortion in this part of the attractor under repeated magnification. Although the attractor is not globally self-similar, there is more here than the simple straightening of curves under repeated magnification. Each of the two pictures consists of groups of *thick lines*; the self similarity is evident in the fact that the structure repeats itself under magnification — it is infinitely complex.

These pictures are constructed using a finite number of dots on a page (or a computer screen), but the attractor is infinitely more complex than that. Recall that there are simple geometrical trapping regions, for example quadrilaterals, which are mapped into themselves under the Hénon map. Denote such a quadrilateral by Q. By any reasonable definition it is two-dimensional and contains an uncountably infinite number of points. Denote also the Hénon map by T; it is a smooth function of the coordinates (x, y), so the image $Q_1 = T(Q)$ is also a two-dimensional region of the plane, containing an uncountable number of points; moreover it is bounded by four smooth curves, albeit not straight lines. This argument may be applied repeatedly, and in this way there is defined a sequence of regions Q_n according to

$$Q \xrightarrow{T} Q_1 \xrightarrow{T} Q_2 \cdots \xrightarrow{T} Q_n \xrightarrow{T} \cdots$$

each of which is two-dimensional and contains an uncountable number of points. Moreover,

$$\mathcal{Q} \supset \mathcal{Q}_1 \supset \mathcal{Q}_2 \cdots \supset \mathcal{Q}_n \supset \cdots$$

Because of the area contraction by the factor $|b|$ per iteration, the regions $\mathcal{Q}_n$ decrease geometrically to zero (in area); due to the strong non-linearity, they also increase rapidly in complexity, a fact reflected in the appearance of the figures.

The attractor is defined as the infinite limit[5]

$$\mathcal{Q}_H = \lim_{n \to \infty} \mathcal{Q}_n = \bigcap_{n=0}^{\infty} \mathcal{Q}_n, \qquad (5.1)$$

and this is the object approximated by finite computation. Obviously $\mathcal{Q}_H$ already complies with points (i) and (iii) on Falconer's list. Shortly, I shall define the *box-counting* dimension of a set, and compute its approximate value ($d_C \approx 1.28$) for $\mathcal{Q}_H$; this is in accord[6] with item (iv). Notice that this value is less than the dimension of any of the sets $\mathcal{Q}_n$, no matter how large the value of n, while it is larger than the dimension of a line, which is why we observe thick lines. A little thought about the rapid increase of complexity of the successive $\mathcal{Q}_n$, as discussed in section 4.9, indicates that this object must comply with point (ii) as well.

The conclusion is that $\mathcal{Q}_H$ is a fractal, constructed by a simple iterative procedure; this is a signal that it is worth while to consider some fractals whose construction is more elementary, and thereby susceptible to straightforward mathematical analysis. A further compelling reason is that at least one property, the dimension, did not survive the infinite limit, being reduced from $d = 2$ to $d_C \approx 1.28$; this immediately raises the question as to what other properties do not survive. In particular, does $\mathcal{Q}_H$ contain an uncountable number of points; indeed, does it contain any points at all?

Exercises

5.1 It should be obvious that $\mathcal{Q}_H$ is not empty. Identify one point which it contains, because the same point is in every set $\mathcal{Q}_n$.

5.2 When $a = 0$ the Hénon map is linear, with an attracting fixed point (x_+^*, y_+^*) (see page 115), furthermore the convergence under two iterations is both uniform and linear. Consider therefore a sequence of circles

---

[5]It is not really possible to avoid using the concepts of the *intersection* and *union* of sets when investigating fractals. The intersection is denoted by the symbol $\cap$, the union by the symbol $\cup$. The meaning is that a point is in $A \cap B$ if it is in both A and B, in $A \cup B$ if it is in either. Equations such as (5.1) have the extra subtlety that there is an infinite set of conditions whose consequence is not readily apparent.

[6]Because each $\mathcal{Q}_{n+1}$ contains only a subset of $\mathcal{Q}_n$, none of the sets $\mathcal{Q}_n$ is contained in $\mathcal{Q}_H$, an indication of the subtlety of the operation of infinite intersection.

D_{2n}, centred at the fixed point, and of radius $|b|^n$. Under the action of the second composition map T_2,

$$D_0 \xrightarrow{T_2} D_2 \xrightarrow{T_2} D_4 \cdots \xrightarrow{T_2} D_{2n} \xrightarrow{T_2} \cdots$$

Show that the attracting set defined by

$$D_\infty = \lim_{n \to \infty} D_{2n} = \bigcap_{n=0}^{\infty} D_{2n},$$

contains only a single point, even though each D_{2n} is an uncountably infinite set of dimension 2. What is the dimension of D_∞? What can you say about the odd-numbered sets D_{2n+1}?

5.2 The Cantor Set

The earliest example of a fractal was the Cantor set, also known as Cantor dust. It is constructed from a closed interval I_0 by recursive deletion of a rapidly increasing number of subintervals. In its most common form $I_0 = [0, 1]$ is the starting set. I_1 is obtained from I_0 by removing the open middle third $(1/3, 2/3)$, and is therefore the union of two closed intervals,

$$I_1 = [0, 1/3] \cup [2/3, 1].$$

At the next step, I_2 is obtained from I_1 by removing the open middle third of each of its two component intervals, that is, we remove $(1/9, 2/9)$ and $(7/9, 8/9)$. It is the union of four closed intervals:

$$I_2 = [0, 1/9] \cup [2/9, 1/3] \cup [2/3, 7/9] \cup [8/9, 1].$$

I_3 is obtained by deleting four open intervals from I_2, namely the open middle third of each of its closed intervals. At the nth step, I_n is the union of 2^n closed intervals, produced from I_{n-1} by deleting the open middle third of each of its 2^{n-1} component intervals. These steps are illustrated in figure 5.2.

There is exact self-similarity here, a great simplification over the Hénon attractor. I_1 consists of two copies of I_0, each linearly scaled by a factor $1/3$, and a similar relation exists in general; I_n is the union of two copies of I_{n-1}, each reduced in size by the factor $1/3$. Obviously the two copies are placed, at each step, so that they adjoin the ends of the original interval I_0. If we continue in this way to (say) I_{100}, and then decide to stop, we will have self-similarity over a range $3^{100} \approx 10^{48}$, i.e., 48 orders of magnitude. To all practical intent this is the same as infinite self-similarity, achieved after only 100 iterations.

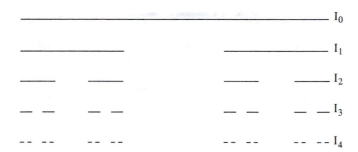

Figure 5.2: Construction of the middle third Cantor set.

The Cantor set itself is defined as

$$I_C = \lim_{n \to \infty} I_n = \bigcap_{n=0}^{\infty} I_n, \tag{5.2}$$

exactly as for the Hénon attractor $\mathcal{Q}_H$. That is, x is in I_C if and only if it is in I_n for all n. Taking the infinite limit removes the problem of defining a point at which self-similarity ceases. The usual limitation is either observational or computational — practical rather than theoretical.

Length of the Cantor set

The length L_n of I_n is naturally defined as the sum of the lengths of its parts. There are 2^n intervals each of length $1/3^n$ so

$$L_n = \left(\frac{2}{3}\right)^n.$$

Thus the only reasonable definition for the length of I_C is that it is zero, since

$$\lim_{n \to \infty} L_n = 0.$$

Evidently I_C has a very complex structure, since it is certainly non-empty, as I shall show. When it was discovered by G. Cantor, there was no known connection with the behaviour of any interesting physical phenomena. In fact, such objects, as they were discovered during the last quarter of the 19th Century, were regarded as *mathematical monsters*. With the advent of personal computers, together with the popularisation of fractals, the same monsters are now regarded more for their intrinsic beauty, a story of rags to riches!

Connection with the tent map

Let's revisit the tent map, removing the previous restrictions on the state variable x and the parameter t, writing simply

$$f(x) = \begin{cases} 2tx, & (x \leq 1/2), \\ 2t(1-x), & (x \geq 1/2), \end{cases} \quad (t > 0).$$

The only requirement is that x and t are real, with t positive.

If $t < 1/2$, then $x_0^* = 0$ is the only fixed point, and all iterations are attracted to it, no matter what the starting point. This is the only basin of attraction in this case. When $t > 1/2$, x_0^* is unstable. Consider what happens to iterations which are outside the interval $[0, 1]$. If $x > 1$, then $f(x) < 0$, so every orbit which starts from $x_0 > 1$ is mapped immediately to $x_1 < 0$. Furthermore, if $x_k < 0$, then $x_{k+1} = 2tx_k < 0$, and with $2t > 1$, these iterations diverge geometrically, being attracted to $-\infty$. The conclusion is that the infinite interval $(-\infty, 0) \cup (1, \infty)$ is part of the basin of attraction of $-\infty$, for all $t > 1/2$. If $t \leq 1$, it is the whole basin, since f is a map of $[0, 1]$ to itself in that case.

What about $t > 1$? Clearly, $f(x) \leq 1$ if $0 \leq x \leq 1/2t$ or $1 - 1/2t \leq x \leq 1$, but $f(x) > 1$ if $1/2t < x < 1 - 1/2t$. So the basin of attraction of infinity includes the open interval $(1/2t, 1 - 1/2t)$ taken from the middle of $[0, 1]$. As for the remaining two subintervals, each is mapped to the whole interval $[0, 1]$ under the first iteration. Therefore, at the next iteration, $x_2 > 1$ for all x_1 in the middle open interval, which is equivalent to x_0 being in the middle part of either of the two ends.

To recover the middle third Cantor set, choose $t = 3/2$. The interval I_0 is the original interval $[0, 1]$. The interval $I_1 = [0, 1/3] \cup [2/3, 1]$ is exactly the set of x for which $f(x)$ is still in I_0, attaining a value > 1 on the middle third. Each of the intervals $[0, 1/3]$ and $[2/3, 1]$ is mapped to the whole of I_0 under f, so f_2 attains a value > 1 on the middle third of each. Alternatively, I_2 is the set of initial values for which the first iterate is in I_1; the second iterate in I_0. In general, I_n is the set of initial values for which the first iterate is in I_{n-1}. Expressed another way, the tent map is the inverse of the self-similarity construction whereby two copies of I_{n-1} are shrunk to produce[7] I_n. Figure 5.3 gives graphs of f, f_2 and f_3, showing the situation.

An infinite set of points

Recall that we found earlier that the tent map with $t = 1$ has infinitely many periodic orbits, among them a period n orbit starting from $x_0 = 2/(1+2^n)$,

---

[7] Since this construction produces two images of the original, it is not a regular function, which is why I did not simply describe it as the inverse of the tent map.

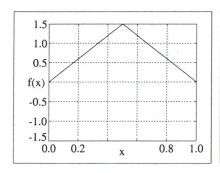 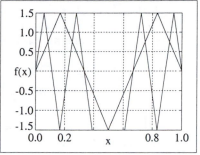

Figure 5.3: Tent map for $t = 3/2$. Graph of f, showing that only the image of I_1 remains in I_0 after one iteration (left). f_2 and f_3, showing the corresponding property for I_2 and I_3 (right).

for every $n \geq 1$. More generally, for arbitrary $t > 1/2$, there is a periodic orbit

$$x_0^* = \frac{2t}{1 + (2t)^n}, \quad x_1^* = \frac{(2t)^2}{1 + (2t)^n}, \quad \cdots \quad x_{n-1}^* = \frac{(2t)^n}{1 + (2t)^n}.$$

The points on this orbit increase steadily from x_0^* to the maximum $x_{n-1}^* < 1$, then start again from x_0^*. All of them are in the Cantor set, since they are not in the basin of attraction of infinity. In fact there are many more periodic and eventually periodic orbits, which is explored in the exercises. All periodic orbits are unstable when $t > 1/2$, so we cannot expect to find them by numerical iteration.

An uncountable number of points

At the expense of a little sophistication we can say more: I_C contains an uncountable number of points. To make the discussion easy, I restrict to the middle third set.

Consider first the set of points in the original interval I_0. I take it as known that the number of such points is uncountably infinite, and that every number $0 \leq x \leq 1$ has a decimal (base 10) representation

$$x = 0.d_1 d_2 d_3 \cdots \tag{5.3}$$

where the d_j are integers between 0 and 9. This representation is not unique, sequences ending with the recurring number 9 are equivalent to a terminating sequence, that is,

$$0.d_1 d_2 d_3 \cdots d_k \, \dot{9} \equiv 0.d_1 d_2 d_3 \cdots (d_k + 1) \, 0.$$

If $d_k = 9$, then $(d_k + 1) = 0$, carry 1; this process continues until the unit can be added without a carry. The extreme example is that $0.\dot{9} = 1.0$.

In the same way, one may represent numbers in I_0 to any base b, with the meaning that

$$0.d_1 d_2 d_3 \cdots = \frac{d_1}{b} + \frac{d_1}{b^2} + \frac{d_1}{b^3} + \cdots$$

The fact that the set I_0 is uncountable is equivalent to the fact that the set of sequences of this form is uncountable. Now it is easy to show that, for the tent map with $t = 3/2$, a number with the base 3 representation $0.d_1 d_2 d_3 \cdots$ is mapped to

$$f(0.d_1 d_2 d_3 \cdots) = \begin{cases} d_1.d_2 d_3 \cdots & (x \le 1/2) \\ \bar{d}_1.\bar{d}_2 \bar{d}_3 \cdots & (x \ge 1/2) \end{cases} \qquad (5.4)$$

where

$$\bar{d}_j = 2 - d_j;$$

this is still in I_0 provided that $d_1 \ne 1$. It follows that the middle third Cantor set is precisely the members of I_0 whose base 3 representation uses only the digits 0 and 2. There is an exact (one-to-one) correspondence (as sequences) between this set and the set of numbers whose base 2 representation is obtained by replacing each digit 2 by the digit 1; that is, the complete (uncountable) set I_0.

Exercises

5.3 Re-examine the arguments which were used to catalogue periodic orbits of the tent map with $t = 1$ (page 37 ff.); in particular show that they still work when $t > 1$. Use this to show that there are an infinite set of periodic orbits, and to investigate the reason they are not dense in I_0, which is a significant difference from the case $t = 1$ (see page 38).

5.4 Write out a proof of equation (5.4); in the process show that if $x = 1/2$, the two formulae agree. (Hint: You will need the fact that $1.0 = 0.\dot{2}$.)

5.5 Show that the points $1/4$ and $3/4$ are in the Cantor set, by identifying the periodic orbit to which they belong. Find also the base 3 representation of this orbit.

5.6 Repeat the previous exercise for the points $1/10$, $3/10$ and $9/10$. Which of these point(s) are on a periodic orbit, which are on an eventually periodic orbit? Are any other multiples of $1/10$ in I_C?

5.7 Recall exercise 2.23, in which orbits of the tent map were investigated using a classification according as successive iterates fell to the left (L) or right (R) of the maximum. Show that if $t = 1$, and if the initial point x_0 of an orbit is represented using base 2 arithmetic, the successive digits $d_j = 0$, 1 determine the sequence L, R and conversely; this will necessitate finding the action of the map on binary sequences. Using the binary representation, show that rational values of x_0 correspond to eventually periodic orbits; irrational values to aperiodic orbits.[8]

5.3 Fractal bifurcation diagrams

Self-similarity and fractal structure have already been noted in bifurcations. In particular, I have discussed in some detail the phenomenon of period doubling, together with the fact that the critical parameter values r_n for the nth bifurcation in any period doubling sequence generally converge to a limiting value r_∞ at a geometric rate, governed by the Feigenbaum constant δ. Associated with this is a certain approximate self-similarity, exhibited, for example, in figure 3.2.

Another feature is evident in figure 5.4. The left hand picture displays the period 5 window which is rather prominent in figure 3.2; two other less prominent windows of period 7 and 9 are also seen. On the right is shown an expanded detail of one of the five legs of that period 5 window. There is clear self-similarity of these two parts of the same diagram; in particular the (now) prominent window with five legs is in reality part of a period 25 window, previously unnoticed.

Periodic windows are associated with tangent bifurcations; in turn these stem from the birth of periodic orbits, of which there are none, for a smooth unimodal map satisfying $f(0) = f(1) = 0$, for sufficiently small parameter value (non-linearity). Typically, at some maximum parameter value, for which the map is completely chaotic, there will be a dense set of unstable periodic orbits. Each of these orbits had its genesis as a periodic window. A little thought leads to a startling conclusion; if there are an infinite number of windows, each of finite width (in parameter value), then the parameter values for which the system is chaotic will be a finite interval with an infinite number of subintervals removed. That is, it will have some similarity to a Cantor set, but it is definitely not so sparse as dust.

---

[8]Because of the conjugacy between the tent map with $t = 1$ and the logistic map with $r = 4$, there must be a corresponding classification of orbits of the latter using symbol sequences L, R. Note that this will not be equivalent to the use of base 2 arithmetic, indicating that symbolic dynamics is a more general technique for the analysis of chaos. There is in general no implication that a recurring group of symbols L, R, which indicates an eventually periodic orbit, corresponds to rational x_0.

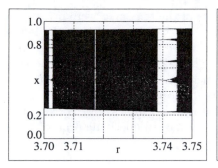
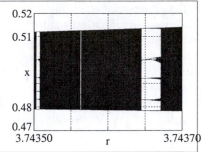

Figure 5.4: Some periodic windows of the logistic map. Sample size 10^3 points, initial 10^3 points discarded (left). Detail, sample size 10^4 points, initial 10^4 points discarded (right).

Sarkovskii's theorem

A proper treatment of the above claims is well beyond the present chapter, however it would be remiss were I not to explain an important result about periodic orbits, which constitutes at least the beginning of the theory. It can be shown that if f is a unimodal map with a period p orbit, then there is a period q orbit for every integer q which precedes p (denoted by[9] $q \leftarrow \cdots \leftarrow p$) in the following sequence:

$$
\begin{array}{ccccccccc}
1 & \leftarrow & 2 & \leftarrow & 2^2 & \leftarrow & \cdots & \leftarrow & 2^n & \cdots \\
\cdots & \leftarrow & 2^m \cdot 9 & \leftarrow & 2^m \cdot 7 & \leftarrow & 2^m \cdot 5 & \leftarrow & 2^m \cdot 3 & \leftarrow \\
\cdots & \leftarrow & 2^2 \cdot 9 & \leftarrow & 2^2 \cdot 7 & \leftarrow & 2^2 \cdot 5 & \leftarrow & 2^2 \cdot 3 & \leftarrow \\
\cdots & \leftarrow & 2 \cdot 9 & \leftarrow & 2 \cdot 7 & \leftarrow & 2 \cdot 5 & \leftarrow & 2 \cdot 3 & \leftarrow \\
\cdots & \leftarrow & 9 & \leftarrow & 7 & \leftarrow & 5 & \leftarrow & 3. &
\end{array}
$$

This result is due to Sarkovskii, therefore named after him. Notice that 1 and 3 are at the ends of the sequence; all other positive integers fall between them in Sarkovskii's ordering. The meaning is that if there is a period 3 orbit, then there are orbits of every period (all other integers occur before 3); equally it is possible to have a period 5 orbit together with orbits of every period except 3. At the other end of the list, a lone fixed point is possible, but a period 2 orbit requires a fixed point as well.

The theorem tells nothing about the stability of the orbits, or the parameter values for which they may be observed. However, for many of the one-dimensional maps we have studied, one sees that periodic orbits, once born via a bifurcation at some critical value r^*, persist for all $r^* < r < r_{\max}$. If this is the case, there must be periodic orbits of every period for all $r \geq r_3^*$, where r_3^* is the critical value at which the period 3 window commences. This

---

[9]Any number of intermediate integers may be in between.

idea was brought to great prominence by a famous paper[10] with the title "Period three implies chaos".

Exercises

5.8 Use the BIFURCATION DIAGRAMS window of CHAOS FOR JAVA to examine the structure of unstable periodic orbits, up to some relatively large period, of the LOGISTIC MAP in its period 3 window. (Recall also that an interior crisis occurs in this window, see pages 98–99.) What does your experimentation suggest about the structure of the set of all periodic orbits, as a subset of $[0,1]$, for parameter values in this range?

5.4 Capacity dimension

One of the more common measures of dimension is the *capacity dimension* d_C. Its definition follows from a consideration of how to place a sufficient number of small boxes so as to contain the whole set, and how the minimum required number of boxes to achieve this increases as their size is decreased.

Given a set A of points in n-dimensional Euclidean space, let $N(\epsilon)$ be the minimum number of n-dimensional cubes of side ϵ needed to cover (contain) every point of A. For a finite set of K points, $N(\epsilon) = K$ once ϵ is sufficiently small that each box can hold only one point. This may be expressed as

$$N(\epsilon) \approx K\epsilon^0, \qquad \epsilon \to 0, \tag{5.5}$$

For an infinite set, it is reasonable to expect that

$$N(\epsilon) \to \infty, \qquad \epsilon \to 0.$$

Let's ask the question, how is this limit approached? For a smooth curve, we expect that

$$N(\epsilon) \approx K\epsilon^{-1}, \qquad \epsilon \to 0,$$

which reflects the fact that we only need boxes which lie along the curve; halving the size approximately doubles the required number of boxes. For a smooth surface,

$$N(\epsilon) \approx K\epsilon^{-2}, \qquad \epsilon \to 0,$$

by a similar argument.

The geometric dimension of these objects is commonly accepted as 0, 1 and 2, respectively; they may be read off as the power of ϵ in the scaling behaviour of $N(\epsilon)$, but this is an unnecessary complication for smooth

---

[10]T. Y. Li and J. A. Yorke, *American Mathematical Monthly*, **82**, 985–992 (1975).

objects. For complex objects, it provides the definition of a new kind of
dimension as follows:

Definition 5.1 (Capacity dimension) *The capacity dimension d_C of a
set A is defined as the exponent in the scaling relation*

$$N(\epsilon) \approx K\epsilon^{-d_C}, \qquad \epsilon \to 0, \tag{5.6}$$

provided it is well defined.

Using logarithms

The simplest way to read off a power is to take logarithms, for example
equation (5.6) takes the form

$$\ln N(\epsilon) \approx \ln K - d_C \ln \epsilon, \qquad \epsilon \to 0. \tag{5.7}$$

One way to extract d_C is to make a log-log plot of $N(\epsilon)$ versus ϵ; the
intercept will give $\ln K$, which is probably of little interest, the slope gives
the all-important dimension. A further reason for making such a plot is to
provide a visual check of the scaling for sufficiently small ϵ.

Another method is to choose a sequence of values ϵ_k that converge to
zero as $k \to \infty$, and then compute the corresponding counts

$$N_1 = N(\epsilon_1), \qquad N_2 = N(\epsilon_2), \qquad \cdots$$

The dimension is recovered as the limit

$$d_C = \lim_{k \to \infty} \frac{\ln(N_{k+1}/N_k)}{\ln(\epsilon_k/\epsilon_{k+1})}. \tag{5.8}$$

Capacity dimension of the Cantor set

Given the above definition, it is straightforward to work out the capacity
dimension of the Cantor set. Suitable boxes are closed intervals whose
length is a power of $1/3$. Let us consider how many such boxes are required
to cover I_n, for increasing n.

(i) Obviously 3^k intervals of length

$$\epsilon_k = 1/3^k, \qquad k = 0, 1, \cdots$$

are required to cover I_0.

(ii) I_1 can be covered by one interval of length ϵ_0, two of length ϵ_1, and
in general by $2 \cdot 3^{k-1}$ intervals of length ϵ_k if $k \geq 1$. The latter conclusion
arises from the fact that we must cover two intervals, each of length $1/3$.

(iii) I_2 can be covered by one interval of length ϵ_0, two of length ϵ_1, four of length ϵ_2, and in general by $4 \cdot 3^{k-2}$ intervals of length ϵ_k if $k \geq 2$.

(iv) The general situation is that for I_n, the required number of intervals is

$$N_{n,k} = \begin{cases} 2^k, & (k \leq n), \\ 2^n \cdot 3^{k-n}, & (k \geq n), \end{cases} \tag{5.9}$$

where the notation $N_{n,k}$ keeps track of the two integers involved.

Now the Cantor set is defined by taking the limit $n \to \infty$, whereas k enters in relation to the length of the covering intervals. Therefore, the box count needed for a capacity dimension calculation is

$$N_k = \lim_{n \to \infty} N_{n,k} = 2^k.$$

This could have been written down immediately, because of the simple structure of the I_n; the question of a double limit, and the correct order, is quite crucial in typical numerical application. Using equation (5.7) to compute d_C from ratios of successive N_k and ϵ_k gives

$$d_C = \frac{\ln 2}{\ln 3} \approx 0.631.$$

The conclusion is that, even though the Cantor set has zero length, it has non-zero fractal dimension.

An asymmetric Cantor set

Start with the interval $I_0 = [0,1]$ as before, but this time construct I_{n+1} from two copies of I_n, one scaled by the factor $1/2$ and placed at the left, the other scaled by the factor $1/4$ and placed at the right. Explicitly, the first few sets are

$$I_0 = [0,1],$$
$$I_1 = [0, 1/2] \cup [3/4, 1],$$
$$I_2 = [0, 1/4] \cup [3/8, 1/2] \cup [3/4, 7/8] \cup [15/16, 1],$$
$$I_3 = [0, 1/8] \cup [3/16, 1/4] \cup [3/8, 7/16] \cup [15/32, 1/2]$$
$$\cup [3/4, 13/16] \cup [27/32, 7/8] \cup [15/16, 31/32] \cup [63/64, 1],$$

To carry out the box counting it is convenient to choose intervals of size

$$\epsilon_k = 1/2^k, \qquad k = 0, 1, \cdots$$

Simple counting gives the following results for $N_{n,k}$ for small k:

$$
\begin{array}{llll}
(k=0) & N_{n,0}=1, & n \geq 0, \\
(k=1) & N_{n,1}=2, & n \geq 0, \\
(k=2) & N_{0,2}=4, & N_{n,2}=3, & n \geq 1, \\
(k=3) & N_{0,3}=8, & N_{0,3}=6, & N_{n,3}=5, \quad n \geq 2.
\end{array}
\tag{5.10}
$$

Our interest is in the limiting values for $n \to \infty$. These begin

$$
N_0 = 1, \qquad N_1 = 2, \qquad N_2 = 3, \qquad N_3 = 5, \qquad \cdots
$$

which is the start of a *Fibonacci sequence*, satisfying

$$
N_{k+2} = N_{k+1} + N_k, \qquad k = 0, 1, \cdots \tag{5.11}
$$

This last observation is a simple manifestation of self-similarity, exact provided that n is much bigger than $2k$ (so that the largest component of I_n is much smaller than the size of the covering intervals). It expresses the fact that the number (N_{k+2}) of intervals of size ϵ_{k+2} required to cover I_n is equal to the sum of the numbers required to cover the left-hand and right-hand ends before they were reduced to produce I_n from I_{n-1}. Since the reduction factors are $1/2$ and $1/4$, respectively, these numbers are N_{k+1} $(2\epsilon_{k+2} = \epsilon_{k+1})$ and N_k $(4\epsilon_{k+2} = \epsilon_k)$.

An exact formula may be given for the numbers in the Fibonacci sequence, but we require only the scaling limit. Substituting[11] $N_k \approx N\alpha^k$ into (5.11), we get the equation

$$
\alpha^{k+2} \approx \alpha^{k+1} + \alpha^k.
$$

Rearranging and cancelling the common factor α^k gives the quadratic equation

$$
\alpha^2 - \alpha - 1 = 0. \tag{5.12}
$$

The number α is unique, and must satisfy this equation; on the other hand the equation has two solutions. Fortunately, one is positive, the other negative, and it follows that

$$
\alpha = \frac{1 + \sqrt{5}}{2}.
$$

The capacity dimension may now be computed by replacing N_k and ϵ_k, in the equation $N_k \approx K \epsilon_k^{-d_C}$, by $N\alpha^k$ and $1/2^k$, respectively. This gives

$$
\alpha^k \approx (1/2^k)^{-d_C},
$$

Taking logarithms, $k \ln \alpha = d_C \cdot k \ln 2$, from which

$$
d_C = \frac{\ln \alpha}{\ln 2} = \frac{\ln(1 + \sqrt{5}) - \ln 2}{\ln 2} \approx 0.694.
$$

---

[11]See exercise 5.10 for justification.

Exercises

5.9 Extend the box counts (5.10) to the next two values of k, and check that (5.11) is satisfied thus far.

5.10 One can find the constant α for the (asymptotic) growth of the Fibonacci sequence by matrix algebra, since equation (5.11) may be expressed as a linear two-dimensional dynamical system:

$$\begin{pmatrix} N_{k+1} \\ N_{k+2} \end{pmatrix} = \begin{pmatrix} 0 & 1 \\ 1 & 1 \end{pmatrix} \begin{pmatrix} N_k \\ N_{k+1} \end{pmatrix}.$$

(i) Solve the eigenvalue problem

$$\begin{pmatrix} 0 & 1 \\ 1 & 1 \end{pmatrix} \begin{pmatrix} \xi \\ \eta \end{pmatrix} = \lambda \begin{pmatrix} \xi \\ \eta \end{pmatrix}.$$

(ii) Show that one of the eigenvalues $\lambda_+ = \alpha$, and that the other λ_- is smaller in magnitude and negative.

(iii) Find the eigenvectors and show that they are independent.

It follows that, for large k, N_k grows as α^k, as claimed above.

5.11 Consider the dynamical system of the previous question. Find its fixed points, and classify their (linear) stability.

5.12 Consider a tent-like map,

$$f(x) = \begin{cases} 2rx, & (x \le s/(r+s)), \\ 2s(1-x), & (x \ge s/(r+s)), \end{cases} \quad (r, s > 0).$$

Find appropriate values of r and s so that the set of orbits which are not attracted to $-\infty$ is the asymmetric Cantor set discussed above.

5.13 Give a description of the asymmetric Cantor set using base 4 arithmetic; find also the action of the map of the previous exercise on this representation.

5.5 Capacity dimension of the Hénon attractor

Computing capacity dimension is a difficult numerical task even for a relatively simple system such as the Hénon attractor. From equation (5.1) one sees that ideally, a box count $N_{n,\epsilon}$ should be computed for each $\mathcal{Q}_n$, using squares of side ϵ. From this data N_ϵ is obtained from the limit $n \to \infty$, after which the required exponent d_C may be extracted from the limit $\epsilon \to 0$. However there is no practical way to do this.

An alternative and practical method is to follow a particular orbit for a large number of iterations, and count how many squares of side ϵ are visited. Assuming that a sufficient number of initial iterations are discarded before commencing the counting process, we expect each point on the orbit to be much closer to the attractor than ϵ, so that each box visited[12] is required for the cover of Q_H. Denote this number by $N_{n,\epsilon}$, where n is the sample length, then

$$N_\epsilon = \lim_{n \to \infty} N_{n,\epsilon}.$$

The infinite limit poses a serious problem; to put it into context, recall that Lyapunov exponents are defined as an infinite limit, but that using $10^4 \sim 10^6$ samples is generally sufficient to obtain good accuracy. In the present case, the error of truncation increases rapidly as ϵ is decreased,[13] which is in conflict with the necessity of taking the small ϵ limit to recover the dimension. Even worse, if n is fixed while $\epsilon \to 0$, then the count will *saturate*, that is, $N_{n,\epsilon} \to n$. This takes us back to the introductory discussion of capacity dimension; that the dimension of a finite set of points is zero is equivalent to the scaling limit (5.5).

Some box-counting numbers for the case $a = 1.4$, $b = 0.3$ are shown in table 5.1; the initial 10^3 points were discarded to give adequate chance for the orbit to approach the strange attractor very closely.[14] The first column gives the length of the sample orbit, the other columns give the number of squares of given size visited by one or more points on it; the side length ϵ of the squares heads each of these columns. The box sizes have been chosen in convenient multiples of powers of 10. The last four columns have certainly not converged, even though the sample length extends to $n = 10^8$; all we know for certain is that the box count cannot decrease as n is further increased, but we need information about how the limit is attained in order to estimate N_ϵ using a reasonable amount of computation. Despite this, it is hard to believe that the counts given here will increase by as much as a further 1% in the infinite limit. Therefore, let's simply use the last count in each column, which is for $n = 10^8$, and compute d_C from the ratio of

---

[12]The number of visits is irrelevant to the question of how many boxes are needed. Clearly information is being discarded about the relative probability of visiting various parts of the attractor. Consideration of this fact leads to the definition of the *natural measure* and the *information dimension*, topics which are not included in this brief chapter. For an introductory account see Ref. [24], pp. 721–744.

[13]There is a scaling relation for this increase; $N_\epsilon - N_{n,\epsilon} \approx K\epsilon^{-\alpha}n^{-\beta}$, with $\alpha \approx$ 2.4 (see exercises 5.14 and 5.15), the relatively large exponent accounts for the rapid deterioration.

[14]The data was obtained using the ITERATE(2D) window of CHAOS FOR JAVA. The explosion in the power of personal computers is well illustrated by this example!

Length	0.016	0.008	0.004	0.002	0.001	0.0005	0.00025
10^5	810	1870	4336	9793	21856	41335	62672
$2 \cdot 10^5$	814	1879	4385	10030	23593	51164	91944
$5 \cdot 10^5$	814	1887	4417	10175	24409	57832	124586
10^6	814	1890	4428	10220	24692	59689	137366
$2 \cdot 10^6$	814	1892	4437	10244	24832	60572	142705
$5 \cdot 10^6$	814	1894	4437	10268	24923	61143	145458
10^7	814	1894	4439	10274	24963	61371	146404
$2 \cdot 10^7$	814	1894	4440	10280	24987	61499	146970
$5 \cdot 10^7$	814	1894	4440	10282	25008	61575	147387
10^8	814	1894	4440	10284	25016	61605	147541

Table 5.1: Box counts, Hénon map, $a = 1.4$, $b = 0.3$. The boxes are squares of side ϵ given at the top of each column; the length of the orbit is given in the first column. Initial 10^3 points discarded.

two adjacent counts N_{n,ϵ_1}, N_{n,ϵ_2}. This gives the sequence of estimates

$$\frac{\ln(1894/814)}{\ln 2} \approx 1.218, \qquad (\epsilon = 0.016, 0.008)$$

$$\frac{\ln(4440/1894)}{\ln 2} \approx 1.229, \qquad (\epsilon = 0.008, 0.004)$$

$$\frac{\ln(10284/4440)}{\ln 2} \approx 1.212, \qquad (\epsilon = 0.004, 0.002)$$

$$\frac{\ln(25016/10284)}{\ln 2} \approx 1.282, \qquad (\epsilon = 0.002, 0.001)$$

$$\frac{\ln(61605/25016)}{\ln 2} \approx 1.300, \qquad (\epsilon = 0.001, 0.0005)$$

$$\frac{\ln(147541/61605)}{\ln 2} \approx 1.260, \qquad (\epsilon = 0.0005, 0.00025)$$

I relegate further investigation of the problem of the infinite limit to the exercises, and make do here with the fact that the dimension is obviously not an integer, and that its value is $d_C \approx 1.28$. But the data also shows just how bad the infinite limit problem is. For example, when $\epsilon = 0.00025$, of the last $5 \cdot 10^7$ iterations only 154 of them fall into boxes not previously counted; this can not be called super-efficient!

Exercises

5.14 An obvious possibility for probing the large n limit of box counting is to look for scaling in both n and ϵ, since scaling seems to be ubiquitous in chaotic systems. Assume therefore that

$$N_{n,\epsilon} \approx N_\epsilon - K\epsilon^{-\alpha}n^{-\beta}, \tag{5.13}$$

a form suggested by Grassberger.[15]

(i) By eliminating the constant K between equations with sample sizes n, $2n$, $4n$, show that

$$2^\beta \approx \left(\frac{N_{2n,\epsilon} - N_{n,\epsilon}}{N_{4n,\epsilon} - N_{2n,\epsilon}} \right).$$

Why will such a formula be of limited use?

(ii) Assuming that β is known, show that

$$N_\epsilon \approx \frac{2^\beta N_{2n,\epsilon} - N_{n,\epsilon}}{2^\beta - 1} = N_{2n,\epsilon} + \frac{N_{2n,\epsilon} - N_{n,\epsilon}}{2^\beta - 1}.$$

5.15 The data of table 5.1 is not in a suitable form for the application of the scaling arguments of the previous exercise.

(i) Use the ITERATE(2D) window of CHAOS FOR JAVA to construct a table of box counts for the HÉNON MAP, in which n and ϵ both increase by factors of 2, starting from minimum values of 10^3 for n and 2.5×10^{-4} for ϵ.

(ii) Use the results of the previous exercise to estimate the value of β.[16]

(iii) Show that

$$\alpha \approx \ln \left(\frac{N_{n,2\epsilon} - N_{n,\epsilon}}{N_{n,4\epsilon} - N_{n,2\epsilon}} \right).$$

and determine an approximate value for α.[17] What light does this throw on the severity of the saturation problem as $\epsilon \to 0$?

(iv) Estimate limiting values N_ϵ and the capacity dimension of the Hénon attractor.

5.16 Apply the methods of the previous exercise to estimate the capacity dimension of the attractor of the LOZI MAP with $a = 1.7$, $b = 0.3$.

---

[15] P. Grassberger, "On the fractal dimension of the Hénon attractor", *Physics Letters*, **97A**, 224–226 (1983). Since ϵ is a continuous variable, it is necessary to write $N_{n,\epsilon}$ rather than $N_{n,k}$; the limit $n \to \infty$ is N_ϵ rather than N_k.

[16] Grassberger's value, obtained by careful fitting of extensive data, is $\beta = 0.89 \pm 0.03$. You cannot expect to do so well without a lot of careful analysis.

[17] Grassberger's value is $\alpha = 2.42 \pm 0.15$.

5.6 Self-similar fractals

A *self-similar set* is one which consists of smaller (possibly distorted) copies of itself; smaller implies that there must be more than one copy (in fact that there must be an infinite number of copies). Denote by $\mathcal{F}$ a self-similar set and by $\mathcal{F}_k$ ($1 \leq k \leq m$) the copies, so that

$$\mathcal{F} = \bigcup_{k=1}^{m} \mathcal{F}_k.$$

I suppose that each copy $\mathcal{F}_k$ is produced by a function ψ_k, that is, $\mathcal{F}_k = \psi_k(\mathcal{F})$; this gives an alternative method to write the construction,[18]

$$\mathcal{F} = \sum_{k=1}^{m} \psi_k(\mathcal{F}). \tag{5.14}$$

This leads to

Definition 5.2 (Contraction mapping) *A function f is called a contraction mapping if there is a constant L, with $0 < L < 1$, such that the distances $|x - y|$ and $|f(x) - f(y)|$ satisfy*

$$|f(x) - f(y)| \leq L|x - y|,$$

for all points x, y in the domain of f.

It is important to note that these maps may be acting in the plane (or even in higher-dimensional space), in which case x stands for a pair of coordinates, etc.

For each of the contraction maps employed in (5.14) I assume that the minimum possible value is chosen for L_k. Given such a set of contractions, with a trapping region U for which

$$\psi_k(U) \subseteq U,$$

it can be shown that there exists a self-similar set $\mathcal{F}$, and that it is the unique limit

$$\mathcal{F} = \lim_{n \to \infty} F_n = \bigcap_{n=0}^{\infty} F_n, \qquad F_{n+1} = \sum_{k=1}^{m} \psi_k(F_n),$$

where F_0 is any subset of U. The parallel with equations (5.1) and (5.2) are obvious.[19]

---

[18]This section follows the book by Yamaguti, Hata and Kigami [31], which contains a concise treatment with full proofs.

[19]I could not resist noting, in passing, that the set $\mathcal{F}$ is an attracting fixed point in a metric space of sets F_0, indicating parallels between the simplicity of fixed points as we first met them in chapter 2, and the sophistication of the contraction mapping theorem in an infinite-dimensional metric space.

Similarity dimension

To motivate the following definition, let's revisit the Cantor set. First, for the middle third set I_C we can use

$$\psi_1(x) = \frac{x}{3}, \qquad \psi_2(x) = 1 - \frac{x}{3}; \tag{5.15}$$

these have the properties that

$$|\psi_k(x) - \psi_k(x)| = {}^1\!/_3|x - y|.$$

There is exact equivalence here, the image produced by ψ_k is an undistorted miniature; such maps are called *similar contractions*.[20] More generally, we can take

$$\psi_1(x) = L_1 x, \qquad \psi_2(x) = 1 - L_2(1 - x),$$

choosing $L_1 = {}^1\!/_2$ and $L_2 = {}^1\!/_4$, for example, gives the asymmetric Cantor set of page 159.

When the functions ψ_k do not introduce distortion, and provided the images $\psi_k(I_0)$ satisfy the *open set conditions* that $\psi_k(I_0) \subseteq I_0$ and that $\psi_k(I_0)$, $\psi_l(I_0)$, $(k \neq l)$, have no overlap, we can apply equation (5.14) to box counting in the limit of small ϵ,

$$N(\epsilon) = \sum_{k=1}^{m} N(\epsilon/L_k). \tag{5.16}$$

Inserting the scaling relation $N(\epsilon) \approx K\epsilon^{-d_C}$ gives a formula for the capacity dimension, for the Cantor sets this is

$$1 = L_1^{d_C} + L_2^{d_C},$$

already employed to calculate d_C.

There is one more preliminary before turning these observations into another definition. Consider the function

$$f(d) = \sum_{k=1}^{m} L_k^d, \qquad 0 < L_k < 1,$$

which results from applying scaling to equation (5.16) for arbitrary m. Now f is a smooth function of d, taking the values $f(0) = m$, $f(\infty) = 0$; it is easy to show that its derivative is negative for all $d \geq 0$. It follows that the equation $f(d) = 1$ has a unique solution, making possible the following:

---

[20]Similar contractions are discussed at length in Ref. [24] under the metaphor of the *Multiple Reduction Copy Machine* (MCRM).

Definition 5.3 (Similarity dimension) *For a self-similar set given by (5.14), the similarity dimension d_S is defined as the unique solution of the equation*

$$\sum_{k=1}^{m} L_k^{d_S} = 1.$$

For the middle third Cantor set this gives $2 \cdot 3^{-d_S} = 1$, $d_S = \ln 2/\ln 3$; for the asymmetric Cantor set $2^{-d_S} + 4^{-d_S} = 1$, which is precisely the quadratic equation (5.12) with $\alpha = 2^{d_S}$.

In conclusion, note that the similarity dimension does not have to coincide, in general, with either the capacity dimension d_C or indeed the Hausdorff dimension d_H. However, $d_S = d_H$ in the case of self-similar contractions which satisfy the open set conditions.[21]

Exercises

5.17 For the Hénon system with $a = 1.4$, $b = 0.3$, find a pair of points (x,y), (x',y'), such that the distance between them is increased under one iteration of the map.

5.18 Show that the contraction maps

$$\psi_1(x) = \frac{x}{3}, \qquad \psi_2(x) = \frac{x+2}{3},$$

produce the middle third Cantor set; comparison with (5.15) shows that the same fractal can be generated by different contractions.

5.19 Calculate the similarity dimension of the middle $1/r$ Cantor set ($r \geq 2$ an integer). What happens in the limit $r \to \infty$ and how does this accord with your expectations? How does the dimension relate to the capacity dimension?

5.7 Lyapunov dimension of two-dimensional maps

Regrettably, the Hénon map is a contortion rather than a contraction, so the considerations of the previous section do not directly apply. Nevertheless they lead, in a natural way, to another type of dimension which has considerable advantage for calculation.

To motivate the idea, consider first a periodic attractor; its Lyapunov exponents L_1 and L_2 are both negative and all nearby initial points are attracted to a finite set of points. Clearly the dimension of such an attractor

---

[21] All of these assertions are proved in Ref. [31].

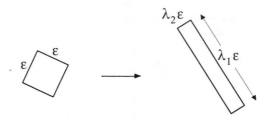

Figure 5.5: Using Lyapunov exponents to approximate the effect of a two-dimensional map on a small square of side ϵ.

is zero. On the contrary, for a strange attractor, $L_1 > 0$ and $L_2 < 0$, which conveys the fact that the attractor is compressed in one direction and expanded in the other, by factors of average value $\lambda_i = \exp(L_i)$ per iteration. One can base a simple argument on this, using approximate self-similarity, which leads to a new dimension definition.

Average scaling behaviour

Let $N(\epsilon)$ be the number of squares of side ϵ required to cover the attractor. After one iteration these squares have undergone an uneven change of scale. Choose the orientation of each small square so that one side is stretched and the other shrunk, to give a rectangle of aspect ratio λ_1/λ_2 (see figure 5.5). One iteration of the map replaces the old covering of N squares by a new covering of $(\lambda_1/\lambda_2)N$ squares having reduced edge size $\lambda_2\epsilon$. This gives a scaling relation, approximate because the actual expansion/contraction factors are in reality position-dependent,

$$\frac{\lambda_1}{\lambda_2}N(\epsilon) \approx N(\lambda_2\epsilon).$$

Assume, as usual in making definitions of fractal dimension, the scaling behaviour

$$N(\epsilon) \approx K\epsilon^{-d_L}.$$

Substituting this formula into the relationship between $N(\epsilon)$ and $N(\lambda_2\epsilon)$, and taking logarithms, gives

$$\ln\lambda_1 - \ln\lambda_2 + \ln K - d_L\ln\epsilon = \ln K - d_L(\ln\epsilon + \ln\lambda_2).$$

Solving for d_L and using the fact that $L_i = \ln(\lambda_i)$, the result is

$$d_L = 1 - \frac{L_1}{L_2}. \tag{5.17}$$

This is the *Lyapunov dimension* of the strange attractor.

Definition 5.4 (Lyapunov dimension) *In the case that the Lyapunov exponent $L_1 > 0$, the Lyapunov dimension of an attractor of a dissipative two-dimensional map is given by the formula (5.17); if $L_1 \leq 0$ the Lyapunov dimension is zero.*[22]

For example, for the Hénon map with $a = 1.4$, $b = 0.3$, simple numerical computation involving orbits whose length is only $10^4 \sim 10^6$ gives

$$L_1 \approx 0.39, \qquad L_2 \approx -1.59,$$

from which

$$d_L \approx 1 + 0.39/1.59 \approx 1.25.$$

Apart from the fact that we do not require excessive computation to get good estimates, there is the advantage that this does not require repeated computations for a range of values of ϵ.

The question of the relation between the Lyapunov dimension and other fractal dimensions has been the subject of much investigation. The *Kaplan-Yorke conjecture*, according to which the Lyapunov dimension d_L and the information dimension d_I are believed to take the same value for a wide range of strange attractors, has received much attention. Although I do not give a treatment of the information dimension herein,[23] it is worth mentioning that it is part of a *continuous spectrum* of dimensions. In particular, d_C and d_I are members of this spectrum, and it is known that

$$d_C \geq d_I,$$

with strict inequality as the normal case. Certainly it appears that $d_C > d_L$ for the Hénon attractor ($d_C \approx 1.28$ — see section 5.5). For further discussion, see, for example, Ref. [21], pp134–144, or Ref. [24], pp736–738.

Exercises

5.20 Recall exercise 5.16, where the capacity dimension of a strange attractor of the Lozi map was found. Use the Iterate(2D) window of Chaos for Java to compute the Lyapunov dimension of this attractor and compare with the capacity dimension.

5.21 A controlled one-dimensional map is two-dimensional, but the original system is recovered in the limit $b \to 0$; in this case $L_2 \to -\infty$ and $L_1 \to L$, the Lyapunov exponent for the original map. What does this suggest about the fractal dimension of attractors of one-dimensional maps?

---

[22] An alternative way to state this is as follows: if $L_1 > 0$, $d_L = 1 - L_1/L_2$, if $L_1 \leq 0$, $d_L = 0 - 0/L_1$; this is a special case of the more general definition given on page 193.

[23] See footnote 12 on page 162 for some information.

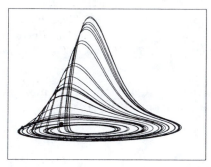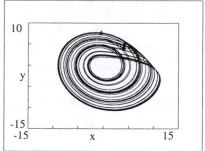

Figure 5.6: A chaotic orbit of the Rössler equations, $c = 5.7$.
Three-dimensional view (left), Projection onto the x-y plane, cir-
culation is counterclockwise (right).

5.22 Investigate the capacity dimension of the attractors of the LOGISTIC
MAP with $r = 3.56$ and $r = 3.57$. (For the counts, select the CON-
TROLLED LOGISTIC MAP in the ITERATE(2D) window of CHAOS FOR
JAVA, set $b = 0$, and expand the y axes as far as possible; this will min-
imise the number of boxes required in the counting process and thereby
enable very small values of ϵ to be used.)

5.8   The Rössler attractor

Rössler's equations (2.6) rated a brief mention in an earlier exercise involving return maps. Like the Hénon map they defy complete mathematical
analysis, yet it is clear from numerical experimentation that they exhibit
many of the typical features of non-linear systems. In particular, there
are chaotic attractors with a single organising centre, this makes for ready
visualisation of the dynamics as a two-dimensional map.

Such a chaotic orbit is displayed in figure 5.6. It is evident that, for
this parameter value, the solution circles the z-axis in a counter-clockwise
direction. The projection of the orbit into the x-y plane has recurrent self
intersections, but the orbit itself cannot intersect because the system is
completely deterministic; each initial value (x_0, y_0, z_0) leads to a unique
orbit. The orbit under consideration is chaotic, a claim that can be supported by Fourier analysis and the computation of Lyapunov exponents;
the largest exponent is positive.

The circulating motion suggests a particularly convenient place to take
a Poincaré section; any vertical half plane, radiating out from the z-axis,
is pierced precisely once per circuit. The plane of section is completely
specified by fixing the angle between the x-axis and the line of its inter-

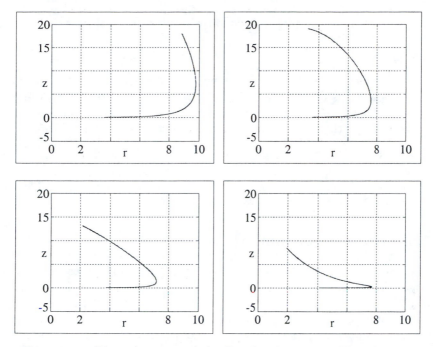

Figure 5.7: Plane sections of the Rössler attractor. The planes progress in 30° increments, starting from a plane parallel to the x-axis (top left) to one parallel to the y-axis (bottom right).

section with the x-y plane. Within this section, suitable coordinates are r (distance from the z-axis) and z. One circuit of the orbit uniquely maps an initial point (r, z) to the next point (r', z'), that is, the differential equations determine a two-dimensional map

$$r' = f(r, z), \qquad z' = g(r, z),$$

although it is not possible to write down explicit formulae for f and g.

The reduction of the Rössler equations to a two-dimensional map enables us to see that the mechanism whereby the strange attractor is produced is precisely the stretching and folding which operates for the Hénon system. This is shown in figure 5.7, which displays the intersection of 10^3 points on the attractor with four different planes of section, spaced 30° apart. The four were chosen so as to sample that part of the attractor where the stretching and folding is most evident. The phenomenon is much better observed, as an animation, using the POINCARÉ SECTIONS window of CHAOS FOR JAVA,[24] which allows one to observe how the points in the

---

[24]See appendix A.10 for documentation on the POINCARÉ SECTIONS window.

section change, as the plane of section is rotated about the z axis.

Exercises

5.23 Use the POINCARÉ SECTIONS window of CHAOS FOR JAVA to view cross sections of the Rössler attractor for $c = 5.7$, observing the way the attractor evolves as the plane of section is rotated about the z-axis. Follow also the sequence of events for the values $c = 5.35, 5.4, 5.5$.

5.24 Use the POINCARÉ SECTIONS window of CHAOS FOR JAVA to view cross sections of the Rössler attractor for $c = 2.0, 3.0, 4.0$. Make certain to discard a sufficient number of initial circuits so that you can identify the nature of each orbit observed in this way.

5.9   The Feigenbaum attractor

Exercise 5.21 suggests that attractors of one-dimensional maps can only be fractal in the marginal case that the Lyapunov exponent makes a transition through zero, although it is hard to make a firm statement because this assumes continuity. In this section I discuss an obvious candidate for observing a one-dimensional fractal attractor, the end of a period-doubling cascade. There are two possible approaches; straightforward numerical experimentation or use of the theory of Feigenbaum scaling, the bare bones of which were sketched in section 3.10. The former is left to the exercises; I choose to explore the latter.

Recall that, associated with the theory of period doubling, there is a universal function g, which satisfies the functional equation

$$g_2(x) = -g(\alpha x)/\alpha, \qquad g(0) = 1.$$

A numerically determined solution was given in equation (3.28); g is a smooth unimodal function which maps the interval $[-1, 1]$ into itself, in which it has a maximum at $x = 0$ and a single unstable fixed point x^*.[25] Graphs of g and g_2 are shown in figure 5.8; one sees immediately that there are unstable orbits of period 1 and 2. A cobweb diagram of the first 500 iterations, commencing from $x_0 = 0$, is also shown; it is clear that they avoid the positions of these unstable orbits.

The map has an attractor which is a fractal somewhat similar to the Cantor set. The intervals which get deleted along the way are created by an unstable period 2^n orbit for each $n \geq 1$, together with the fact that there are no other periodic orbits of the map. The following discussion aims to amplify these claims.

---

[25] Feigenbaum gives the values $x^* \approx 0.5493052461$, $f'(x^*) \approx -1.601191328$; see footnote 20 on page 105 for the reference.

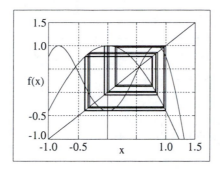

Figure 5.8: The universal function g and its second composition g_2, showing also the first 500 iterations commencing from $x_0 = 0$.

The first step

Consider the orbit which commences from the origin,

$$x_0 = 0, \qquad x_k = g(x_{k-1}) = g_k(0). \tag{5.18}$$

The first few values are

$$x_0 = 0, \qquad x_1 = 1, \qquad x_2 = -1/\alpha \approx -0.3995,$$
$$x_3 \approx 0.7589, \qquad x_4 = 1/\alpha^2 \approx 0.1596, \qquad \cdots$$

Now define the interval $I_0 = [x_2, x_1]$ (see figure 5.9). Using the fact that g is unimodal in $[-1, 1]$, it is clear that after one iteration all points are in I_0, which therefore contains the attractor. We can say more; all points in the interval $[x_2, x_4]$ are mapped to the interval $[x_3, x_1]$ and conversely, that is,

$$[x_2, x_4] \overset{g}{\longleftrightarrow} [x_3, x_1]. \tag{5.19}$$

This leads to the definition of a new interval I_1 as

$$I_1 = [x_2, x_4] \cup [x_3, x_1].$$

Consider the interval (x_4, x_3) which has been deleted in this construction. It contains the fixed point x^*, which is unstable. In fact, it is easy to check that $g'(x) < -1$ for all $x > -x_2$, so all orbits in the interval $(-x_2, x_3)$ will be driven out. But the interval $[x_4, -x_2]$ is mapped into $[x_3, x_1]$, because g is an even function. Consequently, all iterations which commence in I_0, except x^*, eventually enter I_1, after which they are trapped.

This is the first step in a Cantor-like construction of the attractor. Note an important difference; in the Cantor set, all points of I_0 are mapped to

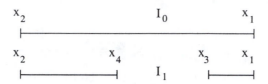

Figure 5.9: The intervals I_0 and I_1 which commence the construction process of the strange attractor.

I_1 by a single application of a contraction map $\psi_1 + \psi_2$, in the present case there are points, arbitrarily close to x^*, which require an arbitrarily large number of iterations of g before they enter I_1, moreover there is one point which is not attracted to I_1.

The recursion

Equation (5.19) shows that there are no orbits of odd period (we needed to show that all orbits except x^* are attracted to I_1 to make this claim). In fact the functional equation implies more than this. First, it is easily shown that

$$g_{2k}(x) = -g_k(\alpha x)/\alpha. \tag{5.20}$$

which implies that a periodic orbit of even length is associated with one of half that length, one cannot exist without the other. So the only allowed periods are the powers of 2; any period may be written as $m \cdot 2^n$, where m is odd, and there are no orbits of odd period except $m = 1$. Differentiating the functional relation,

$$g_{2k}'(x) = -g_k'(\alpha x),$$

which shows that period 2^n orbits are all unstable. I leave aside a proof that there exists such an orbit for each n.

These orbits determine the recursion for the sets I_n. I_2 is obtained by deleting two intervals from I_1, caused by the fact that each of its two subintervals contains a point on the unstable period 2 orbit. These unstable points are, by definition, not in the attractor; more importantly they create the holes, whose end points are related to the special orbit defined in (5.18). Similarly, the 2^n points of the unstable period 2^n orbit lie in the 2^n subintervals which constitute I_n, thus making 2^n holes in it. Since this is an infinite recursive procedure, and each of the sets I_n contains the attractor, the result is the strange attractor

$$I_F = \lim_{n \to \infty} I_n = \bigcap_{n=0}^{\infty} I_n.$$

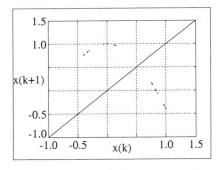 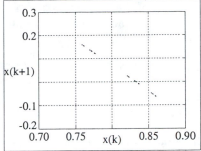

Figure 5.10: First return map for the universal function g. Initial point $x_0 = 0$, sample size 10^4 points, initial 10^4 points discarded.

Points on the orbit (5.18) constitute an obvious numerical approximation to the strange attractor, provided enough initial iterations are discarded. A long sample is displayed in figure 5.10 as a first return map;[26] the holes are clearly seen.

Estimate of fractal dimension

I have already indicated that the dynamics of this attractor is more complex than the self-similarity considered in section 5.6. Nevertheless, it is interesting to compute a kind of similarity dimension, using the structure of the first two intervals determined above. For this purpose, let $l_0 = x_1 - x_2$, $l_1 = x_4 - x_2$, $l_2 = x_1 - x_3$ be the lengths of I_0 and the two pieces of I_1, and define

$$L_1 = l_1/l_0, \qquad L_2 = l_2/l_0.$$

Inserting these into definition 5.3,

$$1 \approx (0.3995)^d + (0.1723)^d;$$

solving numerically gives $d \approx 0.537$, which is close to the most accurately known value $d_C \approx 0.538$ for the capacity dimension of this set.[27]

Exercises

5.25 Recall exercise 5.22. Use the ITERATE(2D) window of CHAOS FOR JAVA in the same way to investigate the capacity dimension of the at-

---

[26] Since the map is one-dimensional this contains no extra information, I used it because it is a convenient method to display the points in the plane rather than on the x-axis.

[27] Given in P. Grassberger and I. Procaccia: Measuring the strangeness of strange attractors, *Physica*, **9D**, 189–208 (1983). Our result is just an estimate, Grassberger obtained precise bounds on the capacity dimension by careful analysis of numerics.

tractor of the LOGISTIC MAP with parameter value $r_\infty \approx 3.5699456\ldots$.
Investigate also how the counts respond to changes of the estimated
value of r_∞ by ± 0.000002.

5.26 Give a proof of equation (5.20).

5.27 If x^* is a point on an orbit of period $2k$, find a related point on an
orbit of period k.

5.28 How does the structure of the periodic orbits of the universal function
g fit in with the classification of Sarkovskii's theorem?

Chapter 6

Non-linear oscillations

Differential equations are an important class of dynamical systems;[1] in this concluding chapter I consider second order equations with linear damping but non-linear restoring term, driven by a periodic applied force. These restrictions have the benefit of permitting easy reduction to a two-dimensional map with constant area-reduction, while encompassing some of the most important examples, although they preclude consideration of the Lorenz and Rössler equations.

6.1 The driven non-linear pendulum

The paradigm,[2] with which I commence, is the driven plane pendulum. As a dynamical model it represents a system consisting of a mass m constrained to move in a vertical plane at a constant distance l from a fixed pivot point. Because the mass moves on a fixed vertical circle, only one coordinate is needed to specify its state, the angular position $x(t)$, measured from the bottom (rest) position. Three forces combine to produce the motion:

(i) Gravity, acting vertically downward with magnitude mg; the tangential component $mg \sin x$ acts as a restoring force. Since $\sin x$ is not proportional to x, it provides the non-linearity.

(ii) A damping force cx', proportional to the angular velocity x'.

(iii) An applied periodic driving force, $g(t)$, acting tangentially and independent of both x and x'.

The equation of motion is given by Newton's second law[3]

$$\text{mass} \times \text{acceleration} = \text{force},$$

---

[1] For an informative account of the mutual origins and development of calculus, differential equations and dynamics, see Acheson's book "From Calculus to Chaos" [2].

[2] The driven non-linear pendulum is the primary model considered in the well-known book by Baker and Gollub [5].

[3] Newton postulated the relation $\dot{p} = \text{force}$ (p the momentum), rather than $m\ddot{q} = \text{force}$ (q the position); since the mass is constant, $\dot{p} = ml\ddot{x}$ here (see also page 5). Another point which I have skated over is that there is a frictionless constraint, consequently it is only necessary to consider tangential components.

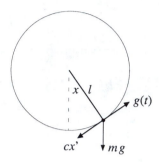

Figure 6.1: Schematic diagram for the driven damped pendulum.

which leads to the second order non-linear differential equation

$$mlx'' + cx' + mg \sin x = g(t).$$

Dimensionless parameters

There are four constants and an arbitrary function here. They do not play an equal rôle, however. One constant just sets the overall scale, since nothing changes if we divide through by (for example) the mass m. Furthermore, if we change the unit of time by the substitution

$$t \rightarrow t\tau,$$

then the equation becomes

$$ml\tau^{-2}x'' + c\tau^{-1}x' + mg \sin x = g(t).$$

The natural choice for the measurement of time is made by setting $ml\tau^{-2} = mg$, giving

$$\tau = \sqrt{l/g}.$$

$2\pi\tau$ is the period of small amplitude oscillations in the case of no damping and no external force, $1/\tau$ the corresponding angular frequency.

Making this choice, and dividing through also by mg, we obtain the equation

$$x'' + cx' + \sin x = g(t), \tag{6.1}$$

which leaves only two important quantities to be chosen, the relative damping factor c and the driving force $g(t)$ (both rescaled from the original).

For simplicity, I restrict attention to the case that $g(t)$ is a trigono-metric function, of angular frequency Ω and amplitude k, and consider the particular form of the driven damped pendulum

$$x'' + cx' + \sin x = k \cos \Omega t. \tag{6.2}$$

With these choices the frequency Ω of the driving force is measured in units of the natural frequency $\sqrt{g/l}$.

Linear approximation

The *small amplitude approximation* which is the subject of many elementary treatments of second order differential equations is obtained by making the linear approximation $\sin x \approx x$ (x small), which gives a constant coefficient equation,

$$x'' + cx' + x = k \cos \Omega t. \tag{6.3}$$

We can find a *particular solution* $x_p(t)$ of this equation by simple guesswork, sometimes called variation of parameters. Since the system is damped, and driven by a trigonometric function, we expect that eventually the motion should be drawn into sympathy with the external force, as represented by

$$x_p(t) = A \cos(\Omega t + \delta). \tag{6.4}$$

A is the *amplitude*, proportional to k, and δ is the *phase shift*, independent of k. Both depend on the damping factor c and the frequency Ω. It is not difficult to check that this is indeed a solution of the equation, and to obtain formulae for A and δ. I leave the details as an exercise, since the linear case is not the object of interest, although we need to understand something about it to set the stage for the non-linear system.

A periodic attractor — linear system

The solution $x_p(t)$ is not just periodic, if $c > 0$ it is a periodic attractor — all nearby solutions are attracted toward it. This is easy to demonstrate precisely because the system is linear; given the particular solution (6.4), substitute the formula

$$x(t) = x_p(t) + x_h(t)$$

into the differential equation. The terms in x_p result in a cancellation of the driving term $k \cos \Omega t$, leaving the *homogeneous equation*

$$x_h'' + cx_h' + x_h = 0.$$

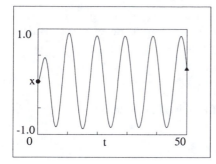
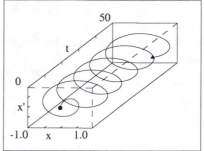

Figure 6.2: A solution of the driven pendulum equations, shown as a function of time (left) and in three dimensions (right). Parameter values $k = 0.5$, $c = 0.5$, $\Omega = 2/3$, initial conditions $x_0 = y_0 = 0$.

This is a constant coefficient equation, with solution[4]

$$x_h(t) = \exp(-ct/2)\big(A\cos(\omega_0 t) + B\sin(\omega_0 t)\big). \tag{6.5}$$

The detailed formulae for ω_0 and the arbitrary constants A, B are of no importance here, what is important is that these additional terms in the solution tend to zero as $t \to \infty$, leaving x_p as the unique attractor for the driven linear system.

A periodic attractor — non-linear system

The above considerations rely on replacing $\sin x$ by x in the differential equation. We expect that the approximation is not too bad provided the system is not driven to large values of x. That is, we expect the full non-linear system should have a periodic attractor for values of k that are not too large. Figure 6.2 shows the solution which starts from $x(0) = x'(0) = 0$, driven at frequency $\Omega = 2/3$, with $c = 1/2$, $k = 1/2$. On the left is a plot of the function $x(t)$ for the first 50 time units, this settles down rapidly to a steady periodic response. The trajectory in three-dimensional space-time is seen on the right.

The butterfly effect

One of the hallmarks of chaos, which is measured by Lyapunov exponents, is sensitive dependence of solutions on initial conditions — the *Butterfly*

---

[4]This assumes that $c < 2$; if $c \geq 2$ the solution consists of decaying exponentials without any trigonometric terms. One also sees that x_p is unstable if $c < 0$.

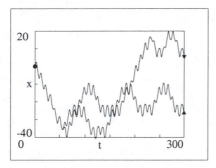

Figure 6.3: Two solutions of the driven pendulum equations. Parameters $k = 1.5$, $c = 0.5$, $\Omega = 2/3$. Initial conditions $x_0 = 0.0$, $y_0 = 1.000$ and $y_0 = 1.001$. The butterfly effect is clearly seen.

effect. I shall discuss the definition of Lyapunov exponents in due course. This will lead to a definition of chaotic orbits for periodically driven systems.

Figure 6.3 shows two solutions with $k = 1.5$, both starting from $x(0) = 0$. The difference between them is that one has initial condition $x'(0) = 1.000$, the other $x'(0) = 1.001$. It was precisely this kind of qualitative difference between two solutions which differed by only a small change of initial condition (sensitive dependence), which gave birth to Lorenz' celebrated results. The paradox is that, even though the two solutions become so unrelated in the sense of direct comparison, there is at every place patterns of behaviour which can almost be matched. This is an indication that the solutions may be under the control of a strange attractor.

Exercises

6.1 Show that the constants which appear in the particular solution of equation (6.4) are given by the formulae

$$A(c, k) = k/\Delta, \qquad\qquad \sin \delta(c, k) = -c\Omega/\Delta,$$
$$\Delta^2(c, k) = c^2\Omega^2 + (1 - \Omega^2)^2, \qquad \cos \delta(c, k) = (1 - \Omega^2)/\Delta.$$

This shows that the response of the linear system is linear in k, and that it has a peak in the vicinity of $\Omega = 1$ (for small c).

6.2 Show that the constant ω_0 which appears in the complementary solution (6.7) is given by

$$\omega_0 = \sqrt{1 - c^2/4}, \qquad c < 2.$$

Show also that x_h is the sum of two decaying exponential functions if $c > 2$.

6.3 Use the ODE ORBITS window of CHAOS FOR JAVA to further investigate some orbits of the driven pendulum system. In particular:

(i) Experiment with initial conditions to test the assertion that the periodic attractor for $k = 0.5$ appears to attract all orbits.

(ii) Use the facilities for rotation of orbits, and for their animation, to gain a firm understanding of the way they evolve in time.

(iii) Examine the system for $k = 1.05$, and experiment with initial conditions to find coexisting attractors.

6.2   Phase Plane

Before proceeding, I want to generalise equation (6.1) slightly to include an arbitrary restoring term, that is, to consider the second order differential equation

$$x'' + cx' + f(x) = g(t), \qquad (6.6)$$

where f is a smooth function of x. A useful example is the *driven Duffing equation*,[5]

$$f(x) = \alpha x + \beta x^3. \qquad (6.7)$$

The behaviour of this system depends critically on whether α is positive, negative, or zero, and also on the sign on β,[6] this is explored further in the exercises.

Solutions of equation (6.6) may be regarded as a single function $x(t)$ determined by a second order equation, but it is extremely useful to put the position and velocity on equal footing. A good reason may be found in the fact that the initial values of both x and x' must be specified in order to uniquely determine the solution. To avoid giving one of the two such a privileged rôle, introduce a separate symbol y for the velocity, whereupon the original equation may be written in terms of two variables as

$$\begin{aligned} x' &= y, \\ y' &= -cy - f(x) + g(t). \end{aligned} \qquad (6.8)$$

This pair of first order differential equations is the preferred form. Its solutions live in a two-dimensional *phase plane* whose coordinates are x, y, or simply x, x'.

---

[5]The driven Duffing equation encompasses a number of important examples including the *two-well oscillator*; it is studied extensively in the book by Moon [19].

[6]Obviously the case that $\beta = 0$ is of little interest.

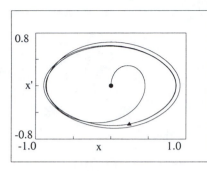
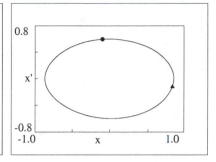

Figure 6.4: Orbit of figure 6.2 in the phase plane (left), after 300
time units have elapsed (right); both have a time span of 50 units.

Properties of orbits

Given an arbitrary initial time t_0, and arbitrary initial values x_0, y_0, the
equations have a unique solution which satisfies

$$x(t_0) = x_0, \qquad x'(t_0) = y(t_0) = y_0.$$

These orbits are smooth curves in three-dimensional space-time, with
coordinates x, y, t. Uniqueness means that they may never intersect, since
a point of intersection would provide a set of initial conditions from which
two different orbits emanate. Viewed in the phase plane, however, the
curves may intersect; such points of intersection are places where $x(t)$ and
$y(t)$ have identical values, but at different values of t.

I return now to the driven pendulum.[7] Figure 6.2 (right), shows an
orbit in which the three-dimensional form is apparent. What is not quite
so apparent is the rapid convergence to a periodic attractor, seen more
clearly in a phase plane view such as those of figure 6.4, particularly the
right hand one which shows the solution in the time interval $300 \le t \le 350$.

It is important to realise that all the views of this solution were produced by looking at the same data from different aspects,[8] two of which
were chosen to be exactly along one of the axes in three-dimensional space,
providing a two-dimensional projection.

---

[7]The theoretical discussions of this chapter all apply to the general equation (6.6),
but the driven pendulum will continue as the particular example under consideration.

[8]Specifically, they were obtained in the ODE ORBITS window of CHAOS FOR JAVA
which provides for rotation of axes in three dimensions.

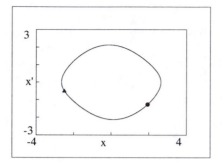 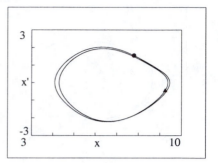

Figure 6.5: Phase plane diagram for the driven pendulum, after solutions they were allowed to converge to a periodic attractor. $k = 1.0$, period 1 orbit (left), $k = 1.07$, period doubled (right).

Period doubling

For sufficiently large k, the non-linearity causes qualitative changes to the behaviour of the solutions. In order to concentrate on the attractor, one looks for evidence that the solution has converged and discards as transient the solution thus far. I have done that in figure 6.5 for $k = 1.0$ and $k = 1.07$, with the same values of c and Ω as before. The results show clear evidence of period doubling, demonstrating the ubiquitous nature of that bifurcation.[9]

Exercises

6.4 The plane pendulum has an obvious symmetry, since it cannot matter which direction from the bottom is chosen as positive. This is reflected in the fact that the undriven pendulum equation $x'' + cx' + \sin x = 0$ is unchanged by the substitution $x \to -x$. Now the right hand side of equation (6.2) has its own special property,

$$g\left(t + \pi/\Omega\right) = k\cos(\Omega t + \pi) = -k\cos\Omega t = -g(t).$$

(i) Show that, if $x(t)$ is a solution of (6.2), then so is $-x(t+\pi/\Omega)$. This gives a classification of orbits according to their symmetry; an orbit for which

$$x(t + \pi/\Omega) = -x(t), \qquad y(t + \pi/\Omega) = -y(t), \qquad (6.9)$$

will be called *symmetric*, the significance is that if a point (x, y) of phase space visited by the orbit, then so is the symmetrically placed point $(-x, -y)$, a half period later.

---

[9]Actually, it will not seem surprising once the system is reduced to a two-dimensional map of the phase plane.

(ii) Show that, if an orbit $x(t)$ is not symmetric, then it and $x_1(t) = -x(t + \pi/\Omega)$ form a pair of distinct orbits.

6.5 The previous exercise was concerned with symmetric and non-symmetric orbits, this exercise is an exploration using the ODE ORBITS window of CHAOS FOR JAVA.

(i) Using the value $k = 1.05$, display two orbits in the phase plane starting from $(-2.2, 1.4)$, $(-0.3, 2.0)$, respectively. Set the time interval to $94.2478 \approx 30\pi$ (approximately 10 periods of the driving term at the frequency $\Omega = 2/3$).

(ii) Using the tool in the ODE ORBITS window which computes a new solution starting from the previous final position, verify that the two solutions converge to distinct periodic orbits which appear to be related by the inversion $x \rightarrow -x$, $y \rightarrow -y$.

(iii) Decrease the value of k in increments of 0.01 down to $k = 1.01$. At each stage, discard the transient as in (ii) before making further change to k.

(iv) Continue as in (iii) from $k = 1.01$ using increments of 0.001. Evidently there is a bifurcation taking place; what type do you believe it to be?

6.6 In the previous exercise you observed a bifurcation by commencing with a pair of orbits, observed for $k = 1.05$, and then decreasing the value of k. Starting with the same pair of orbits, what bifurcations are observed as k is increased in steps of 0.01?

6.7 The driven Duffing equation, as expressed in equations (6.6, 6.7), has two more parameters (α and β) than the driven pendulum; both may be eliminated by scaling. The case that $\alpha = 0$ is obviously special. Show that, by a suitable rescaling of the amplitude $x \rightarrow Kx$, the equation reduces in this case to

$$x'' + cx' \pm x^3 = g(t).$$

where the choice of sign depends on the sign of β. The case that $\beta < 0$ is totally unstable, and therefore of no interest. I shall call the other case the *Ueda oscillator*,[10] it is also implemented in CHAOS FOR JAVA, with driving term $g(t) = k \cos \Omega t$ as for the driven pendulum.

---

[10] This seems less confusing than *driven cubic oscillator* since there have been several *cubic maps*, while *driven Duffing equation* hides the fact that there is no linear term, which is usual in that case. This particular form of the equation was investigated in some detail by Y. Ueda and collaborators — see Moon [19] for further details.

6.8 Use the ODE ORBITS window of CHAOS FOR JAVA to examine orbits
of the Ueda oscillator

$$x'' + cx' + x^3 = k\cos\Omega t. \qquad (6.10)$$

with $c = 0.1$ and a selection of values of $k \le 10$.

6.3   Poincaré sections

Even the phase plane picture is complicated, in fact you can examine chaotic
orbits in the phase plane without gaining much insight, except for the
obvious complication.

Let's step back and ask why we are looking at orbits are all. Since
the system is deterministic, an extreme point of view is that we only need
specify the initial position in the phase plane (x_0, y_0), and the time t_0, after
which the equations reveal all. The problem is that this gives no insight
whatsoever, it is just the *clockwork universe* philosophy of Laplace revisited
(page 6).

For differential equations of the type under consideration, it is easy to
implement the method of *Poincaré sections*. In general, the difficulty is
to find a suitable surface which the orbit must pierce repeatedly;[11] for a
periodically driven system the phase plane provides such a surface. It is
pierced once, and once only, for each value of the time, allowing us to record
the positions at a convenient sequence of times.

There is an obvious choice for these times, namely once per cycle of
the applied force, always at the same point of the cycle. Expressed as a
formula, that is, $t_n = t_0 + 2\pi n/\Omega$. Each increment of n corresponds to
increasing the phase of the periodic driving force by 2π radians, therefore
it is customary to measure the initial time t_0 in these units also, writing
$t_0 = \phi_0/\Omega$ and

$$t_n = \frac{\phi_0 + 2\pi n}{\Omega}, \qquad n = 0, 1, \cdots.$$

ϕ_0 is the *phase* of the section, which may be varied to get different sections.
Examining the changes as ϕ_0 is taken through a complete range from 0 to
2π gives an impression of the structure of the orbit.

The period map

Taking snap-shots of where the system is in the phase plane, at some sequence of times, will always produce a set of points in the plane. What
is so special about the choice made here is the relation to the frequency

---

[11]The fact that we already viewed some sections for the Rössler equations (page 170)
seems to belie this assertion; see however exercise 6.12 for an indication of the difficulties.

of the external disturbance. It comes from an important property of the differential equations (6.8), namely

if $(x(t), y(t))$ is a solution, then so is $(x(t + 2\pi/\Omega), y(t + 2\pi/\Omega))$.

This follows from the fact that if we change the time variable by $t \to t' = t + 2\pi/\Omega$, nothing changes in the equations. On the left hand sides $d/dt = d/dt'$, while c is constant. On the right hand sides, the driving force is unchanged because

$$k \cos \Omega t' = k \cos \Omega(t + 2\pi/\Omega) = k \cos \Omega t.$$

In general, the two solutions will not be the same. To investigate the connection between them, let's call them $(x_0(t), y_0(t))$ and $(x_1(t), y_1(t))$; they are related by the simple formulae

$$x_1(t) = x_0(t + 2\pi/\Omega), \qquad y_1(t) = y_0(t + 2\pi/\Omega).$$

The first pair, $(x_0(t), y_0(t))$, is the unique solution with initial values

$$x_0(t_0) = x_0, \qquad y_0(t_0) = y_0,$$

and after one time step they have the values

$$x_1 = x_0(t_0 + 2\pi/\Omega), \qquad y_1 = y_0(t_0 + 2\pi/\Omega).$$

These are the initial values for the solution $(x_1(t), y_1(t))$, starting from $t = t_0$; the two solutions are in fact part of the same (infinite) orbit, one period out of step.

Reviewing the arguments leading to this conclusion shows that it applies to any periodically driven system, of period Ω, not just the case that the driving term is trigonometric.

Phase of section

Let's recast the preceding considerations in a different way. An initial time t_0 is equivalently specified by an initial phase $\phi_0 = \Omega t_0$, which may be incremented by any integer multiple of 2π. This leads to:

Definition 6.1 (Phase of section) *Given an initial time t_0, the corresponding phase of section is given by*

$$\phi_0 = \Omega t_0, \qquad \mathrm{mod}\ 2\pi, \tag{6.11}$$

meaning that ϕ_0 is reduced by an integer multiple of 2π so as to lie in the range $0 \le \phi_0 < 2\pi$.

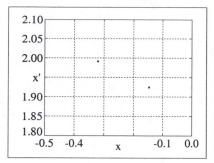 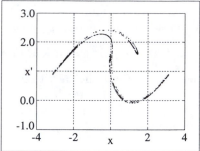

Figure 6.6: Poincaré sections for the driven pendulum. $k = 1.07$, period 2 (left), $k = 1.5$ strange attractor (right). Sample size 10^3 points, initial 10^2 points discarded.

For any initial point (x_0, y_0), starting at initial time $t_0 = \phi_0/\Omega$, the differential equations determine a unique orbit, which arrives at a point

$$(x_1, y_1) = (x_0(t_0 + 2\pi/\Omega), y_0(t_0 + 2\pi/\Omega))$$
$$= (x_1(t_0), y_1(t_0)),$$

after one period of the driving force. The time has been incremented by $2\pi/\Omega$, but the phase remains the same. This is a two-dimensional map of the phase plane to itself, in which the phase appears as a parameter. The vital point is that this map contains complete information about the dynamics of the system. This is the consequence of periodicity of the driving force; solutions remain solutions under the translation $t \rightarrow t+2\pi/\Omega$ and the effect of such a time translation on the initial point is $(x_0, y_0) \rightarrow (x_1, y_1)$. The conclusion is that, for periodically driven systems such as the pendulum, we may replace an investigation of orbits in three-dimensional space by investigation of a two-dimensional map.

Definition 6.2 (Poincaré sections) *Given a phase of section ϕ_0, the orbit of the map*

$$(x_0, y_0) \rightarrow (x_1, y_1) \rightarrow \cdots \rightarrow (x_k, y_k) \rightarrow \cdots$$

generated by sampling positions in the phase plane at the sequence of times

$$t = t_0 \rightarrow t_1 = t_0 + 2\pi/\Omega \rightarrow \cdots \rightarrow t_k = t_{k-1} + 2\pi/\Omega \rightarrow \cdots$$

is a Poincaré section of the corresponding orbit of the differential equation.

One consequence of the above is that, in order to specify the initial condition for a periodically driven system, it is sufficient to specify x_0, y_0,

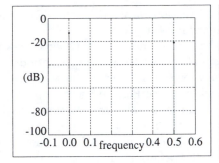 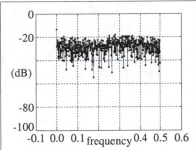

Figure 6.7: Fourier analysis, driven pendulum, using Poincaré section data. $k = 1.07$, period 2 orbit (left), $k = 1.5$, strange attractor (right). Sample size 10^3 points, initial 10^2 points discarded.

while restricting t_0 by $0 \leq t_0 < 2\pi/\Omega$. This convention is followed when setting initial conditions for such systems in CHAOS FOR JAVA.

Poincaré sections for the period-doubled solution of figure 6.5(right) and the chaotic solution of figure 6.3 are shown in figure 6.6. It is immediately clear that there is an intimate connection with two-dimensional maps, and that there is a strange attractor in the chaotic case.

Periodicity

Any orbit which is periodic, with the same period as the driving force, will obviously be a fixed point of the Poincaré section. Conversely, if an orbit is a fixed point of the Poincaré section, then it is periodic as a function of time, satisfying

$$x(t + 2\pi/\Omega) = x(t), \qquad y(t + 2\pi/\Omega) = y(t),$$

because the new initial conditions (after one period) are identical with the original. More generally, if a solution determines a period n orbit of the Poincaré section (as a map), then it is periodic as a function of time, satisfying

$$x(t + 2\pi n/\Omega) = x(t), \qquad y(t + 2\pi n/\Omega) = y(t),$$

and conversely.

This means that Poincaré sections contain complete information about the periodicity or otherwise of the corresponding full solution, although the frequency information is restricted to frequencies no greater than $\Omega/2$. Naturally, the full solution will have higher frequency components which are lost if we investigate the Poincaré section rather than the differential equations, but this may be of secondary importance.

A crucial question for chaos is the definition of a chaotic orbit as one which is not periodic (nor in the basin of attraction of a stable periodic orbit) and which has a positive Lyapunov exponent. We see that the question of long term periodicity can be settled from the Poincaré section alone. In particular, if the discrete Fourier spectrum of the Poincaré section contains non-zero amplitudes at all frequencies in the range $0 \le \omega \le 1/2$, even after discarding a sufficiently long initial transient, then the orbit cannot be of this type. Figure 6.7 displays Fourier spectra corresponding to the Poincaré sections of the figure 6.6. The period 2 nature of the one, and the aperiodic nature of the other, are clearly evident.

Exercises

6.9 Exercise 6.5 was concerned with symmetric and non-symmetric orbits of the driven pendulum. Using two POINCARÉ SECTIONS[12] windows of CHAOS FOR JAVA and the initial conditions found previously, locate the two periodic orbits at $k = 1.05$, one in each window. By moving the phase of the section through $180°$ and measuring positions on the screen, check that the positions of the two orbits satisfy (6.9).

6.10 Use the FOURIER ANALYSIS window of CHAOS FOR JAVA to investigate the periods of the orbits observed in exercises 6.5 and 6.6.

6.11 Investigate the Ueda oscillator (6.10) with $c = 0.1$. Some suggestions are:

(i) Commence by using the ODE ORBITS window of CHAOS FOR JAVA with $k = 2.5$ to observe the two distinct orbits which result from the initial conditions $(1.54, 1.89)$ and $(1.77, -1.41)$.

(ii) Follow the structure of these orbits to smaller values of k, and classify the bifurcations from which they emanate.

(iii) Follow the orbits to larger values of k, and obtain evidence of a period doubling cascade to chaos.

(iv) Look for evidence of a tangent bifurcation to a period three orbit at $k \approx 5.563$.

6.12 Use the ODE ORBITS window of CHAOS FOR JAVA to examine orbits of the Rössler equations with $a = 0.2$, $c = 12$; in particular check whether the projection in the x-y plane always circles in the same direction. Examine the Poincaré sections of these orbits also.

---

[12]See appendix A.10 for documentation on the POINCARÉ SECTIONS window.

6.13 Use the available tools of CHAOS FOR JAVA to classify the behaviour of the Rössler equations with $a = 0.2$ in the range $6.6 \leq c \leq 6.8$.

6.4 Lyapunov exponents

Lyapunov exponents may be defined for the solutions of differential equations and for Poincaré sections, in the latter case there are two independent Lyapunov exponents, in the former case three. Numerical calculation of either is rather complicated.

Lyapunov exponents for Poincaré sections

For a discrete map Lyapunov exponents are average contraction/expansion factors per iteration; this is essentially a time average using a single iteration as time unit. Differential equation are formulated with their own intrinsic time scale, used in the definition of time derivative; it is therefore natural that Lyapunov exponents for differential equations should be expressed as averages per unit time. This leads to the following definition:

Definition 6.3 (Lyapunov exponents of Poincaré section) *Given an initial point* (x_0, y_0), *the Lyapunov exponents* $L_1(x_0, y_0)$, $L_2(x_0, y_0)$ *of a Poincaré section are given by the formulae*

$$L_1(x_0, y_0) = \lim_{k \to \infty} \frac{1}{T_k} \left(\lim_{\delta_0 \to 0} \ln |\delta_k^{\max}/\delta_0| \right),$$

$$L_2(x_0, y_0) = \lim_{k \to \infty} \frac{1}{T_k} \left(\lim_{\delta_0 \to 0} \ln |\delta_k^{\min}/\delta_0| \right),$$

where T_k *is the elapsed time for the* k *iterations.*

For the systems under consideration, the time is given by

$$T_k = \frac{2\pi k}{\Omega},$$

so the difference between this definition and the previous one (definition 4.6, page 129) is rescaling by the factor $\Omega/2\pi$.[13]

There is an important feature in common between Poincaré sections of the driven non-linear system (6.8) and the generalised Hénon map (4.8); both are dissipative maps, with constant area contracting factor. For the

---

[13] At first sight it may seem strange that Lyapunov exponents do not have an absolute scale; of course only ratios of exponents occur in the definition of Lyapunov dimension which cannot depend on the choice of time scale.

Hénon map, this factor is the absolute value $|b|$, in the present case it is given by

$$\exp(-2\pi c/\Omega). \tag{6.12}$$

A justification of this claim is given in appendix C. An important consequence is that the two Lyapunov exponents are simply related, since the product of the two scaling factors $\lambda_1 = \exp(L_1)$ and $\lambda_2 = \exp(L_2)$ has to equal the area reduction factor. Taking into account the time rescaling, equation (6.12) gives the relation

$$L_1 + L_2 = -c.$$

Lyapunov exponents for differential equations

The differential equations under consideration are three-dimensional, therefore proper definition of Lyapunov exponents should involve three contraction/expansion factors for an evolving three-dimensional ellipsoid. The necessary theory starts from the fact, which I state without proof, that to linear approximation a small ellipsoid is continuously transformed as a succession of small ellipsoids, with ever changing principal axes and directions.[14]

The evolution of a small ellipsoid must be traced along the particular orbit which has initial conditions $x(t_0) = x_0$, $y(t_0) = y_0$, $t = t_0$, the factors in the linear approximation come from considering *variational derivatives* of the differential equations themselves. This is treated briefly in appendix C; the point is to find how other orbits, which start close to the orbit under investigation, evolve in time. An important claim which is proved in the appendix is that the volume contraction factor for a three-dimensional ellipsoid over one time period is the same as the area contraction factor (6.12) for an ellipse in the Poincaré section.

Now there is one direction of variation for which it is easy to state and solve the variational equations, namely when t_0 is varied by δt_0, while (x_0, y_0) are varied so as to stay on the same orbit. Obviously this nearby solution generates the same orbit, and the nearby point is always where the actual point is at a time difference of δt_0. The conclusion is that one of the contraction/expansion factors is equal to unity, its logarithm zero, making one Lyapunov exponent exactly zero. Moreover, the principal axis associated with the non-trivial exponents are in the phase plane.[15] It follows that the other two Lyapunov exponents of the differential equation match those of the corresponding Poincaré section. Note that there are many systems for which matters are much more complicated.

---

[14]The proof is essentially along the lines of exercises 4.25 – 4.27.

[15]More precisely, the third variational equation (page 226) tells us that $\delta t = \delta t_0$ as the orbit evolves, so the size of the ellipsoid in the direction orthogonal to the phase plane remains constant in the linear approximation used to compute Lyapunov exponents.

Lyapunov dimension

Lyapunov dimension is defined in an arbitrary number of dimensions; given the n Lyapunov exponents of an n-dimensional system, written in decreasing numerical order

$$L_1 > L_2 > \cdots > L_n,$$

let k be the largest integer for which the sum of the first k satisfies

$$S_k = L_1 + L_2 + \cdots + L_k \geq 0,$$

then the Lyapunov dimension is defined as

$$d_L = k - S_k/L_{k+1}.$$

For two-dimensional maps this is equivalent to the previous definition 5.4.

For differential equations of the type being studied, the importance of the relationships among the Lyapunov exponents, and the fact that one is zero, becomes clear. Since the orbits are continuous curves joining successive points of a Poincaré section, it is natural to expect that the dimension $d^{(3)}$ of any attractor,[16] viewed as an object in three-dimensional space, should be simply related to the dimension $d^{(2)}$ of its Poincaré section by $d^{(3)} = d^{(2)} + 1$.

For the Poincaré section, if $L_1^{(2)} > 0$, dissipation ensures that $L_1^{(2)} + L_2^{(2)} < 0$, and the Lyapunov dimension is

$$d_L^{(2)} = 1 - L_1^{(2)}/L_2^{(2)}.$$

For the corresponding three-dimensional orbit $L_1^{(3)} = L_1^{(2)}$, $L_2^{(3)} = 0$ and $L_3^{(3)} = L_2^{(2)} < 0$, so the Lyapunov dimension is

$$d_L^{(3)} = 2 - L_1^{(3)}/L_3^{(3)} = d_L^{(2)} + 1,$$

as expected. In the case that $L_1^{(3)} = L_1^{(2)} < 0$, $d_L^{(2)} = 0$ and $d_L^{(3)} = 1$, since $S_1^{(3)} = 0 \geq 0$ giving $k = 1$ in that case.

In conclusion, note that there are two possibilities for the Lyapunov dimension of an attractor:

(i) A periodic attractor, which is a one-dimensional curve in three-dimensional space, or a zero-dimensional set of points in the phase plane. This has both (non-zero) Lyapunov exponents negative.

---

[16]To keep the discussion clear, I introduce a cumbersome notation whereby the superscript (2) or (3) is added to everything to indicate the context.

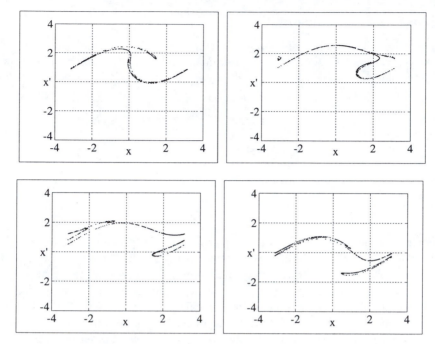

Figure 6.8: Poincaré sections, driven pendulum $c = 0.5$, $k = 1.5$. Sample size 10^3 points, initial 10^2 points discarded. The phase of section varies from $0°$ (top left) in increments of $45°$.

(ii) A strange attractor, which has $L_1^{(2)} > 0$, $L_2^{(2)} < 0$, and Lyapunov dimension $d_L^{(2)} = 1 - L_1^{(2)}/L_2^{(2)} > 1$. Since $L_2^{(2)}$ is finite, this is a strict inequality.

The missing possibility is for an attractor with $d^{(3)} = 2$ or $d^{(2)} = 1$, that is, an attracting solution which traces out a smooth surface in three-dimensions; this would appear in the Poincaré section as a smooth curve. The crucial point is that solutions which are restricted to such a surface will not be allowed to intersect, a far more restrictive condition in two dimensions than in three. Such possibilities lead to consideration of maps of a smooth closed curve in the phase plane to itself (equivalently, maps of a circle), but that is the beginning of another story.

Strange attractor of the driven pendulum

For the driven pendulum, we can readily observe the stretching and folding mechanism in the Poincaré sections. Some typical pictures, generated by the POINCARÉ SECTIONS window of CHAOS FOR JAVA, are shown in figures

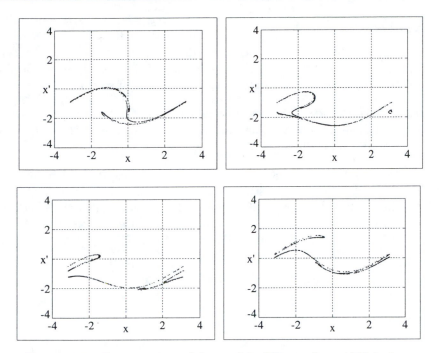

Figure 6.9: Continuation of figure 6.8. Phases from 180° in increments of 45°. Sections at ϕ_0 and $\phi_0 + 180°$ are mirror images, indicating the symmetry of the attractor under $\phi_0 \to \phi_o + \pi$.

6.8 and 6.9. The stretching and folding, as the phase ϕ_0 is increased, is clearly seen, as is the symmetry of the attractor.[17]

Using a facility in the window, estimated values of the Lyapunov exponents, calculated on the same orbit data (sample size 10^3, initial discard 10^2), were

$$L_1 \approx 0.117, \qquad L_2 \approx -0.617.$$

Note that the sum of the two is $-c = -0.5$ (to the quoted accuracy); any failure would be of the numerics rather than the theory. From these values

$$d_L \approx 1 + 0.116/0.616 \approx 1.19.$$

Increasing the sample size to 2×10^3 changes these estimates to

$$L_1 \approx 0.112, \qquad L_2 \approx -0.611, \qquad d_L \approx 1.18,$$

an indication of the difficulty of accurate numerical estimation. Taken together with the Fourier spectrum (figure 6.7), this data leaves little doubt that the observed behaviour is chaotic, the attractor strange.

---

[17]Were it not for this, there would needs be a pair of coexisting attractors.

Exercises

6.14 Use the POINCARÉ SECTIONS window of CHAOS FOR JAVA to make some estimates of the Lyapunov dimension of the Rössler attractor observed in figure 5.6, as an attractor in the plane of section.

6.15 Use the POINCARÉ SECTIONS window of CHAOS FOR JAVA to investigate the effect of damping on the Lyapunov dimension of the attractors of the driven pendulum, with $k = 1.5$ and $\Omega = 2/3$.

6.16 Use the POINCARÉ SECTIONS and FOURIER ANALYSIS windows of CHAOS FOR JAVA to investigate and classify the attractor of the Ueda oscillator (6.10) for $k = 10.0$, $c = 0.1$. Examine also the effect of increasing the damping constant c for these values of k and Ω.

Appendix A

Chaos for Java Software

This appendix,[1] while providing documentation for the use of CHAOS FOR JAVA, is not intended to be read in isolation. In particular, because each feature of the software has specific uses directly related to various sections of the text, no further explanation of technical terms is given here. The main text may be read sequentially, this appendix should be consulted as necessary. Additional information may be found in the READ ME file which comes with the software.

A.1 Installation

CHAOS FOR JAVA is provided as JAVA[2] class files, together with other documents; they are available free for non-commercial use. It is possible to run CHAOS FOR JAVA either as an APPLET or as a JAVA APPLICATION. For information use a browser to visit[3]

http://sunsite.anu.edu.au/education/chaos

or commence a search from the publisher's website. There are links to pages from which the software may be downloaded, with a variety of options for download and deployment, and to pages in which the software may be run in a Java-enabled brower, perhaps to explore before downloading. Some of the information in this appendix may become out of date; the Web pages will be updated as necessary, as will the software.

You will need a run-time environment for the platform you are using. There are a number of options. The simplest is to use a JAVA enabled browser such as MICROSOFT INTERNET EXPLORER or NETSCAPE NAVIGATOR, which run on many platforms. Once you have installed all the files

---

[1] This is a corrected and updated version for the 2nd printing.

[2] All software and hardware will be referred to by their commonly known names; in many cases these are trade marks which are the property of their registered owners, including APPLE COMPUTER INC., MICROSOFT CORPORATION, NETSCAPE COMMUNICATIONS CORPORATION and SUN MICROSYSTEMS INC.

[3] This particular SUNSITE is maintained by the Australian National University and I would like to acknowledge their support in providing these facilities. Other SUNSITES may choose to mirror the software; links will be added as and when this occurs.

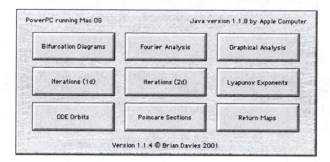

Figure A.1: The main panel of CHAOS FOR JAVA.

in a suitable location, simply open Chaos.html as a local file, which will run it as an APPLET in a page with the name EXPLORING CHAOS.

Because of the computational intensity of many of the operations, it is vital to use a JIT (Just-in-time) VIRTUAL MACHINE, otherwise some operations will be quite slow.[4] The latest versions of the two recommended browsers both provide such a VIRTUAL MACHINE, in fact MICROSOFT INTERNET EXPLORER gives the user a choice, and it is your responsibility to select the appropriate option. Indeed it is a good idea to try all options available to you and decide which is the most convenient and/or efficient.[5]

It is also possible to run CHAOS FOR JAVA as a JAVA APPLICATION, which avoids the security restrictions placed on an APPLET; it also allows for extended features (not documented in this appendix) such as saving and restoring the current states, saving pictures, setting and saving preferences, and printing. In this case you will have to install a suitable JAVA run time environment, although these are currently available without charge for all the popular platforms. For more information on download options and currently available versions visit the download page; for more information on JAVA visit

http://java.sun.com/products/jdk/

---

[4]It seems to be a common belief that JAVA is intrinsically slow. My experiments indicate that there is little cost in computational speed of a JIT VIRTUAL MACHINE over the use of native code, although graphics do incur quite a penalty. The former factor is the critical one for investigating dynamical systems. CHAOS FOR JAVA uses off-screen drawing to avoid duplicating graphical operations when windows change their position or front-to-back order on the screen. For this reason, it requires adequate memory in order to have a number of windows concurrently open.

[5]There can be considerable speed differences between various modes of use.

A.2   General features

The illustrations used in this appendix were all produced using the recommended browsers, by screen capture,[6] on an iMAC computer; in some cases running MAC OS 8.5, in other cases running WINDOWS 95. Regardless of the method of utilising the software, running it as an APPLET will result in a window with the appearance shown in figure A.1.

The principal operations of CHAOS FOR JAVA are initiated by a single click of the appropriate button.[7] After a delay, during which time the button will remain depressed, an independent window will be created. The one shown in figure A.2 is a ITERATE(1D) window of CHAOS FOR JAVA window. Because it was created by an APPLET, the browser has appended a security warning to the window.

The main areas of the window will be briefly described. The *tool panel* contains *tools* for controlling various operations, such as starting and stopping a computation, setting zoom modes, and choosing particular features which are specific to the window. The *prompt panel*, and the associated *disclosure triangle*, is used to display a variety of messages and information. In figure A.2, it shows a prompt about the tool under the cursor. The *control panel* is used to make various choices and for the input of parameters and other numerical data. Details vary with the chosen window and will be described in later sections. With the exception of the ODE ORBITS window, the *scrollbars* are used in the obvious way.

Prompt panel

This panel has a number of different functions, all related to feeding back information to the user. The following is a list of uses:

(i) When the cursor is moved over a tool, a brief description of its function is displayed, similarly when it is moved over a data entry field.

(ii) *Warnings* or *alerts* are displayed, in red (other messages are in black). A short history of alerts is kept; it may be reviewed by clicking in the *disclosure triangle* on the right hand side of the prompt panel.

(iii) When the cursor is moved within the bounds of the graph, its coordinates are displayed,[8] as in figure A.3. Coordinates are calculated to

---

[6]The figures in the main text were produced with an application version of the program, with font and colour options chosen so as to give output suitable for high resolution printing; consequently they have a somewhat different appearance from the screen images used in this appendix.

[7]This is replaced by menus in the application version.

[8]The exception to this is that there is no facility in the ODE ORBITS window for displaying coordinate positions of the mouse relative to three-dimensional orbits.

Tool Panel   Prompt Panel   Disclosure triangle   Control Panel

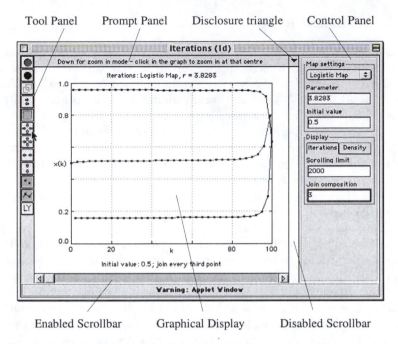

Enabled Scrollbar   Graphical Display   Disabled Scrollbar

Figure A.2: An ITERATE(1D) window of CHAOS FOR JAVA, showing the main parts and their layout, which are typical. The prompt
panel displays information about the tool under the cursor.

the accuracy allowed by the pixel resolution of the screen; the number
of decimal places used for the display reflects this limitation.[9]

(iv) Certain numerical computations may be made using special tools.
As an example, figure A.7 shows the GRAPHICAL ANALYSIS window
being used to calculate a fixed point of map.

Messages displayed in the prompt panel stay there until the mouse is
moved some distance. When the current coordinates are being displayed,
they are updated as often as possible. In other circumstances the information remains for a little longer — exactly how long will depend on the
circumstances and the platform.

---

[9]The values shown in figure A.3 are accurate in the first two decimal places. Moving
the mouse very slightly will reveal that one pixel changes the position by about 0.003.
Making the window bigger will increase the resolution, as will zooming in.

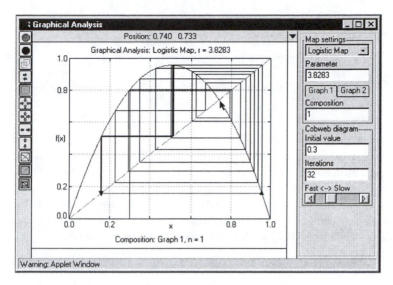

Figure A.3: A GRAPHICAL ANALYSIS window of CHAOS FOR JAVA, showing the use of the prompt panel to display the coordinates of the current cursor position. Both scrollbars are disabled.

Axes and scrolling

It is important to be able to move around graphical information both by scrolling and zooming. To understand the precise result of any particular attempt at either, it is necessary to understand how the axis scales and subdivisions are chosen.

Each axis has a *maximum range* of values over which results may be viewed. A visual indication that this limit has been reached is afforded by the fact that the relevant scrollbar[10] is *disabled* (displayed as an empty rectangle). This is the case in figure A.2 for the vertical scrollbar, indicating that the maximum range of values of f is 0 to 1 for the logistic map in the ITERATE(1D) window. In the same figure the horizontal axis is the iteration number. The limit is presently 2000, set in the *data entry field* labelled *Scrolling limit*. Only the first 100 iterations are displayed, but the remaining 1900 may be viewed using the horizontal scrollbar, which is therefore *enabled*.

Axes also have a minimum resolution beyond which zooming in will be refused. Within these limitations, axes are always chosen so that the

---

[10]The application version has a choice of scrollbar appearance; the default depends on the platform, but may be changed.

Line Down   Page Down   Scroll Box   Page Up   Line Up

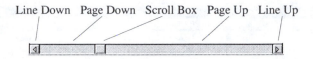

Figure A.4: An enabled scrollbar — standard appearance.

subdivisions are a multiple of 1, 2 or 5 times a power of 10, while the
number of subdivisions is kept between 4 and 7 if possible. This is reflected
in figure A.2 by the fact that the horizontal axis has subdivisions of 20,
the vertical axis of 0.2. Zooming in, which is described below, can make
the axis subdivisions smaller, but the same rules apply. For example, an
attempt to select a vertical axis range of 0.157 to 0.356 will result in it
being set to 0.15 to 0.40 with five divisions in steps of 0.05.

Scrollbar behaviour

A typical enabled scrollbar, and its parts, is shown in figure A.4. To guar-
antee consistent behaviour, CHAOS FOR JAVA has its own scrollbars, so
the appearance will not match the platform's standard. Nor will the behaviour necessarily match your expectation; in particular scrolling using
the line/page up/down boxes is *synchronised*, which means that the next
increment is made only after the full effect of the previous one has been
computed and displayed. During synchronised scrolling operations the triangle in the corresponding line up/down box is highlighted.

Depressing the mouse button[11] while the cursor is in the *line up* box
will cause the range to be increased by one subdivision, and this will repeat
so long as the button is kept depressed. So, in figure A.2, the range will
change from $0-100$ to $20-120$, then to $40-140$, etc. Pressing the button in
the *page up* box will cause the range to be incremented by the full width less
one subdivision. In the same figure this results in the sequence of ranges
$0-100 \rightarrow 80-180 \rightarrow 160-260$, etc. The line/page down boxes work in an
analogous way.

Finally, moving the scrollbox itself will result in no action, other than
in the scrollbar itself, until after the mouse button is released. This kind
of scrolling is not synchronised because that could lead to very annoying
pauses once a sequence of long computations had been triggered.

---

[11]The number of buttons is platform dependent — in general the left button should
be correct.

General tools

The top nine tools shown in figures A.2 and A.3 are common to all two-dimensional plots; the remaining three are peculiar to the ITERATE(1D) window and will not be described here. Each tool carries a prompt which is displayed in the prompt panel when the mouse is moved over it. Each of the nine will be described in turn.

The first two are for starting and stopping a computation.

Start: Pressing this button will cause all the relevant data entry fields to be checked for new data. Changes will result in a fresh computation being made and displayed. If there are no changes to the data, the graph will simply be refreshed and an alert displayed.

Stop: Pressing this button should cause long computations to stop, possibly after a small delay. Usually, the progress of longer computations is obvious from a progress indicator which will appear during their progress.

The next two have simple functions; pressing either of them causes an immediate action, provided that such action is possible.

Revert: This button will revert the axes to the standard choice for the selected map — the *default view*. An alert will show if this is the current view.

Undo: This button will undo the last zoom. Only one previous zoom can be undone, otherwise an alert will show.

Zoom modes

The five remaining tools set the zoom modes. They are *linked checkboxes*; one of them always remains down, it determines the current *zoom mode*, depressing another releases the one which is down. These tools do not result in any immediate action, actual zooms are triggered by appropriate use of the mouse and the mouse button.

Set Framed Zoom Mode: The mouse must be used to make the selection rectangle.

Set Zoom In Mode: Clicking at any point decreases the range of both axes by a factor of approximately[12] 2.15.

Set Zoom Out Mode: Clicking at any point increases the range of both axes by a factor of approximately 2.15.

Set Horizontal Zoom Out Mode: Clicking at any point increases the range of the horizontal axis by a factor of approximately 2.15.

Set Vertical Zoom Out Mode: Clicking at any point increases the range of the vertical axis by a factor of approximately 2.15.

---

[12]This is followed by the setting of new axes, which means that the final factor can never be exactly 2.15.

Zooming

A framed zoom uses a selection rectangle chosen by clicking at one position within the bounds of the graph and dragging to another position before releasing the button. The selection rectangle, whose opposite corners are at the positions of clicking and releasing, will show while the button is still down. Once it is released a zoom will occur, or an alert will be given.[13] A visual cue that framed zoom mode is selected is the fact that the cursor changes from an arrow to a crosshair whenever it is within the bounds of the graph.

Other types of zoom are effected by a single mouse click. The point at which it is clicked becomes (as far as is possible within the constraints of choosing new axes) the centre of the new view. A visual cue that one of these modes is selected is the fact that the cursor retains its default form of an arrow even within the bounds of the graph.

Control panel and data entry

Not surprisingly, this panel is the vehicle for setting the parameters of a given calculation. Generally there are one or more *groups*, with the first group devoted to the map or equations under investigation and setting the main parameters. In figure A.5, for example, the CUBIC #1 MAP has been chosen, but this may be changed by clicking on the *choice* item (which is a pop-up menu or selection list, depending on the platform) and dragging the cursor to the new choice before releasing the button. The selected map has one initial value, which is set to 0.666667 in the displayed figure. For details of the other settings, refer to the section on the BIFURCATION DIAGRAMS window.

Group tabs

Some groups include a *tab*, such as the *Display* group in figure A.2 and the *Map settings* group in figure A.3. These work in the obvious way, in that clicking in the tab switches the visible fields for data input. It is important to note, however, that quite a number of operations which are specific to data under the control of a tab (such as initial values) are switched when the tab is switched. As an example, switching the tab in figure A.3 from *Graph 1* to *Graph 2* will not only expose the relevant composition field, it will also result in an immediate update of the cobweb diagram.

---

[13]Both can result if it is possible to zoom in one direction but not the other.

Data entry fields

Input to data entry fields in the control panel is achieved by typing in numerical data. Each field has an associated *minimum* and *maximum* numerical value, and a numerical *type* (integer or decimal number). Entering data that is out of range will result in the relevant limit being substituted; entering data of the wrong type (for example, 1a00 for 1000) will produce results which are platform dependent, and almost certainly unintended. Either circumstance should result in an alert being shown.

Pressing the return or enter key while the text entry cursor is active in a data entry field is a signal to start a new computation using the current data.[14] As with the *Start button*, all the data entry fields will be checked, not just the one in which the return/enter key was pressed. Fields which have been hidden will be checked if they are relevant to the computation.

The usual features of word processing are supported under JAVA for data entry fields; they are editable text. Entries may be copied or pasted both within CHAOS FOR JAVA itself, and to other running applications via the system clipboard, for example to a word processor or calculator. The tab key should move the insertion point from one field to the next, and shift-tab should work in the reverse direction.[15]

A.3 BIFURCATION DIAGRAMS

An example of this window is shown in figure A.5. For one-dimensional maps, bifurcation and final state diagrams[16] may be computed, either separately or superposed, as in the figure. There are tools for switching each option on or off independently, immediately below the zoom tools. The top one controls whether or not final states are displayed, the bottom one serves the same purpose for periodic orbits (bifurcation diagrams). Bifurcation diagrams are not supported for two-dimensional maps, moreover final state diagrams display values of x_k (see page 111 for a discussion of the reason).

Final states are shown when the appropriate tool is down. A detailed description of how they are constructed is given in section 3.2. The number of iterations discarded and the sample size are set in the *Iterations* group. Pressing return or enter while in either of these data entry fields will initiate a new computation; it will also cause the appropriate tool to be depressed if it is currently up. After determining which pixels contain one or more points on the orbit, they are displayed, using a colour which depends on whether or

---

[14]Precise details are dependent on the hardware/software combination being used, check to see how it works!

[15]Unfortunately, this behaviour is not implemented in all JAVA VIRTUAL MACHINES.

[16]See sections 3.1 and 3.2 for an explanation of terms used in this section.

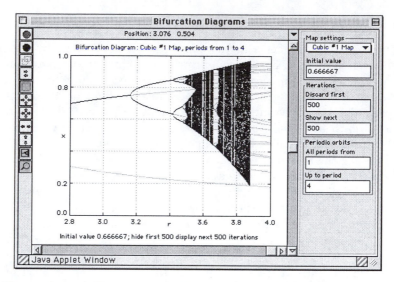

Figure A.5: A BIFURCATION DIAGRAMS window, showing final states and numerically computed orbits of period 1 to 4 inclusive.

not the same pixel is required for displaying part of the bifurcation diagram. If this is not the case, the pixel is painted dark grey. However, if the point coincides with a stable or unstable orbit, the pixel is painted a dark blue or dark red, respectively.

Bifurcation diagrams are shown when the appropriate tool is down, in which case a search is made for orbits whose periods are within the limits set in the *Periodic orbits* group. Pressing return or enter after entering data in either of these fields will initiate a new computation; it will also cause the appropriate tool to be depressed if it is currently up.

The method is as follows. For each vertical pixel position, which represents a particular value of x, a search is commenced, at the value $n = 1$, for a fixed point of f_n within a one-pixel interval, and terminated as soon as one is found (or aborted once the selected maximum value is exceeded). As explained on pages 34–35, such a fixed point determines the period of an associated orbit. If the period is in the selected range, the orbit is displayed. Stable orbits are displayed in blue, unstable in red. In the event that the same pixel position is required for the final state diagram, a dark hue is used, otherwise a light one. In this way it is possible to distinguish the exact behaviour at each point on the screen when the information is superposed on the same diagram.

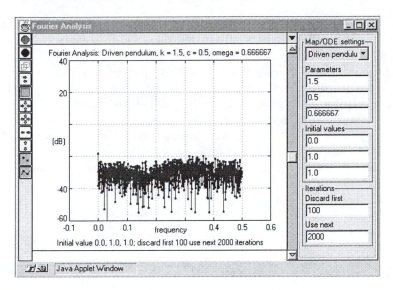

Figure A.6: A FOURIER ANALYSIS window. All spectra are calculated from a discrete map, in this case 2000 iterations of a Poincaré section of the driven pendulum equations.

A.4   FOURIER ANALYSIS

This window calculates the fast Fourier transform[17] of a sample of iterations, then displays the amplitude of the Fourier components using decibels as the vertical scale. Both one and two-dimensional maps may be investigated, including Poincaré sections of selected differential equations. In all cases, the spectrum is taken from the sequence of x_k values.

The example shown in figure A.6 is for the driven non-linear pendulum, whose Poincaré section is a two-dimensional map of the phase plane. There are three parameters and three initial values, which are set in the *Map/ODE settings* and *Initial values* groups. The arrangement of these groups changes to suit the selected dynamical system.

The initial number of iterations which are discarded, and the sample size, are set in the *Iterations* group. Factors which should be taken into account in selecting these numbers are discussed in page 49. A brief account of the theory is given in appendix B.

Fourier transforms of discrete systems are themselves discrete, so the data should be displayed simply as a set of discrete points. This can make it rather difficult to understand a particular spectrum if most of the data is out of range. There are two special tools associated with the display of

---

[17]See section 2.8 for an explanation of terms used in this section.

discrete points which appear also in some other windows.[18] These tools toggle between their on and off states in response to a click. One controls whether or not points are joined, the other changes their size. They permit discrete data to be joined by lines, and to be displayed as large or small points. A large point is 3 pixels square, centred on the actual position, a small point is a single pixel. Joining the points is only a guide to the eye — the data really is discrete. For example, a system which has converged to a stable period 3 orbit will have only two amplitudes greater than -200dB, namely A_0 and $A_{1/3}$, this is seen in figure 2.14 (page 49).

A further important point to note is that the discrete Fourier transform of a Poincaré section, although related to the more usual transform of the continuous system, can only detect frequency components which are less than one-half the frequency of the periodic driving force. This is discussed on page 190.

A.5   GRAPHICAL ANALYSIS

An example of this window has already been shown in figure A.3. The full capabilities are as follows:[19]

(i) Draw one or two graphs of a one-dimensional map f or selected compositions f_n of it. In the event that two graphs are displayed, they will both be for the same parameter value; the only permitted difference is the composition numbers n.

(ii) Draw the line $y = x$ and calculate the fixed points of f_n (which are seen on the graph as intersections) and the associated derivative.

(iii) Display animated cobweb diagrams for the maps. These are not particularly informative for higher compositions, so they are not displayed for values of $n > 8$, which is indicated by an alert.

Switching the tab

One of the controls in the *Map settings* group is a tab for switching between the two graphs. One purpose of switching is to enter new data; since it may be required to enter new data in both fields before initiating a new computation, switching the tab does not enter the data. Numerical values entered into the composition fields must be greater than zero for Graph 1; entering blank data under Graph 2 is a signal that the second graph is not

---

[18]The large points tool is in the POINCARÉ SECTIONS, ITERATE(1D) and RETURN MAPS windows; the ITERATE(1D) window has the join points tool.

[19]See pages 17, 19 and 34 for an explanation of terms used in this section.

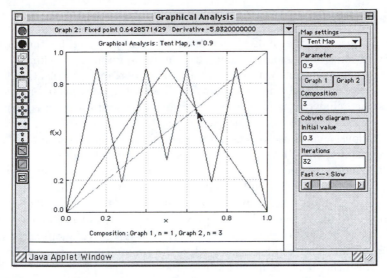

Figure A.7: Finding a fixed point and derivative of f_3. Once the tool is depressed, clicking nearby displays the information in the prompt panel for the graph whose tab is selected.

required. This is a fundamental difference of behaviour which is used in some other windows of CHAOS FOR JAVA.

Cobweb diagram and animation

By default the drawing of the cobweb diagram is animated and there is an associated control in the *Cobweb diagram* group for controlling the speed of the animation, which may be changed while the animation is in progress. Animation may be switched off by choosing the fastest setting. The number of iterations displayed in the cobweb diagram, and the initial value, are set in the *Cobweb diagram* group.

Obviously the cobweb diagram will be different for different compositions of the same map, but it may only be displayed for one graph at a time.[20] For this reason, the choice of composition for the cobweb diagram is determined by the state of the tab, furthermore switching results in an immediate change.

Note that, if the cobweb diagram is displayed, then it will be hidden if the line $y = x$ is hidden. Conversely, showing the cobweb diagram will also show the line $y = x$. The state of the tools changes to reflect this.

---

[20]The alternative seems to lead to considerable confusion.

Fixed points

The line $y = x$ is shown or hidden using the tool provided for the purpose. A fixed point and associated derivative may be found by clicking near an intersection of the line with the graph. It is important to notice that, if two graphs are displayed, the fixed point will be for the one selected in the tab, the same behaviour as for cobweb diagrams. This information is displayed in the prompt panel (see figure A.7).

Obviously such use of the mouse conflicts with its use for zooming. Consequently, the GRAPHICAL ANALYSIS window has an extra tool which sets the mode for finding fixed points.[21] After depressing the *set fixed point mode* tool, a single click will initiate solution of the equation $x = f_n(x)$ by a method of interval searching followed by an iteration.[22] This locates the nearest zero to the selected point, provided there are not two or more zeros within one pixel of each other. It may be necessary to zoom in to avoid this problem. The result is displayed in the prompt panel, and will remain there until the mouse is moved a little way.

A.6   ITERATE(1D)

An example of this window has already been shown in figure A.2. The full capabilities are as follows:

(i) Show successive iterations x_k of a map as a function of k.

(ii) Show how these iterations are connected under a selected composition of the map.

(iii) Compute and display the orbital density of an orbit.[23]

(iv) Compute a numerical value of the Lyapunov exponent of an orbit.[24]

Display group

There are two modes of display, selected by the tab in the *Display* group; the *Map settings* group is common to both. The first time an ITERATE(1D) window is opened it is in the mode for displaying iterations (see figure A.2). An example of the orbital density mode is shown in figure A.8. Note

---

[21] This tool is a checkbox linked with the zoom mode tools, it remains down until one of them is selected.

[22] Specifically, values of $\phi_n(x) = x - f_n(x)$ are computed at each horizontal pixel position, starting from where the mouse was clicked, and continuing for 50 pixels each side, until a change of sign is found. The interval in which it lies is refined iteratively.

[23] See page 60 for the definition.

[24] See page 51 for the definition.

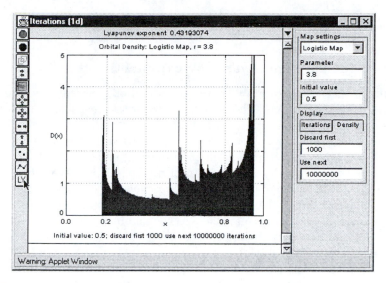

Figure A.8: Orbital density and Lyapunov exponent in the ITER-
ATE(1D) window, after setting the *Display* tab to Density mode.

that Lyapunov exponents may only be computed in this mode. Changing
the display mode also changes the relevant data entry fields; since they
are for different computations, the hidden fields are not checked before
commencing a new computation.

Displaying iterations

The first data entry field in the *Display* group affects the way iterations
are joined. This is particularly useful to indicate the action of a selected
composition of the map. For example, at the parameter value chosen in
figure A.2 the logistic map is in an intermittent period 3 state. Joining
every third point shows the action of f_3 on three different initial values,
namely x_0, $x_1 = f(x_0)$, $x_2 = f(x_1)$. Since the horizontal axis is set to view
100 iterations in figure A.2 there are three distinct sub-sequences under
iteration of f_3, $(x_0, x_3, x_6, \cdots)$, $(x_1, x_4, x_7, \cdots)$ and $(x_2, x_5, x_8, \cdots)$. These
are joined separately to indicate this.

The second field simply sets the limit for horizontal scrolling. The only
purpose of this is to ensure that the scroll box actually moves by a percep-
tible amount during scrolling, which requires that there be a finite limit.

To make the visual presentation clearer, the point size may be changed
and/or successive points may be joined by straight lines, using the tools

provided. As with the FOURIER ANALYSIS window, this is only a guide to
the eye; there are no intermediate values such as $x_{5/3}$!

Orbital density and Lyapunov exponents

Changing to the *Density* tab causes normalised orbital densities to be calculated — see figure A.8. The map is iterated from the chosen initial value
for the number of iterations in the first data entry field, then further iterated for the number in the second field. Statistics are collected for the
latter sample, converted to a normalised density, and displayed.

In the density mode, the special tool marked LY is active. Pressing it
results in a calculation of the Lyapunov exponent, as a simple average over
the displayed sample. The result is shown in the prompt panel, presented
to the same number of decimal places as the number of digits in the sample
size. For example, 100000 requires six digits so the Lyapunov exponent is
displayed to six decimal places. This is shown in figure A.8. This does not
mean that the estimate will be that accurate, but it can hardly be more
accurate since the number 100000 has been substituted for an infinite limit!
The numerical value will disappear when the mouse is moved a little, it may
be redisplayed (not recomputed!) by depressing the LY tool again.

A.7   ITERATE(2D)

An example of this window is shown in figure A.9. The full capabilities are
as follows:[25]

(i) Show successive iterations of one or two orbits of a two-dimensional
map as points in the plane.[26]

(ii) Show the basins of attraction of displayed orbit(s), of infinity, and
initial points which do not appear to be in any of these basins.

(iii) Count boxes for displayed portion of an orbit(s), using squares of
selected edge size for the covering.[27]

(iv) Calculate Lyapunov exponents of displayed orbit(s).[28]

Most of these features are illustrated in figure A.9, which is for the
CONTROLLED LOGISTIC MAP map with parameter values for which there
are coexisting attractors.

---

[25] Chapter 4 and section 5.4 contain explanations of the terms used in this section.

[26] The point sizes are selected automatically; large size is used for 16 or less displayed
points, small size otherwise. The effect may be seen in figure 4.5.

[27] See section 5.4 for the treatment of box counting and capacity dimension.

[28] See section 4.5 for the treatment of Lyapunov exponents of a two-dimensional map.

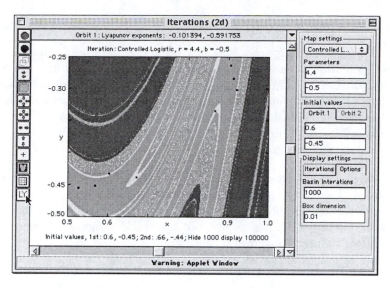

Figure A.9: A ITERATE(2D) window. For the selected parameter values, the CONTROLLED LOGISTIC MAP map has two co-existing orbits of period 4 and 6, respectively. All four points on the first orbit are in view, only four of the six points on the second orbit.

Initial value group

Two-dimensional maps frequently have two or more coexisting attracting orbits, which may be found by starting the iteration from any initial point within the corresponding basin of attraction. There is provision in the ITERATE(2D) window to display either one or two orbits, using different initial values. Figure A.9 has two orbits; the initial value settings for the first orbit are shown under the *Orbit 1* tab. Blank data is not accepted for this orbit. Initial value settings for a second orbit are made by first switching to the *Orbit 2* tab and then entering non-blank data. A blank entry indicates that no second orbit is required. The first orbit is coloured blue, as is the corresponding tab, green is used for the second orbit and its tab.

Box counts and Lypanunov exponents may be computed for either orbit (see below), the choice corresponds to the tab settings. Thus, in the figure, the Lyapunov exponents which are displayed in the prompt panel are for Orbit 1, as indicated.

Display settings group

The *Display settings* group also has a tab. The *Iterations* tab allows the discard and sample sizes to be set in the usual manner. (In figure A.9, the discard size is 10^3 points, the sample size 10^5 points; this was used for the display of both orbits and for the computation of the Lyapunov exponents, but the data entry fields are obscured.)

Settings for basin and box counting operations are under the *Options* tab, as displayed in the figure. It allows for two important settings.

(i) For computing basins of attraction a Basin iterations number is required. This is the maximum number of iterations used, for each initial condition in turn, before the search for an attractor is abandoned. The basin colours match the orbits, but the shade is lighter. Points in the basin of infinity are shown in dark grey. This may leave points whose basin is undecided, these are shown in light red.

(ii) For box counting, the size of the squares is set in the Box dimension field.

More on basins

It is important to note that the algorithm used for computing basins of attraction is restricted to examination of the displayed portions of the orbits only. Moreover, the computation of undecided areas can be quite unreliable unless a relatively large basin iteration number is selected; you should experiment with this. In particular, if you choose not to display the second orbit in figure A.9, red areas will indicate initial conditions which may be used to find the missing orbit, but this is only reliable if the iteration count is in the order of several hundred. As a further consequence, if a close up is selected which does not include any of the points on one of the orbits, the corresponding basin will display as red, indicating that it could not be located.

More on box counting

Once again, the algorithm used for box counting is restricted to the displayed portions of the orbits only, modified by the fact that the display area is tiled, from bottom left, by squares of the selected size, which may cause a small overlap with the top and/or right.[29] Thus a box count of the

---

[29] For example, if a box dimension of 0.03 were selected for the displayed figure, the boxes would cover from $x = 0.5$ to $1.01 = 0.5 + 17 \times 0.03$, and from $y = -0.5$ to $-0.23 = -0.5 + 9 \times 0.03$.

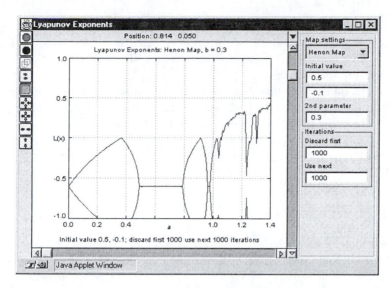

Figure A.10: A LYAPUNOV EXPONENTS window, giving a global picture of parameter dependence. Because a calculation is made for each horizontal pixel position, large samples are impractical.

orbits as displayed in figure A.9 will return 4 for both orbits, despite the fact the the first orbit is period 4, the second period 6.[30]

A.8 LYAPUNOV EXPONENTS

There are several options in CHAOS FOR JAVA for calculating Lyapunov exponents.[31] The preferred option of calculation for a single orbit of a one or two-dimensional map is to use the LY tools in the ITERATE(1D) or ITERATE(2D) window, respectively. For differential equations there is an LY tool in the POINCARÉ SECTIONS window; note that differential equations are not included in the LYAPUNOV EXPONENTS window, only one and two-dimensional maps are implemented for it.

The LYAPUNOV EXPONENTS window displays numerically estimated Lyapunov exponents as a function of just one map parameter. An example is shown in figure A.10; because it is for the HÉNON MAP map the second parameter is set in the *Map settings* group, whilst the range of values of the parameter a is controlled by the horizontal scrollbar. The data entry

---

[30]This is not a recommended way to investigate the periodicity of orbits — it is intended for estimating capacity dimension, which makes it even more important to have the complete orbit in view.

[31]See sections 2.9, 4.5 and 6.4 for the definitions of Lyapunov exponents.

fields for the *Map settings* group depend on the map. In the example shown
there are two initial values x_0 and y_0. For other maps a second parameter
may not be needed; nor a second initial value; the arrangement of the *Map
settings* group changes to suit.

All Lyapunov exponent calculations are made by first discarding a selected number of iterations, starting from a prescribed initial value, after
which the estimate is based on a selected sample size. These two numbers
are set in the *Iterations* group. Because the calculation must be made at
several hundred different parameter values, using large numbers of iterations may be prohibitively slow.

A.9   ODE ORBITS

An example of this window is shown in figure A.11. One or two orbits of
a differential equation may be shown in three-dimensional view, under the
control of the scrollbars, which have a completely different function in this
window than in all other windows. The displayed figure has only one orbit,
whose initial values have been set under the *Orbit 1* tab of the *Initial values*
group. As in the ITERATE(2D) window, a second orbit is shown when non-
blank initial values are entered under the *Orbit 2* tab, conversely it is not
shown if one or more of those fields is blank. The initial point(s) are shown
as small circles, the final point(s) as small triangles.

Parameters are set in the *ODE settings* group, initial values in the *Orbit settings* group. For *autonomous systems*,[32] these are initial coordinate
positions, for *non-autonomous systems* the first field is the time, reduced
by an integer multiple of $2\pi/\Omega$ so as to lie in the range $0 \le t_0 < 2\pi/\Omega$.

Rotations of the orbit point are determined as follows.

(i) The horizontal scrollbar controls the *azimuth*, rotating the orbit
about the vertical axis. This axis is always assigned to the third variable, z for the Lorenz and Rössler systems, x' for periodically driven
systems.

(ii) The vertical scrollbar controls the *elevation*, which is the angle above
or below the x-y plane (or the t-x plane) from which the orbit is viewed.

(iii) The increments for these scrollbars is $15°$ for page up/down, $3°$ for
line up/down; the position of the scrollbox is rounded to the nearest $3°$.

---

[32]I did not discuss the distinction between autonomous and non-autonomous systems
in the main text. The Lorenz and Rössler equations are autonomous, meaning that
the instantaneous velocities depend only on the instantaneous positions; time has no
absolute meaning for them. Periodically driven systems are non-autonomous, so that
the initial time is relevant only to within integer multiples of a period.

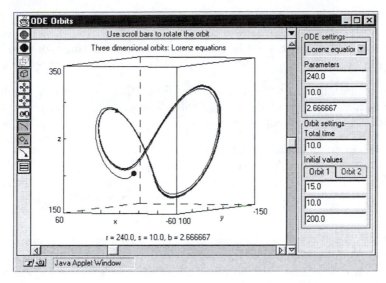

Figure A.11: A ODE ORBITS window. Settings controlled by the special tools are at their initial defaults.

(iv) It is actually the *view point* which is rotated; clicking the left-hand part of the horizontal scrollbar in figure A.11 is equivalent to moving yourself to further to the left.

There are a number of tools which are unique to the ODE ORBITS window, apart from the top three which are the usual start, stop and default view tools. From top down, they are

(i) Default resize on rotation. When this tool is depressed (the default) the scale of the projection is recomputed every time the orbit is rotated. Turning this off will result in the rotation being treated as a rigid body.[33]

(ii) Expand scale. Unlike the zoom in and zoom out tools of the other windows, this takes effect immediately, changing the horizontal and vertical scales by approx 20%.[34]

(iii) Contract scale, opposite of the previous tool.

(iv) Bounding box tool. The default, as shown in figure A.11, is to display the orbit within a rectangular box with the axes labelled. Depressing the tool will give views such as were shown on page 9.

---

[33] Note that perspective is not applied to three-dimensional views.

[34] Because the scrollbars have a different function, this has limited use once the orbit exceeds the viewing area; it may be preferable to maximise the window for more detail.

(v) Smooth orbits. The data for displaying orbits is sampled at relatively large time intervals, which may result in the orbit appearing as quite obvious straight line segments. Depressing this tool turns on a spline algorithm for smoothing displayed orbits, it also slows the display.

(vi) Mark initial and final positions. When this tool is down, the initial positions are indicated by small coloured circles, the final positions by small coloured triangles.

(vii) Animate orbits. When this tool is clicked, the orbit(s) are redrawn as an animation. The initial points are displayed first, as small coloured circles, then the orbit is drawn a small section at a time, with the evolving points shown as small moving triangles, rather like kites on the end of string.

(viii) Reset initial conditions. Clicking this tool causes the current values of the variables to be inserted into the initial value fields, after which a new orbit calculation is initiated. The effect is to compute a new orbit starting where the previous one finished. Remember that, for periodically driven systems, the initial value of the time is reduced to the interval $0 \le t_o < 2\pi/\Omega$.

A.10   Poincaré Sections

An example of this window is shown in figure A.12; there are similarities with the Iterate(2D) window.[35] Like it, points on an orbit of a two-dimensional map are displayed, but there is provision to view only one orbit, and no facility to compute basins of attraction.[36] However, because the map is a section of a continuous system, the phase is a free parameter, set by a small scrollbar in its own *Phase* group. This allows for animated viewing of the effect of changing the phase. Because of the large amounts of orbit data which must be stored, the increments are in the relatively coarse amounts of 15°.

As in the Iterate(2D) there is provision for controlling the selection of points for display, under the *Display* tab of the *Orbit settings* group. The other tab, labelled *Starting*, reveals fields for setting initial conditions. This will be required in a regime where there are multiple attractors, so as to observe the desired orbit.

There are three special tools:

(i) A tool which determines whether the default axis ranges are changed after each calculation. This tool should be de-selected in a situation

---

[35]See section 6.3 for an explanation of terms used in this section.
[36]These restrictions may be removed in a some future version of Chaos for Java.

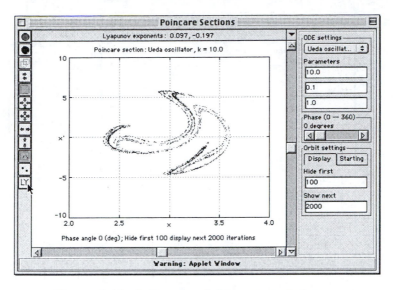

Figure A.12: A POINCARÉ SECTIONS window.

where it is required to view the effect of small parameter changes without changing the display.

(ii) The large points tools as in some other windows.

(iii) The LY tool which operates as in the ITERATE(1D) and ITER-ATE(2D) windows.[37]

One final comment: there is no provision for box counting; whilst this would be simple to implement it could be exceedingly time consuming.

A.11   RETURN MAPS

An example of this window is shown in figure A.13; it is used to display plots of points (x_k, x_{k+d}) as discussed on page 136; in fact the figure shown here should be compared with figure 4.12.

The *Map/ODE settings* group is similar to that in the FOURIER ANAL-YSIS window; in this instance only two-dimensional maps and selected differential equations are allowed. The *Orbit settings* group is similar to the one in the POINCARÉ SECTIONS window, with the addition of a data entry field for the delay d. Initial values are set by switching to the *Starting* tab.

Once again, there are three special tools:

---

[37]It must be emphasised that this computation is for the Poincaré section as a discrete system, using the section at zero phase — see section 6.4.

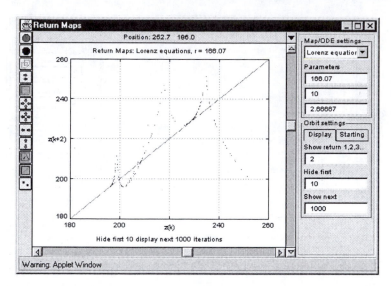

Figure A.13: A RETURN MAPS window, showing second return of the Lorenz equations — compare with figure 4.13 (page 138).

(i) A tool which determines whether the default axis ranges are changed after each calculation, whose effect is the same as in the POINCARÉ SECTIONS window.

(ii) A tool for showing or hiding the line $x_{k+d} = x_k$, useful for examining close returns near to tangent bifurcations of for making comparisons with behaviour observed in the GRAPHICAL ANALYSIS window.

(iii) The large points tools as in some other windows.

Appendix B

Discrete Fourier Transform

The purpose of this appendix is to sketch some of the considerations involved in computing discrete Fourier transforms,[1] to explain thereby the reasons for the restrictions placed on sample sizes in CHAOS FOR JAVA, and to assist in interpretation of results.

B.1 Complex roots of unity

To begin, let $\omega = \exp(2\pi i/N)$; this is a primitive Nth root of unity, having the properties $\omega \neq 1$, $\omega^2 \neq 1$, $\cdots$, $\omega^{N-1} \neq 1$, $\omega^N = 1$. Its connection to the purpose at hand is given by the representation

$$\omega = \cos(2\pi i/N) + i\sin(2\pi i/N),$$

and the related *de Moivre's theorem*

$$\omega^n = \cos(2\pi in/N) + i\sin(2\pi in/N).$$

Given a sequence x_k, $(0 \leq k < N)$, it is required to find the coefficients $a_{m/N}$ and $b_{m/N}$ of the representation (2.24). For simplicity, write $\alpha_m = a_{m/N}$, $\beta_m = b_{m/N}$, and

$$x_k = \sum_m \big(\alpha_m \cos(2\pi km/N) + \beta_m \sin(2\pi km/N)\big).$$

Let's replace this with the more general question of finding complex coefficients γ_m such that

$$x_k = \sum_{m=0}^{N-1} \gamma_m \exp(2\pi ikm/N) = \sum_{m=0}^{N-1} \gamma_m \omega^{km}. \tag{B.1}$$

For each k, this is an equation for a complex number; the requirement that the data is real imposes N conditions on the coefficients γ_m, which has important consequences.

---

[1] Extensive treatments may be found in a number of books devoted to the subject.

B.2   Discrete orthogonality

Equations (B.1) constitute a set of N linear equations for the N unknowns γ_m. They are readily solved using a simple trick. Start with the polynomial factorisation

$$1 - z^N = (1 - z)(1 + z + z^2 + \cdots + z^{N-1}),$$

and rewrite it as the sum of a finite geometric progression:

$$\sum_{n=0}^{N-1} z^n = \frac{1 - z^N}{1 - z}.$$

Now substitute $z = \omega^m$, $(0 \le m < N)$, to obtain[2]

$$\sum_{n=0}^{N-1} \omega^{nm} = N\delta_{m,0} = \begin{cases} N, & (m = 0) \\ 0, & (m \ne 0). \end{cases} \tag{B.2}$$

This is a rather compact way of expressing the *discrete orthogonality* of trigonometric functions. To see this, use de Moivre's theorem, and take the real and imaginary parts of the resulting expressions. This gives the relations

$$\sum_{n=0}^{N-1} \cos\left(\frac{2\pi nm}{N}\right) = N\delta_{m,0}, \qquad \sum_{n=0}^{N-1} \sin\left(\frac{2\pi nm}{N}\right) = 0.$$

B.3   Fourier amplitudes

If we multiply equations (B.1) by ω^{-kn}, sum over n, reverse the order of summation and use orthogonality, there results

$$\sum_{n=0}^{N-1} x_n \omega^{-kn} = \sum_{n=0}^{N-1}\sum_{m=0}^{N-1} \gamma_m \omega^{(m-k)n} = \sum_{m=0}^{N-1} \gamma_m \delta_{k,m} = N\gamma_k,$$

giving an explicit formula for the Fourier coefficients

$$\gamma_m = \frac{1}{N} \sum_{n=0}^{N-1} x_n \omega^{-mn}. \tag{B.3}$$

N coefficients are required for the Fourier representation, for each the evaluation of this formula requires a sum over N terms; it follows that straightforward use will require an amount of computation proportional to N^2.

---

[2]If $m = 0$ the formula $(1 - z^N)/(1 - z)$ is tricky; it is easier to note that every term in the sum has the value 1 and just add.

Since $\omega^N = 1$, the left hand side of (B.3) is unchanged by the substitution $m \to m + N$, giving the periodicity condition

$$\gamma_{m+N} = \gamma_m,$$

where now the restriction $0 \leq m < N$ is removed. In addition, complex conjugation has the effect $\overline{\omega}^n = \omega^{-n}$; taking the complex conjugate of (B.3) gives

$$\overline{\gamma}_m = \gamma_{-m} = \gamma_{N-m}, \qquad \overline{x}_k = x_k.$$

In the event that the data is pure imaginary, the corresponding relation is

$$\overline{\gamma}_m = -\gamma_{-m} = -\gamma_{N-m}, \qquad \overline{x}_k = -x_k.$$

These two symmetries allow one to recover the Fourier amplitudes of the real and imaginary parts of a complex data set separately; given such a set $z_k = x_k + iy_k$, with Fourier amplitudes $c_m = a_m + b_m$,

$$2a_m = c_m + \overline{c}_{N-m}, \qquad 2ib_m = c_m - \overline{c}_{N-m}. \tag{B.4}$$

B.4   Using real and imaginary parts

Thus far there is no condition on the choice of N, from here on I assume that it is divisible by 2 and write $N = 2M$. This done, let's examine equation (B.3) more closely, writing it out term by term and rearranging:

$$\begin{aligned} N\gamma_m &= x_0 + x_1\,\omega^{-m/N} + x_2\,\omega^{-2m/N} + x_3\,\omega^{-3m/N} + \cdots \\ &= \left(x_0 + x_2\,\omega^{-m/M} + \cdots + x_{N-2}\,\omega^{-(M-1)/M} \right) \\ &\quad + \omega^{-m/N}\left(x_1 + x_3\,\omega^{-m/M} + \cdots + x_{N-1}\,\omega^{-(M-1)/M} \right). \end{aligned} \tag{B.5}$$

The vital point is that the two bracketed terms are the same discrete transform, operating on the even and odd data points separately. This suggests that we define a new complex data set by

$$z_0 = x_0 + ix_1, \quad z_1 = x_2 + ix_3, \quad \cdots \quad z_{M-1} = x_{N-2} + ix_{N-1},$$

and consider its discrete Fourier transform, which will involve ω^2 rather than ω because $1/M = 2/N$.

Let the Fourier coefficients of this new set be c_m, and let the corresponding coefficients for the real and imaginary parts of z_k be a_m and b_m; the latter are precisely the combinations which occur in (B.5), so it is clear that

$$2\gamma_m = a_m + \omega^{-m/M} b_m,$$

and on using (B.4) we recover the Fourier coefficients for the original real data set of length N from the Fourier coefficients of c_m. This is one of the (standard) tricks used in CHAOS FOR JAVA, which is why N must be even.

B.5   Fast Fourier Transform

I have explained the previous trick in some detail because the method of subdividing data is at the heart of the Fast Fourier Transform. Assume that the data has been reduced to a complex set z_k, whose length $N = pM$ is divisible by a prime number p, and whose Fourier coefficients are γ_m. Equation (B.4) is hardly changed, becoming

$$
\begin{aligned}
N\gamma_m &= z_0 + z_1\,\omega^{-m/N} + z_2\,\omega^{-2m/N} + z_3\,\omega^{-3m/N} + \cdots \\
&= \left(z_0 + z_p\,\omega^{-m/M} + \cdots + z_{N-p}\,\omega^{-(M-1)/M}\right) \\
&\quad + \omega^{-m/N}\left(z_1 + z_{p+1}\,\omega^{-m/M} + \cdots + z_{N-p+1}\,\omega^{-(M-1)/M}\right) \\
&\quad \vdots \\
&\quad + \omega^{-m(p-1)/N}\left(z_{p-1} + \cdots + z_{N-1}\,\omega^{-(M-1)/M}\right).
\end{aligned}
$$

Just as before this reduces the computation of the γ_m to a process of assembling the Fourier amplitudes for each of the p subsequences. The principle difference is that each must be computed separately; it is not possible to use the real and imaginary parts as placeholders since the data was complex from the outset.

   The reasons that this procedure is so powerful are easy to see. First, suppose that it is applied just once; the time required for the original computation is of order N^2, after the above rearrangement it is of order $p(N/p)^2 = N^2/p$. Second, the computation of the p new Fourier transforms are exactly parallel to each other; all that is required is to sort the data into the order

$$
z_0, z_p, z_{2p}, \cdots, z_1, z_{p+1}, \cdots, z_2, z_{p+2}, \cdots, z_{N-1},
$$

which requires exactly the same amount of storage, followed by the appropriate computation. Finally, the new computation can be further broken down provided that the number N/p is itself divisible by a small prime. In fact, given the factorisation

$$
N = p_1 p_2 \cdots p_n, \tag{B.6}
$$

the time required will be roughly proportional to $N n p_n^2$, since the number of stages is n, the final transform will be of size p_n, assumed small, and the total data set retains its original length N at each stage. The most efficient choice is $N = 2^n$, for which the time grows as $Nn = N\ln N$.

   These considerations indicate why CHAOS FOR JAVA, for reasons of efficiency, refuses to accept sample sizes which do not factor in the form (B.6) with small prime factors p_j.

Appendix C

Variational equations

C.1   Derivation and meaning

For computing Lyapunov exponents we need to know about the relative evolution of neighbouring orbits, to linear approximation.

Suppose that we have a solution $(x_0(t), y_0(t))$ of equations (6.8), and that we want to know about a nearby orbit

$$x(t) = x_0(t) + \delta x(t), \qquad y(t) = y_0(t) + \delta y(t).$$

We may write down the equation which these two solutions satisfy and take the difference. For the angular velocity this gives

$$\frac{d\delta y}{dt} = y' - y_0' = -c(y - y_0) - \big(f(x) - f(x_0)\big).$$

Now for the approximation. First, $f(x) = f(x_0 + \delta x) \approx f(x_0) + \delta x f'(x_0)$, from which

$$\frac{d\delta y}{dt} \approx -c\delta y + f'(x_0)\,\delta x.$$

The other equation requires no approximation,

$$\frac{d\delta x}{dt} = x' - x_0' = y - y_0 = \delta y.$$

These equations are known as *variational equations*, since they determine solutions which are near to a known solution. They have the important property of being linear, although one of the coefficients is not constant, so that numerical methods are required in general.

C.2   The area contracting property

Now let's consider a parallelogram in the phase plane,[1] one corner of which is the solution (x_0, y_0). The two adjacent corners, assumed to be close so

---

[1]This is just the argument used in section 4.3, albeit at a more sophisticated level.

that linear approximation applies, are at $(x_0 + \delta x_1, y_0 + \delta y_1)$ and $(x_0 + \delta x_2, y_0 + \delta y_2)$. The area of the parallelogram is given by

$$A(t) = |\delta x_1(t)\delta y_2(t) - \delta x_2(t)\delta y_1(t)|\,,$$

by a standard formula from vector calculus, which gives the area of a parallelogram whose sides are the vectors $\mathbf{a}$, $\mathbf{b}$ as $|\mathbf{a} \times \mathbf{b}|$. Differentiating the formula with respect to time gives

$$\frac{dA}{dt} = \left| \frac{d\delta x_1}{dt}\delta y_2 + \delta x_1 \frac{d\delta y_2}{dt} - \frac{d\delta x_2}{dt}\delta y_1 - \delta x_2 \frac{d\delta y_1}{dt} \right|.$$

When we substitute from the variational equation, the dependence on the unknown function $x_0(t)$ completely vanishes, to give $dA/dt = -cA$. This result is amazingly simple, the solution completely trivial, $A(t) = A(t_0)\exp[-c(t-t_0)]$. From this, the area reduction factor claimed in equation (6.12) follows by the substitution of $2\pi/\Omega$ in place of $t - t_0$.

C.3   Three-dimensional case

For the full three-dimensional case, we need only add the third variational equation for δt:

$$\frac{d\delta t}{dt} = 0.$$

By another standard formula from vector calculus, the volume $V(t)$ of a rectangular box whose sides are the vectors $\mathbf{a}$, $\mathbf{b}$, $\mathbf{c}$ is $|\mathbf{a} \times \mathbf{b} \cdot \mathbf{c}|$; since $\mathbf{c}$ (which comes from the solution δt) is orthogonal to the vectors $\mathbf{a}$ and $\mathbf{b}$, it follows that[2]

$$\frac{dV}{dt} = -cV.$$

These results imply that one Lyapunov exponent is zero, that an evolving small ellipsoid has principal axes for expansion/contraction in the phase plane, and that the volume contraction matches the area contraction, as claimed on pages 192ff. Denote the magnification factors by $\lambda_1^{(3)}(t)$, $\lambda_2^{(3)}(t)$, $\lambda_3^{(3)}(t)$, with $\lambda_2^{(3)}(t) = 1$; their logarithms are the Lyapunov exponents, which we can relate to the exponents $\lambda_1^{(2)}$, $\lambda_2^{(2)}$ of the Poincaré section,

$$\lambda_1^{(2)} = \lambda_1^{(3)}(2\pi/\Omega), \qquad \lambda_2^{(2)} = \lambda_3^{(3)}(2\pi/\Omega).$$

It must be reiterated that this result follows from the very special nature of the equations.

---

[2] A result which could also be deduced using the Gauss divergence theorem.

Appendix D

List of Maps and Differential Equations

This final appendix lists all of the maps and differential equations which occur in the text, and which are built in to CHAOS FOR JAVA, together with a cross reference to their first appearance. Strictly speaking this is redundant, but it seems appropriate to assemble the information here for easy reference. The order matches their order of appearance in windows of CHAOS FOR JAVA.

D.1 One-dimensional maps

LOGISTIC MAP (page 14)

$$f(x) = rx(1 - x), \qquad (0 \leq r \leq 4)$$

SINE MAP (page 12)

$$f(x) = q\sin(\pi x), \qquad (0 \leq q \leq 1).$$

CUBIC #1 MAP (page 17)

$$f(x) = 27rx^2(1 - x)/16, \qquad (0 \leq r \leq 4)$$

CUBIC #2 MAP (page 18)

$$f(x) = rx(1 - x^2)/\sqrt{3}, \qquad (0 \leq r \leq 4.5)$$

CUBIC #3 MAP (page 19)

$$f(x) = x(1 - p + px^2), \qquad (0 \leq p \leq 4).$$

TENT MAP (page 14)

$$f(x) = \begin{cases} 2tx, & (x \leq 1/2), \\ 2t(1 - x), & (x \geq 1/2), \end{cases} \qquad (0 \leq t \leq 1).$$

TENT #2 MAP (page 55)

$$f(x) = \begin{cases} t\left[\frac{3}{2}x + x^2\right], & (x \le \frac{1}{2}), \\ t\left[\frac{3}{2}(1-x) + (1-x)^2\right] & (x \ge \frac{1}{2}). \end{cases}$$

TENT #3 MAP (page 41)

$$f(x) = \begin{cases} 3t(x + \frac{2}{3}), & (x \le -\frac{1}{3}), \\ -3tx, & (-\frac{1}{3} \le x \le \frac{1}{3}), \\ 3t(x - \frac{2}{3}), & (x \ge \frac{1}{3}), \end{cases}$$

D.2   Two-dimensional maps

HÉNON MAP (page 107)

$$f(x, y) = 1 - ax^2 + y, \qquad g(x, y) = bx,$$

LOZI MAP (page 113)

$$f(x, y) = 1 - a|x| + y, \qquad g(x, y) = bx,$$

CONTROLLED LOGISTIC MAP (page 140)

$$f(x, y) = rx(1 - x) - bx + y, \qquad g(x, y) = bx;$$

CONTROLLED CUBIC MAP (page 144)

$$f(x, y) = rx(1 - x^2)/\sqrt{3} - bx + y, \qquad g(x, y) = bx;$$

D.3   Differential equations

LORENZ EQUATIONS (page 8)

$$\frac{dx}{dt} = \sigma(y - x), \qquad \frac{dy}{dt} = rx - y - xz, \qquad \frac{dz}{dt} = xy - bz.$$

RÖSSLER EQUATIONS (page 18)

$$\frac{dx}{dt} = -y - z, \qquad \frac{dy}{dt} = x + ay, \qquad \frac{dz}{dt} = a + z(x - c).$$

DRIVEN PENDULUM (page 179)

$$x'' + cx' + \sin x = k \cos \Omega t.$$

UEDA OSCILLATOR (page 186)

$$x'' + cx' + x^3 = k \cos \Omega t.$$

Bibliography

[1] R. Abraham and C. Shaw, *Dynamics: The Geometry of Behavior. Part I: Periodic Behavior, Part II: Chaotic Behavior*, Arial Press, Santa Cruz, California, 1982.

[2] D. Acheson, *From Calculus to Chaos*, Oxford University Press, 1997.

[3] K. T. Alligood, T. D. Sauer and J. A. Yorke, *Chaos: An Introduction to Dynamical Systems*, Springer, 1997.

[4] D. K. Arrowsmith and C. M. Place, *An introduction to Dynamical Systems*, Cambridge University Press, 1990.

[5] G. L. Baker and J. P. Gollub, *Chaotic Dynamics, an Introduction*, Cambridge University Press, 1990.

[6] J. Barrow-Green, *Poincaré and the Three-body problem (History of Mathematics, volume 11)*, American Mathematical Society, 1997.

[7] P. Bergé, Y. Pomeau and C. Vidal, *Order within chaos*, Hermann, Paris, France, 1984.

[8] J. M. Blatt, *Dynamic Economic Systems*, M. E. Sharpe Inc. NY, 1983.

[9] J. Creedy and V. Martin (eds), *Chaos and Non-linear Models in Economics*, Edward Elgar Publishing, 1994.

[10] R. L. Devaney, *Chaotic Dynamical Systems, 2nd ed.*, Addison-Wesley, 1989.

[11] K. Falconer, *Fractal Geometry: Mathematical Foundations and Applications*, Wiley, 1990.

229

[12] J. Frøyland, *Introduction to Chaos and Coherence*, Institute of Physics Publishing, 1992.

[13] J. Gleick, *Chaos: Making a New Science*, Viking Press, NY, 1987.

[14] R. A. Holmgren, *A First Course in Discrete Dynamical Systems*, Springer-Verlag, 1994.

[15] H. Lauwerier, *Fractals. Endlessly Repeated Geometrical Figures*, Penguin, Princeton University Press, 1991.

[16] E. N. Lorenz, *The Essence of Chaos*, University of Washington Press, USA, 1993.

[17] B. B. Mandelbrot, *The Fractal Geometry of Nature*, W. H. Freeman, NY, 1983.

[18] M. Martelli, *Discrete dynamical systems and chaos*, Longman Group UK, 1992.

[19] F. C. Moon, *Chaotic Vibrations*, Wiley, 1987.

[20] T. Mullin (ed.), *The nature of Chaos*, Clarendon Press, Oxford, 1993.

[21] E. Ott, *Chaos in Dynamical Systems*, Cambridge University Press, 1993.

[22] E. Ott, T. Sauer and J. A. Yorke, *Coping with Chaos*, Wiley, 1994.

[23] H. O. Peitgen and P. H. Richter, *The beauty of Fractals*, Springer-Verlag, Berlin, 1988.

[24] H. O. Peitgen, H. Jürgens and D. Saupe, *Chaos and Fractals: New Frontiers of Science*, Springer-Verlag, NY, 1992.

[25] E. E. Peters, *Chaos and Order in the Capital Markets*, Wiley, 1991.

[26] I. Peterson, *Newton's Clock: Chaos in the Solar System*, W. H. Freeman, NY, 1993.

[27] N. Rasband, *Chaotic Dynamics Nonlinear Systems*, Wiley, 1990.

[28] C. Robinson, *Dynamical Systems: Stability, Symbolic Dynamics, and Chaos*, CRC Press, Boca Raton, 1995.

[29] P. T. Saunders, *An introduction to catastrophe theory*, Cambridge University Press, 1980.

[30] H. G. Schuster, *Deterministic Chaos: An Introduction*, 2nd. ed., VCH Publishers, Weinheim, Germany, 1988.

[31] M. Yamaguti, M. Hata and J. Kigami, *Mathematics of Fractals*, (Translations of Mathematical Monographs, vol. 167) Americal Mathematical Society, 1997.

Index

Acheson D., 177
Alligood K. T., 59, 135, 147
area contracting, 118, 133, 191
asymptotic stability, 19, 25, 109
attractor, 19, 109
   chaotic, 64, 68, 96 – 98
   coexisting, 112, 142, 182
   Feigenbaum, 172 – 176
   Hénon, 108, 145, 148
   Lorenz, 8, 15, 26
   periodic, 34, 112, 142, 179
   Rössler, 170 – 172
   strange, 8, 108, 145, 174, 194
   symmetric, 193
   three-band, 98

Baker G. L., 177
Barrow-Green J., 6
basin, 19
   boundary, 111, 132 – 134
     and unstable point, 132
     fractal, 142
   of attraction, 19, 110
   of infinity, 110
Baumol W. J., 4
behaviour, 8
   chaotic, 8, 11, 89, 97, 195
   intermittent, 92 – 95, 137
   regular, 11
   universal, 87, 104
Benhabib J., 4
bifurcation, 65 – 67, 111
   diagram, 23, 65
   flip, 66
   period doubling, 66, 75 – 77, 111,
     122, 184

pitchfork, 102, 145
reverse, 77
   period doubling, 137
   tangent, 91, 137
tangent, 89 – 91, 111, 137, 190
transcritical, 66, 101, 144
Blatt J. M., 4
boom and bust, 3
boundary, 111
   fractal, 142
   of basin, 111, 132 – 134
box counting, 157, 161
   dimension, 158
butterfly effect, 9 – 11, 180

Cantor G., 151
Cantor like attractor, 172
Cantor set, 150 – 154
   asymmetric, 159
   base 3 representation, 154
   capacity dimension, 158
   self-similarity, 160
   similarity dimension, 166
capacity dimension, 157 – 160, 167,
   169, 175
   Cantor set, 158
   Hénon attractor, 161
celestial mechanics, 5
chaos, 1, 4, 6 – 11, 27, 56, 180
   and period three, 157
   control of, 143
   numerical evidence, 20, 56
   period doubling route, 71
chaotic, 3, 170
   attractor, 64, 68, 96 – 98
   behaviour, 8, 11, 89, 97, 195